INSIDE INFO

For Keir
With love and appreciation

Words of thanks

I want to thank all the people who helped
me to write this book, including the many
whose generous criticism both encouraged
and obliged me to improve it. In particular,
thanks are due to Mike Bacon who vetted
the whole manuscript for technical accuracy, and to John Izat, Pete Twining, and
David R F Walker for unstinting technical
advice by telephone, often at un-social
hours. My debt to Charlotte Hanbury, who
compiled the index, is immense.

At BBC Publications I am very grateful to
Jennie Allen for her superb editorial work,
to Frances Abraham for the picture
research and to Roger Fletcher and his
team for working well beyond the call of
duty on the design and illustrations.
Thanks also to people involved in the other
parts of the *Inside Information* project for
their comments: Christopher Stone,
who produced the radio series, Charly
Loveland, who masterminded the software
pack, and Anthony Coles, who co-ordi-
nated the input from the City and Guilds of
London Institute. I also thank Bob Salkeld,
who involved me in the *Inside Information*
project in the first place.

For their generous practical help I am very
grateful to Jessie and Ada, and also to Dave
who proof-read and sub-edited large
amounts of the manuscript in addition. I
appreciate the efficient and courteous help
of the library staff at Jordanhill College of
Education. Above all, I am grateful to my
husband for his tactful mixture of
encouragement and candid commentary,
together with the unfailing support that
allowed me to complete the task despite
Sandy's and Helen's attempts to help.

INSIDE INFORMATION

COMPUTERS, COMMUNICATIONS AND PEOPLE

JACQUETTA MEGARRY

British Broadcasting Corporation

This book accompanies the BBC Radio series *Inside Information*, first broadcast in OPTIONS on Radio 4 VHF from 12 May to 14 July 1985 and repeated from 13 October to 15 December 1985. The series was produced by Christopher Stone.

Within this book the term 'BBC Micro' refers to the microcomputer manufactured by Acorn Computer plc under licence from the British Broadcasting Corporation.

The book forms part of BBC Radio 4's IT project which includes the City and Guilds of London Institute 444 'Inside Information' assessment (see page 220 for further details).

Published to accompany a series of programmes prepared in consultation with the BBC Continuing Education Advisory Council.

This book is typeset in 9/10 Ehrhardt by Phoenix Photosetting, Chatham and printed and bound in England by Mackays of Chatham Limited Cover and colour separations by Belmont Press, London

The cover illustration and that on page 8 are by Brian Robins.
The diagrams throughout the book are by Mike Gilkes with additional material by John Gilkes.

First published 1985
Published by the
British Broadcasting Corporation
35 Marylebone High Street,
London WIM 4AA
ISBN 0 563 21102 4

Picture Credits

Colour
Page 49 *both top* Science Photo Library, *bottom* John Izat; 50 *top* IBM United Kingdom Ltd, *bottom* Science Photo Library; 67 Micronet 800, Telemap Ltd; 68 Microvitec PLC; 86 Aspect Advertising Ltd; 103 Texas Instruments; 121 Roger Fletcher; 122 *top* RH Electronics Ltd, *bottom* ITT Consumer Products (UK) Ltd; 139 Nippon Telegraph & Telephone Corporation, Tokyo; 173 British Telecom; 174 Nelson Trowbridge, Hampshire County Education Dept.

Black and white
Page 11 *left* STC Telecommunications Ltd, *right* British Telecom; 13 *both* British Telecom; 14 Micronet 800, Telemap Ltd; 15 Jacquetta Megarry; 16 Rediffusion Simulation Ltd; 17 Jacquetta Megarry; 19 *top* British Museum, *centre* Epigraphical Museum, Athens, *bottom* National Museum of Wales; 22 Barnabys Picture Library; 23 Midland Bank; 25 *left* Comark Electronics Ltd, *right* BBC; 26 *all* BBC Research Dept; 28 BBC; 32 *left* Data General Ltd, *right* Hewlett Packard Ltd; 33 IBM United Kingdom Ltd; 36 *left* University of Edinburgh, *right* Dallas Independent School District; 37 *left* Allied Business Systems Ltd, *right* Acorn User Magazine; 38 Micro Control Systems Inc.; 39, 40, 41, 44 *top* & *centre* BBC; 44 *bottom* Penman Products Ltd; 46-7 Austin Rover Ltd; 48 Barnabys Picture Library; 53 BBC; 56 British Telecom; 57 Data General Ltd; 58 & 63 BBC; 81 Jessop Microelectronics Ltd; 88 Apple Computers Ltd; 92 *centre bottom* Racal Electronics Ltd, *others* British Telecom; 101 British Telecom; 106 Science Museum; 107, 112, 115 & 116 British Telecom; 117 3M United Kingdom PLC; 135 & 136 BBC; 138 Prestel, British Telecom; 142 BBC; 145 Daily Telegraph Colour Library; 151 Austin Rover Ltd; 152 & 153 *top* Thorn EMI; 153 *bottom* Philips Electronics; 165 BBC; 169 *top* J. Sainsbury plc, *bottom* Channel 4 Television; 181 BBC; 188 Redifusion Simulation Ltd.

Contents

Part 1

Part 2

Part 3

Part

Information world
Information and communication
Inside the computer
Some computer systems in action
How programs work
Systems software and applications software
The changing telephone
The video revolution

Chapter 1: Information world

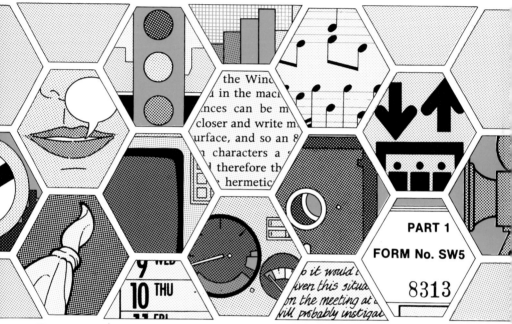

Figure 1 Information can be coded in many different ways.

This book takes you inside the world of information and the new ways of handling and transmitting it. Although modern technology, especially computing, plays a leading role, this book is not mainly about equipment (*hardware*). It pays more attention to *software*, the all-important instructions that control the hardware and make it seem clever or stupid, friendly or hostile. Above all, it explains how the new information systems affect the people who use or control them and how they indirectly affect each and every one of us. Technologies are nowadays developing and converging so fast that no-one can escape their influence. This book is both about exciting new opportunities and unprecedented dangers.

Humans have always depended on their ability to gather and transmit information. At first, we relied upon word of mouth, so that news only spread when people moved around and talked directly to others. Stories and skills had to be passed down orally from generation to generation; sometimes they became changed or were forgotten in the process.

Then we began to develop ways of storing messages permanently: in paintings on cave walls, in marks chipped onto tablets of stone, or in words written on slates, papyrus scrolls and, later, paper. The invention of writing was a breakthrough; it offered a way of coding information so that messages could not only be stored permanently, but also passed on without distortion. Of course, the system depends on the person receiving the message being able to decode it: writing is useless without its counterpart skill of reading.

In the Middle Ages, reproducing a written manuscript was a laborious process, the skills of reading and writing were confined to the educated few and books were very scarce and expensive. But the arrival of the printing press meant that once the words in a manuscript had been set up in type, any number of copies could be produced mechanically: quickly, cheaply and correctly. The foundations of modern publishing – the worldwide spread of books, newspapers, magazines – had been laid.

Nowadays the publishing industry is big business and caters for a mass market. It also embodies a clear division between those who write (the authors of books and articles) and those who read (the literate masses), with the publishers making the decisions about whose ideas are made available. We shall see how electronic media not only create a need for widespread computer (as opposed to book) literacy, but also challenge the assumptions and economics of publishing.

The computer is playing a central role in the information revolution. In fact, the word 'computer' is a bit misleading, for much computer usage concerns numbers only incidentally. Although computers *can* be used to compute, ie perform complicated calculations at superhuman speed, that is of significance only to a few people. The primary reason why computers are so revolutionary in their impact on human life is that they are information machines. *Any* information that can be represented – whether in words, in pictures, or in some other way – can be fed into a computer as *data*. There it can be processed as long as definite rules can be laid down as to how the computer should treat the data. This is the whole art of designing *programs*. If we can explain how we do something – anything – in enough detail for a programmer to turn it into instructions for a computer, then (in principle, at least) a computer can do the job for us – and do it accurately, reliably, at great speed, 24 hours a day.

Figure 2 Letters and numbers have been used to code information for centuries.

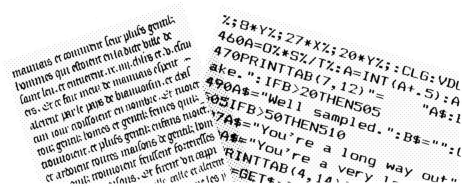

In practice, of course, it doesn't always make sense to computerise: various human, technical and economic factors must be weighed up carefully. Computers are more suited to doing some tasks than people are, but if their introduction increases unemployment the social cost may be too high. For other tasks computers may be too inflexible. For example, computers are still rather limited in their ability to handle pictorial information. Even on large and expensive systems, computer graphics tend to be crude compared with photographs, often showing colour only at the price of having less fine detail, and demanding a lot of computer memory and processing power to display even simple *animation* (movement). Recent changes in methods of storing television pictures and transmitting computer and video information provide ways of overcoming these limitations by combining the best features of computer and video systems and making them accessible from a distance.

The term *information technology* (IT) is sometimes used for the whole rapidly con-verging field of computing, video and tele-communications. Part One of this book begins with fundamental ideas about coding and transmitting information (Chapter 2), and then examines the basics of computer systems, hardware and soft-ware (Chapters 3 to 6). Chapters 7 and 8 explain the principles behind recent advances in telecommunications and video and how they marry with computer systems. Part Two shows how information technology affects us as individuals, both as employees and citizens. Part Three is a reference section; it contains further information which you may want to refer to as you read – especially the Glossary (page 198), which explains a wide range of techni-cal words connected with IT.

Information technology is at work in many different ways in the developed countries throughout the world. The six examples which follow here are typical of systems which you might find in day-to-day use. I only have space to describe them briefly, but after you have read this book you should be able to come back to them and understand the simple principles on

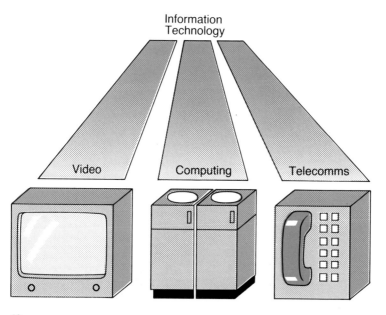

Information Technology

Video   Computing   Telecomms

which they are based. There is no mystery or magic about the equipment, but a lot of ingenuity is needed to plan what should be done and to make sure that the systems serve human needs – not the other way around.

Information unlimited – in the living-room

Susie and Charlie Taylor were fairly typical owners of a home microcomputer – they started out with great ideas of learning to program, but soon dropped into the habit of just playing arcade games on it. What changed the picture was when Susie discovered from her bank that an equally cheap device (called a *modem*) could connect the computer to the telephone and allow it to communicate with a vast information network called Prestel. The Prestel computers contain 250 000 'pages' of business, travel and general informa-

tion, any of which can be displayed on a television set just by typing out the page number on the keyboard. Unlike broadcast television, Prestel communication is two-way: by pressing different keys on the computer keyboard it is possible to send messages, order goods and catalogues and even buy computer software.

Susie's bank has linked up with a large firm of travel agents to offer their customers free access to Prestel for a trial period. The bank and travel agent's computers can be linked to the Prestel network, so customers can check their bank balances, find out about last-minute package holiday availability, and even make bookings and pay for them – all without stirring from their living-rooms. They can even 'talk to' the computer controlling the local airport arrivals board so they can find out if a flight is delayed before setting out to meet a friend. Picture Prestel allows users to see photographs of the holiday resorts and accommodation superimposed on the normal computer-type display – a feature that is also popular with house-hunters and estate agents (Figure 4).

Figure 3 Converging technology: a desktop computer with built-in telephone and screen.

Figure 4 Picture Prestel can display still photographs along with text.

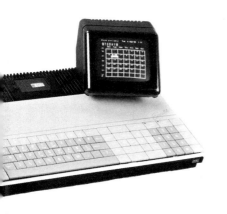

An intelligent card index

The detective was exhausted. He was interviewing a prime suspect in connection with yesterday's armed robbery at a high-street bank, but he was getting nowhere. The man continued to profess his innocence and seemed to have a watertight alibi. The detective had no way of disproving the man's story, but he had an odd feeling of familiarity about the crime. Where had he heard of a similar case a few months ago . . .?

He let a partner take over the questioning and tried a different approach. Taking his incident report, the eye-witness accounts and the details from the interview down to the computer room, he fed them all into the common bank of information that is being built up by police forces all over the country. This *database* contains details such as suspects' names, addresses, physical description (sex, height, weight, age and colouring), accent, any known aliases and associates, vehicles owned and driven, sightings at or near incidents and crimes, any criminal record, and a mass of other information including free space for any comments the detective wants to make. There are already thousands of facts held on dozens of witnesses and suspects in this investigation.

The detective decided to ask questions about previous crimes in his area. He looked first for any robberies in the previous 10 years which shared certain features with the one in hand: took place during daylight opening hours; use of a sawn-off shotgun; one of the robbers tall, thin and with a slight accent; use of a hired van as the getaway vehicle; and the crime coinciding with a street demonstration elsewhere in the town. No matches were found, but when he connected his mini-computer to the national network via the telephone, three similar-sounding crimes with most or all of these features were unearthed. Two of the three were in a town where his suspect had lived at the time, and the third report revealed a description pro-

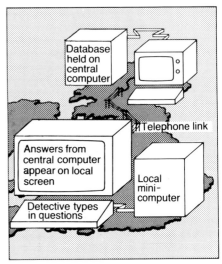

Figure 5 Information held in a central database can be made instantly available to detectives all over the country, using the telephone network to link computers.

vided by a van rental salesman that tallied closely with the suspect's own.

Further searches in this massive database revealed other connections and suspicious details. Armed with these, he returned to the interview room and, after further questioning, extracted enough information to get a search warrant for the man's home. Directly incriminating evidence connecting the man with the hiring of the getaway vehicle was found, and eventually the suspect confessed.

The computer database did not 'know' any facts that were not previously available on cards and paper at the various different police regional headquarters. But what it did do was make all of that information instantly accessible to each police force. It also enabled detectives pursuing different investigations to interrogate it by asking questions, and combinations of questions, about previous incidents and convictions.

Where time is money

Chris Morley is a currency dealer in a major banking capital. He does all his business by telephone, sending telexes to confirm major deals. Since he has many overseas customers, and prices can change from minute to minute, fast and efficient communications are vital to him: the seconds ticking away not only pile up the telephone bill, they can also make the difference between profit and loss on a currency exchange.

At one time, he had a number of separate telephones on his desk, a shared secretary in an outer office to dial outgoing calls, accept incoming calls, operate the telex machine and type the odd letter. He had to phone a broker for up-to-date exchange rates and to consult the daily newspapers, weekly magazines and other sources for background information on the state of the economies and currencies in various countries. The arrival of push-button telephones helped speed things up a bit, especially the ones with memories so that he could store the most-used numbers – useful for the long overseas dialling codes. A telephone-answering machine was another time-saving purchase, especially for receiving informa-

tion from contacts in different parts of the world, whose time zones made it hard for both parties to communicate during working hours. But still he needed a lot of separate devices: telephones, typewriter, telex, answering machine, and sometimes he still found he had missed an important call.

Now he has a single small *touch-screen* built into his desk-top with a separate keyboard that he sometimes uses as well. The screen has 64 squares, each of which can be activated by a finger-touch. By touching different squares he can use his screen as a telex machine, a telephone, a computer terminal and an electronic letter-sender, or a combination of these machines all at the same time. After noticing an incoming call from Japan or France, he can speak to his client and simultaneously call up information on the top half of the screen from a vast computer database (to which he subscribes) to quote exchange rates between any two world currencies, whether for immediate dealing or for an agreed date in the future. Pressing a different square on the screen gives him telex facilities to confirm the deal in writing – with part of the screen always reserved to advise him of any urgent incoming messages.

Figure 6 The City Business System in use. Touch screens allow users to control telephone, telex and computers with ease.

Teacher's friend in the corner

Although it's long past 4.00 pm, Laura Stewart is still in the classroom of the primary school where she teaches. She is working late in order to put the finishing touches to her project on whales with her class of nine-year-olds. It's due to begin next week and she has a large range of audio-visual resources, workcards and stories ready to arouse the children's interest. Because the pupils were keen to try out the school's recently acquired microcomputer, she wants to check what computer programs are available that could be integrated into the work that they are going to be doing.

The school has a trial membership of Micronet 800, a computer club within Prestel. Laura loads in the software, puts the telephone handset into the *acoustic coupler* and types out a *password*. After passing through the Prestel Welcome frame and main index page, she quickly finds herself roaming around the Micronet database. She locates the section labelled 'Education', and finds a number of possible programs suitable for the particular microcomputer that her school has bought. The

system allows her to try out demonstration programs free, although if she wants to store a program permanently, so that the school's computer can run it at any time, the school's account will be charged automatically by the Prestel computer.

The one she likes best is called ANIMAL. The pupil thinks of an animal and the program tries to guess what it is. Every time the program is unable to guess the animal, it asks the pupil to type in a question that would distinguish this animal from the ones the program already has details on. For example, if the program only 'knows' about fishes, the first time a pupil thinks of a whale, the program will, after exhausting its options, produce a message saying 'I give up. Tell me a question to distinguish whale from . . .?'. The pupil might type in 'Does it breast-feed its young?'. Then the program responds by asking 'What is the answer for whale?' and the pupil types 'Yes'. So the program actually starts by 'knowing' very few animals, but it has been designed to store all the details that are fed into it. Realising that it will 'learn' wrong answers as well as correct ones, Laura plans to check through the stored answers from time to

time. However, she likes the idea that the pupils will have to think up good questions, not just give the right answers, and also the fact that the computer program gradually increases the repertoire of animals that it 'knows' about. Of course, it doesn't really *know* about animals; it only appears to because it can repeat the questions it has been taught and compare the answers with those it has stored.

She types in the instruction to *download* the program into the computer's memory, and confirms her intention after she has been reminded of the price that the school will be charged (which is substantially less than the normal mail order price). Screens full of meaningless-looking characters are sent down the line and Laura then disconnects herself from the Prestel system. Rather to her surprise, she is able to load the program at her first attempt and it runs perfectly. The following week she is slightly disappointed to find that the pupils don't seem particularly impressed by her *telesoftware*, as it is called. However, they do take a delight in devising subtle questions to distinguish whales from other mammals, other sea-living creatures and other large animals.

```
Have you chosen an animal?
YES
Does it live in water?
YES
Is it a herring?
NO
Is it a whiting?
NO
Is it a salmon?
NO
```

```
NO
I give up. What is it?
WHALE
Tell me a question to distinguish
WHALE from the others.
DOES IT BREAST-FEED ITS YOUNG?
And the answer for whale is...?
YES
Another game?
```

Figure 7 Conversation between the user and the computer. The program presents the questions (lower case letters) and the user the answers (upper case letters).

Crash landing?

Co-pilot MacGregor is beginning to sweat. The tiny landing strip is looming up at alarming speed, but he daren't cut the throttle back any harder or he will risk stalling the engines. Night is falling quickly, and he knows there are steep hills ahead. One of his passengers is seriously ill and the ambulance is waiting at the airfield. With a strong tail-wind he is approaching the point of no return. Either he must try to climb out of this predicament, or go in to land, hoping to skid himself to a halt before the end of the runway . . . or else he'll have to take this whole course of instruction again!

For the aircraft that Co-Pilot MacGregor is flying is entirely imaginary. The cockpit controls are realistic to the last detail and every fine adjustment he makes affects not only the view on the wide-angle screen but also the seat-of-his-pants feelings provided by the motion of the mobile cockpit. However, the whole apparatus is mounted safely on the ground at a pilot training school where he is doing a conversion course in order to fly lighter planes than he had previously been qualified for.

The equipment uses advanced technology to recreate really convincing pilot's eye-views, showing the terrain surrounding the airport, the runway landing lights, foul-weather conditions and changing lighting/visibility conditions suitable to the time of day and latitude of the airport selected. The cockpit instruments show realistic readings for altitude, electrical measurements, warning lights, dials and radar screens, and are directly controlled by the same computer that generates the screen graphics.

Flight *simulators* like these are not only safer than letting trainee pilots fly real passengers. They also expose the pilot to a greater range of operating conditions and airports, give him more practice in less time, cost far less to run than real aircraft and are available for up to 20 hours a day without disrupting or endangering other day-to-day passenger or freight flights. Similar equipment is used to train pilots for helicopters and for military aircraft. The training is so effective that pilots do not always need to fly the real plane before being passed out as qualified!

Call in the expert

John is just setting off for a day's fishing when he finds that his car won't start. He lives in a remote village, miles from the nearest garage. Fortunately, his home is equipped with a videodisc player, and his wife recently bought him a new disc: the *Videodisc Manual of Motor Car Maintenance.* He puts the disc into the player, which is connected to an ordinary television set. He scans through the disc using a remote-control keypad and within a second or two has located the section on starting troubles.

The first question is about the noise the engine makes when he tries to start it. It plays different engine noises said to be typical of 'starter motor not engaging', or 'poor power supply'. Although he has no idea what the starter motor is, he is prepared to believe the disc when it informs him that it is this that has jammed, since that noise sounded just like the one his car made. The next question it asks is whether his gearbox is automatic or not. He knows the answer to that one: manual. The disc tells him to switch off his ignition, put the car into third gear and rock it back and forth with the handbrake off. He then tries the ignition again and is delighted to find that the engine starts first time.

Thinking this over while waiting for the fish to bite, John wonders why he always felt so helpless with car engines in the past. He reflects that the problem began when as a teenager his friends all seemed very knowledgeable about bikes and cars. John hadn't known what half the words meant and was shy of asking questions. He had tried looking at repair manuals, but the inside of his engine never looked much like the tidy diagrams and even when he knew what part was at fault, he often found it hard to know where to look for it – or even which way round to hold the manual!

Back at home he starts to explore other 'branches' of the videodisc sequence. He finds that in some cases he would have had to get professional help (for example, if he had had an automatic gearbox). In others, he could have followed simple instructions illustrated by film clips and animated diagrams. If the battery had been at fault, he is shown not only how to use jump leads to get started from another car engine, but also how to look after the battery and prevent trouble in the first place by routine maintenance. The commentary is simple to follow and friendly in tone, though at the touch of a button he finds a more technical commentary is available as an alternative.

Browsing through a section about possible problems with distributors, John is delighted to find an illustrated list of all the tools he would need first. A separate section on the major items illustrates the correct way to use them: for example, he sees a feeler gauge being used to check a gap between contact points – and also learns that he can use a credit card as a makeshift. The reference section explains more about how all the major systems operate, with practical advice about maintenance and repair. He takes a ten-question self-test on what he has learned, responding by pressing keys on the keypad, gets eight answers right and is directed to a revision sequence on the wrong answers.

Figure 8 Screen shot from *The Videodisc Manual of Motor Car Maintenance.* The user hears different engine sounds on the soundtrack and has to choose which one applies.

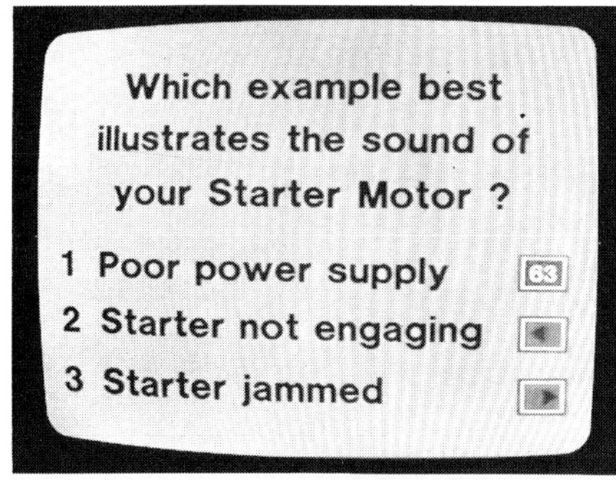

Which example best illustrates the sound of your Starter Motor ?

1 Poor power supply [⚏]
2 Starter not engaging [◀]
3 Starter jammed [▶]

Chapter 2: Information and communication

Data and information

Data is the word used for known facts, especially facts that are stored in a computer system or processed in some way. Computer data often looks pretty meaningless taken in isolation, like a fragment of printed music, some lines of code, or a knitting pattern. Unless you know the conventions, it is impossible to extract the information. To take a simple example, 310884 just looks like any old large number – an example of data; but if I tell you that it is a code for today's date, you can probably deduce the information that I am writing this on 31 August 1984. Data *becomes* information once it has been communicated and made meaningful to someone.

We receive information via a tremendous variety of means: words (spoken or written), pictures, symbols, music, numbers and gestures. This chapter is about changing methods of coding information and communicating it over long distances – telecommunications.

Roman alphabet and Arabic numerals

No-one knows exactly when human beings first developed spoken language, but since that immense leap forward in our ability to communicate, there have been surprisingly few milestones. Early attempts to leave or transmit permanent messages were based on pictures and pictographs, adequate for representing images, events and things, but hopelessly limited for communicating abstract ideas. Around 1000 BC, the Phoenicians made a breakthrough by inventing an alphabet. Later the Greeks and then the Romans developed different alphabets, but the principle of making letters or signs corres-

pond with spoken sounds revolutionised our ability to record and transmit ideas. Nowadays, although countries in the Middle East, the Soviet Union and the Far East do have different systems, the Roman alphabet of 26 letters and a space is an international standard.

Figure 9 Many different alphabets have been used through the ages but the Roman alphabet is now internationally accepted.

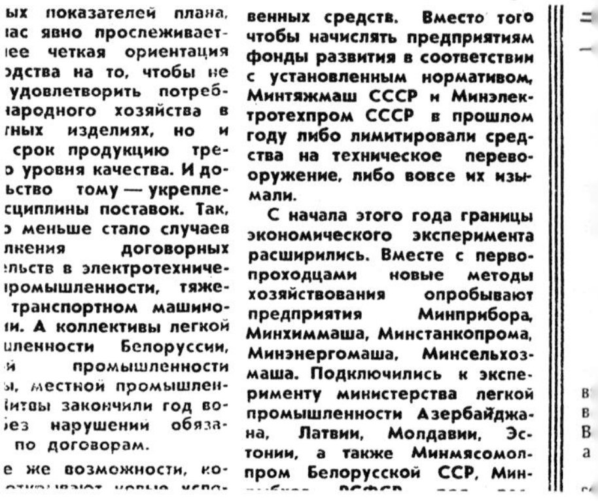

ых показателей плана, iac явно прослеживает- iee четкая ориентация эдства на то, чтобы не удовлетворить потреб- iародного хозяйства в гных изделиях, но и срок продукцию тре- э уровня качества. И до- ьство тому — укрепле- сциплины поставок. Так, э меньше стало случаев лкения договорных iльств в электротехниче- iромышленности, тяже- транспортном машино- iи. А коллективы легкой iленности Белоруссии, и промышленности iI, местной промышлен- iнты закончили год во- iез нарушении обяза- по договорам.

е же возможности, ко-

венных средств. Вместо того чтобы начислять предприятиям фонды развития в соответствии с установленным нормативом, Минтяжмаш СССР и Минэлектротехпром СССР в прошлом году либо лимитировали средства на техническое перевооружение, либо вовсе их изымали.

С начала этого года границы экономического эксперимента расширились. Вместе с первопроходцами новые методы хозяйствования опробуют предприятия Минприбора, Минхиммаша, Минстанкопрома, Минэнергомаша, Минсельхозмаша. Подключились к эксперименту министерства легкой промышленности Азербайджана, Латвии, Молдавии, Эстонии, а также Минмясомолпром Белорусской ССР, Мин-

Факт и комментарий

АКОМЬТЕСЬ:
ОНОМЕТР

...тся прибор, созданный казанскими специали-
...образный советчик начинающего автолюби-
...к для тех, кто еще не слишком «чувствует»

...деть нашу но-
...4? — предлагает
...уктор проекта
...авайте сядем в

...конструкторско-
...прибор, устрем.

...вать в потоке машин. — Если
стрелка в зеленом секторе, зна-
чит, двигатель работает нор-
мально, потребление топлива
наименьшее. Красное поле пре-
дупреждает о чрезмерной на-
...грузке на мотор и перерасходе

Испытания в Центральном науч-
но-исследовательском автомо-
бильном и автомоторном инсти-
туте показали, что, умело поль-
зуясь прибором, автолюбитель
сберегает до 20 процентов топлива. Прибор косвенно сигнали-
зирует и об отдельных неис-
правностях, например, о подго-
рании клапанов. Очень важна и
природоохранная функция эко-
...нометра: благодаря плавной ез-

В результате работ по конст-
рукторскому и технологическо-
му совершенствованию узлов и
систем, по увеличению надеж-
ности и долговечности автомо-
билей их пробег без капиталь-
ного ремонта уже достиг
150 тысяч километров.

Недавно на автозаводе вве-
ден в действие второй конвей-
ер, на котором собираются
75- и 110-тонные самосвалы.
Впереди у заводских конструк-
торов новые задачи: создание
машин грузоподъемностью 230
—250 тонн для особо крупных
карьеров.

Слава о белорусских автоса-
мосвалах давно перешагнула
границы республики. Сегодня
«БелАЗы» трудятся в 700 авто-
хозяйствах СССР и 35 государ-
ствах. Завод в Жодино стал
одним из крупнейших в Европе

Австри
«третьк

К гак
Институт
лем резу
им исслед
го мнени
выборы в
веденны в
ворится
то две но
рассчиты
восьми

ИТАЛ

Выс

РИМ. 7
Серия м
ций проти
стоялась
Они были
довщине

The Roman system of writing down numbers, however, was a major barrier to progress in arithmetic and all the advances that depended on it, like navigation, astronomy and physics. Roman numbers are still used sometimes – on old-fashioned clock-faces, marking volume numbers on books and journals, or even giving the copyright date on television credits! Translating a long Roman date is bad enough, but most people would find doing a complex calculations in Roman numbers almost impossible (Figure 10).

In the first 1000 years AD, while Western countries were still labouring away with Roman numerals, the modern decimal system of using different symbols (0 to 9) for numbers with zero also showing place value was perfected in India. As a result, by 500 AD Indian mathematicians had solved problems which had baffled the greatest Greek and Roman scholars. Between 800 and 1500 AD, the Indian method spread to the West, at first through the Hindu traders' ancient caravan route through Baghdad. Rather unfairly, the symbols 0 to 9 are usually called Arabic numbers after the Arabs who transmitted the invention from India to Europe.

Most people in the Western world learn these two coding systems – the Roman alphabet and Arabic numerals – as children. If they learn to type, the same letters and numbers appear on the keyboard, which is arranged in a roughly similar way whatever the language though some need special accents and some countries use slightly different lay-outs. If they travel abroad they will still be able to read (if not pronounce!) street signs, prices and telephone numbers almost anywhere.

Modern international communication methods depend on electronic handling of data expressed in these two coding systems. The general name given to a letter, number or punctuation mark – anything of a kind you might find on a typewriter keyboard – is *alphanumeric* character.

(a) (b) (c)

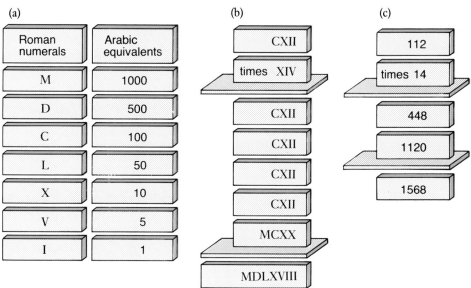

Figure 10 (a) The Roman system of representing numbers held back progress in arithmetic and mathematics for centuries. (b) A simple multiplication sum Roman-style. (c) The same sum in Arabic numerals: (d) (*opposite page*) Roman numerals are still sometimes used for clock faces and dates.

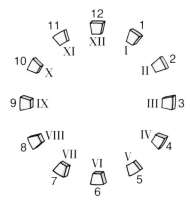

MDCCCCLXXXVII stands for 1987

There is a widely accepted convention called *ASCII* (pronounced 'askey') for coding alphanumeric characters as numbers. It is explained on page 196. For the present, the important thing is that any message that can be expressed in ASCII characters can be turned into a unique set of numbers – and back again.

One-way and two-way communication

Face-to-face conversation is a two-way process: you speak to me, I reply to you, and so on. Telephone conversations are two-way too, but written forms of communication, such as letters or newspapers, are normally one-way only. Although the person who receives the letter may send a reply later, at the time it is sent the sender doesn't know if it will even be received safely. Broadcast television and radio are inherently one-way: transmissions may be seen and heard, but not responded to – other than by changing channel or switching off.

Computer experts call communications in both directions *duplex*, and in one direction only *simplex*. Some links allow data to travel in both directions but not at the same time – for example, a walkie-talkie set that has to be switched between 'listen' and 'send'. This is known as *half-duplex* (Figure 11).

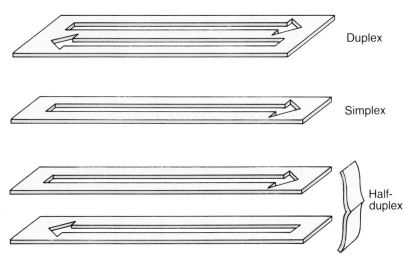

Duplex

Simplex

Half-duplex

Figure 11 A link may allow communication in both directions at once (duplex), in one direction only (simplex), or in both directions but not at the same time (half-duplex).

Codes and conventions

Two-way communication depends on having a coding system that is understood both by sender and receiver, and an agreed convention about signalling the beginning and end of the message. In speech, the coding system is a language like English or Spanish; the convention that one person speaks at a time may seem too obvious to mention. In fact, the signals that people use in conversations and meetings are often non-verbal; 'body language' varies from culture to culture. For example, lowering the pitch of the voice may mean the end of a sentence or dropping the eyes the end of a contribution; a sharp intake of breath may signal the desire to interrupt; catching the chairman's eye or raising one's hand may indicate the desire to speak in a formal setting like a debate; a clenched fist may indicate anger.

When these visual signals are not possible, more formal signals may be needed. The confusion created on the telephone by a 'crossed line' demonstrates how dependent we are on knowing whose turn is next. Over an intercom set or radio link, signals like 'Are you receiving me?' and 'Hearing you loud and clear' may be needed to establish contact, and 'over and out' to mark that the conversation is over. The technical convention required for a communications link is called a *protocol*. Communications protocols have to be strictly observed for contact to be made and messages to be exchanged.

Whenever computer terminals can give humans access to sensitive information, agreed conventions and special passwords are used to prevent unauthorised people from getting access. To get money or account information using a high-street cash-dispenser you need not only a special card but also the right Personal Identification Number (Figure 12). You have to type in your number correctly and you must follow the exact procedure for confirming the amount and removing your card before the money is dispensed. The exchange of signals between the user and the cash-dispenser program has to follow the rules strictly, otherwise it will be aborted (for example, the cash-dispenser will keep the cash card and withhold the money). This is an example of an agreed protocol between human and machine.

Figure 12 The exchange between a customer and a bank's computer is regulated by strict conventions.

Overcoming distance

Having invented an alphabet which meant that messages could be written down, the peoples of the Ancient World began to transmit them over increasing distances using runners, horses or boats. For urgent short-distance messages, other principles were devised: during the Persian Wars in 480 BC soldiers reflected sunlight off their shields to send a warning signal. The same principle is used in the heliograph, which reflects flashes of sunlight off a moveable mirror. It is, of course, useless at night or in bad weather.

In 1588 in Britain, a chain of beacon fires was used to spread the news of the threatened invasion by the Spanish Armada. Other visual methods include smoke signals, Aldis lamps and semaphore. For all of these, you need to know when to expect a signal, where to look for it, and to have the source in your direct line of sight. Long-distance communication is only possible in good lighting conditions and depends on a chain of manned look-out posts.

In order to transmit messages in code, sender and receiver must first agree on a coding system and a protocol. Many codes represent each letter and number by a combination of long and short signals: these could be dashes and dots, flashes of light, or sounds. In a visual system, each look-out post would have to record the message and relay it to the next one – a time-consuming and error-prone process. Although light itself travels incredibly fast, visual communications are very slow and primitive because of the time it takes to code each letter and the rate at which human beings can detect and decode them. Short flashes have to be long enough to be seen and long flashes long enough to be noticeably different from short ones. Even a skilled operator might take an average of a couple of seconds to code each word.

However, once the letters and numbers have been coded, the message can be transmitted quickly as electric impulses

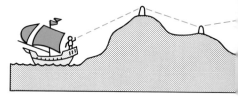

Figure 13 In the past, urgent messages were sent using beacon fires and flashing lights. These methods depended on good weather and a clear line of sight.

along metal cables without needing human intervention. By 1900, organisations that needed fast communication between continents were using the electric telegraph which worked on this principle. But telegraphy was expensive then and only worked between suitably equipped stations linked by special cables and manned by trained operators. In addition, electrical impulses had the disadvantage of fading as they travelled down a wire, and they suffered from distortion due to stray electro-

Figure 14 Signal, noise and the effect of transmission over long distances.

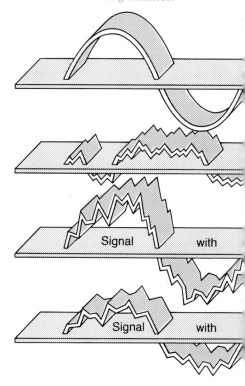

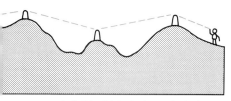

magnetic fields. *Noise* is the technical term for any unwanted effects that may mask or distort any signal, whether it consists of electrical impulses, light or actual sound. In a noisy channel, parts of the signal may be lost or altered (Figure 14). (A good communications channel is said to have a high *signal-to-noise ratio*.) So it was the invention of the telephone which marked the real beginnings of a profound revolution for ordinary citizens. Operating a telephone requires no special skills nor knowledge of a special coding system. It transmits ordinary speech using a quite different principle from telegraphy (Chapter 7). And this brings us to one of the most fundamental choices in information-handling: *analogue* versus *digital*.

Analogue and digital

Everyday quantities like light, sound, time, pressure and temperature exist in some *amount*. They can be measured and represented by *analogy* – by the movement of a pointer on an exposure meter, the trace of the sound-wave on a screen, the sweep of a seconds hand round a clock-face, the movement of a barometer dial, the rise and fall of a column of mercury as it expands and contracts with temperature. These are all *analogue* methods of measuring analogue quantities.

A *digital* watch measures time in a quite different way from a traditional (analogue) one. It counts the exact number of vibrations of a tiny crystal within one second, and turns that into a digital display of minutes and seconds. There are many digital instruments for measuring analogue quantities (Figure 15). Because most electronic devices work on digital principles, converting analogue into digital and back again is a vital process in modern information processing.

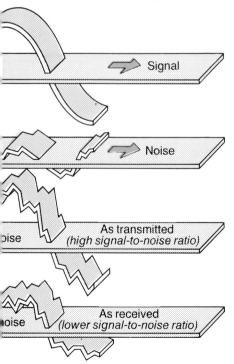

Signal

Noise

As transmitted
(high signal-to-noise ratio)

As received
(lower signal-to-noise ratio)

(a)

(b)

Figure 15 (a) A digital thermometer displays the temperature directly in numbers. (b) The mercury in an analogue thermometer rises and falls with changes in temperature. The user reads its length against a fixed scale marked with numbers.

Speech is an analogue signal consisting of complicated sound waves. Telephones transform these sound waves into electrical waves of a similar shape and size (see Figure 16. But the further the electrical waves have to travel, the weaker the signal becomes and the worse the noise (distortion). We will see in Chapter 7 how modern telephone systems can combat these problems – once the analogue signals have been turned into digital ones. As in computing, the digital signals used in modern telephone systems are handled as numbers of a special kind called *binary* numbers.

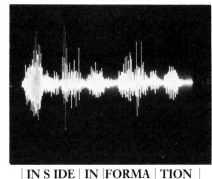

'HELLO'

| H | ELL | O |

'INSIDE'

| IN | S | I | DE |

'INSIDE INFORMATION'

| IN S IDE | IN |FORMA | TION |

Figure 16 Electrical waves produced by words spoken into a telephone.

The binary system

Most human counting systems have the number 10 at their base. We count everyday numbers in powers of 10: ones, 10s, 100s, 1000s. . . . Perhaps this evolved because our 10 fingers made a convenient counting aid. For some purposes, other bases are more convenient: counting bottles in dozens and grosses (units of 12 and 144) may have arisen because packing cases with holes arranged three times four are a convenient shape to handle. The 24-hour period of the earth's rotation makes 12s and 60s important for measuring time.

Yet other everyday things suggest a number base of two. A light switch is either on or off, a padlock is locked or unlocked, a question is answered yes or no, a gate is open or closed. Things with only two possible states are most easily represented by arithmetic based on the number two. Computers use the binary system because their components are either 'on' or 'off', corresponding to the binary numbers 1 and 0.

If you are interested in how to turn ordinary numbers eg 14 (base-10), into their binary equivalents, ie 1110 (base-two), you can find out on page 195. But you don't *need* to be able to do binary arithmetic in order to grasp the importance of the system for modern information handling.

Redundancy and feedback

Redundancy is a technical word for the extent to which parts of a message can be predicted from a knowledge of other parts. Ordinary English has a high degree of redundancy. If you try to read a newspaper story after someone has blacked out one word in two, you may be surprised at how little of the meaning has been lost (Figure 17a). But if you try the same trick on a tele-message or telex, you will find it almost impossible – unless the sender has been very extravagant – because most of the redundant words will have been left out.

Messages with no redundancy would be vulnerable to the least bit of noise. If there is an important change of plan someone might send a message saying:

DO NOT REPEAT NOT MEET PLANE 0900 TOMORROW

The words REPEAT NOT are, strictly speaking, redundant; but if the con-

sequences of losing the first two words of the shorter message 'DO NOT MEET PLANE 0900 TOMORROW' are important enough, then it is certainly wise to include them.

Any message consisting of normal sentences actually contains lots of built-in redundancy. To test this, try getting someone to strike out one letter in two throughout a sentence and see whether you can still guess its meaning (Figure 17). (It gets *much* harder if the spaces between words are taken away.) Anyone who can read a language has unconsciously picked up a lot of information about the frequencies of various letters in the alphabet and uses this knowledge to fill in the most probable letters. In different languages, different letters crop up with different, but characteristic frequencies. For example, in English the commonest letter is an 'e' and nearly all words contain at least one vowel. Try recording a speaker's words by writing down only the consonants in what is said.

Figure 17 Redundancy: (a) Although one word in every three has been deleted in this newspaper paragraph you can probably guess the gist of the story. (b) Can you read this sentence in which every other letter and all the spaces have been removed? (c) A clue: the same sentence with the spaces restored.

You will probably find that you can reconstruct this improvised 'shorthand' quite easily. Cn y ndrstnd ths sntnc?

Redundancy can only preserve the accuracy of a message if the person on the receiving end has the necessary knowledge to capitalise on it. You can only supply the missing letters or words in the experiments suggested above if you are familiar with the language they are written in. Imagine trying to take a dictated message in an unfamiliar foreign language.

Electronic communications depend on machines to code, transmit, forward, boost and decode messages written in languages that the machines do not speak or write. Generally such machines have no information about the likely structure of the words or sentences, nor even any idea that spaces or full stops are different in kind from other letters that make up the message. Compared with a human operator who might be able to guess a replacement for a missing or incorrect character, machines tend to be both unintelligent and uninformed. (This makes them impartially so for all messages and all languages, which may be an advantage for international communications.) To prevent transmission errors they therefore need to build redundancy of a different kind into the message.

Check digits are a useful way of doing this for a system that depends on numbers. The last digit of any International Standard Book Number (ISBN – see page 2) is a check digit, calculated in a set way from all the other digits so that if an error is made in copying the number, the sum no longer checks and the ISBN can be queried. When using binary numbers to represent ASCII characters, up to seven digits are needed to represent each one (Figure 19): thus 'C' can be shown as 1000011. An eighth digit can be added as a check, so as to make all the digits add up to

Figure 18 Speed writing is a quick method of recording a speaker's words, taking advantage of the redundancy built into the language.

Figure 19 The letters BBC can be represented as a string of binary 1s and 0s according to a widely accepted code called ASCII.

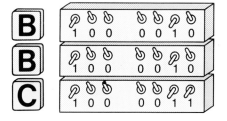

an even number; this is called a *parity check*. For example, the rule could be 'If the number of 1s is odd, add a 1; if the number of 1s is even, add a zero.' That way if a 1 were turned into a 0 by mistake, the sum would not check and the error could be detected and put right.

Even with each character having a built-in parity check, severe noise could lead to two mistakes that might cancel each other out. Other checks can be added, so that each group of characters and each chunk of data is checked as it is transmitted. Digital communications links maintain continuous checking of the incoming data. The whole process of querying a discrepancy and having part of the message retransmitted can be done automatically: the human users of the system may never even realise that it is going on.

Measuring information

The smallest unit of information that can exist in computing is one binary digit, 0 or 1, called a *bit* for short. This is the basic building-block from which characters, words and messages are constructed. A group of eight bits is commonly called a *byte*. Since 11111111 (base-two) equals 255 (base-10), one byte can represent any of the 256 combinations possible (from 0 to 255).

A keyboard based on the Roman alphabet has 26 upper-case letters, 26 lower-case letters, 10 numerals and 34 punctuation marks, making a total of 96 characters. The ASCII system also allows for 32 other characters (eg to signal the beginning or end of text, a carriage return or line feed, a backspace or delete function). To represent these 128 different combinations, the ASCII system allocates a number from 0 to 127 to each one. This takes up seven out of the eight bits in a byte, leaving one free for parity checking (page 196).

Information can be measured in bits or bytes, though both units are rather small for everyday use. Each page of this book can store around 350 words averaging seven characters each (including spaces). That makes around 2450 characters per page of solid text, requiring 2450 bytes or roughly 20 000 bits. Table 1 shows how some other methods of storing information compare.

Table 1:
Amount of data stored in various forms

	No of bits
Telemessage (50 characters)	400
Office memo (350 words)	20 000
Newspaper-quality photograph	100 000
Single frame of colour television	1 000 000
High-quality colour photograph	2 000 000

These numbers are only a rough guide, but they give an idea of the varying magnitudes involved.

Measuring data transfer

The rate of transferring data from one place to another can be measured in bits per second (Table 2). Transmission speeds on the existing public telephone network vary widely. On an ordinary *voice-grade* line, transmission might be at 1200 bits per second (bps), or even at 2400 bps. On the newer digital systems (page 108) speeds of up to 64 000 bps are possible.

Even on the analogue network, computer data can be transmitted by telephone using a gadget called a *modem* (page 105). Modem speeds are usually quoted in *baud*; for most practical purposes, 1 baud equals one bit per second. A home computer enthusiast might have a 300-baud modem: it can receive or transmit data at 300 bps, or around 43 bytes per second. This means sending text at 43 characters, or about six words, per second, so it would take about a minute to transmit a page of text from this book. Faster modems can handle up to 1200 baud on voice-grade lines, and even up to 9600 baud on certain lines, reducing transmission times correspondingly. Further gains in speed tend to make both modems and telephone lines disproportionately expensive.

Why should faster tranfer speeds be desirable? It isn't just a question of keeping telephone bills down: the nature of the message may *demand* a faster method. Pictures, for example, demand far more bits to code and store their contents than the same area of text. Even a low-quality black-and-white newspaper photograph may need 1 000 000 bits, and a high-quality colour photograph perhaps 20 times as many. *Facsimile transmission* (page 116) allows still pictures to be sent down telephone lines at speeds of up to 9600 baud. For moving pictures a completely different principle is needed. To view normal-speed colour TV pictures requires a transmission speed of around 90 million baud – far beyond the capacity of a telephone cable.

The huge figures for colour television and cinema reflect the wastefulness of coding detailed and moving pictorial information point-by-point (see Chapter 8). Furthermore, data transmission speeds tell you nothing about the rate at which information is received or digested. If the television is constantly switched on but paid no more attention than the wallpaper, or if the cinema audience is not watching the film, then no matter how many millions of bits of data are transmitted, the rate of *information transfer* may be negligible.

Table 2: Transmission speeds for different kinds of data in bits per second.

Morse operator	30
Touch typist	40
Telex machine	50
Slow dictation	100
Cheap computer modem	300
Silent reading	400
Expensive computer modem	9600
High-speed digital telephone line	64 000
Hi-fi music broadcast	400 000
Compact disc player	700 000
Colour television	90 million
Cinema moving pictures	900 million +

Figure 20 Three ways of sharing out the band width available in a coaxial cable.

(a) Three hi-fi music bands at 500 000 baud each.

(b) Twenty-four telephone lines at 64 000 baud each.

(c) More than 30 000 telex lines at 50 baud each.

Communication channels and bandwidth

Communication channels vary in their capacity to carry information. The telephone system uses a network of copper cables each of which *could* carry over 15 million baud. Normally these cables are used to carry 24 simultaneous telephone lines of 64 000 baud each. The same capacity could be shared out differently, eg over 30 000 telex lines at 50 baud or three hi-fi music channels at 500 000 baud, carrying a much larger range of frequencies. However, there would not be enough room for even a single television channel.

Laying lots of cables to link everyone who wants to receive all these different kinds of signal would be quite impracticable. Fortunately, the discovery of radio waves in the nineteenth century brought the possibility of communication without wires. In 1901, Marconi succeeded in sending a wireless telegraph across the Atlantic, less than half a century after the first transatlantic telegraph cable had been laid; countries all over the world set up radio transmitting stations soon afterwards and the new radio receivers were called 'wireless' sets. The age of public broadcasting had arrived.

Radio waves form part of the spectrum of electromagnetic waves (page 192). Their wavelength is measured in metres and their frequency in cycles per second or *Hertz* (Hz) (see page 196 for fractions and multiples of these units). The shorter the wavelength, the higher the frequency. It was soon found that high-frequency waves could carry more information since more 'space' (technically known as *bandwidth*) is available at higher frequencies.

Analogue voice-grade telephone lines only carry frequencies between 300 Hz and 3300 Hz, the range traditionally considered adequate to reproduce the human male voice. This cuts out most of the higher frequencies that are present, especially in female voices. Anyone who has listened to a radio phone-in programme knows how much lower in quality the tele-phone voices sound; radio broadcasts can carry up to 18 000 Hz allowing more faithful reproduction of voices and music. Chapter 7 explains how light waves offer vastly more bandwidth than radio waves.

Electronic information

We have seen how their new counting system revolutionised the work of the Indian mathematicians. The Roman alphabet led to the publishing industry and also created the condition of illiteracy, ie the inability to communicate through reading and writing. The ability of modern electronic techniques to code, store, transmit and decode alphanumeric characters both quickly and cheaply could have even more profound long-term effects on our patterns of work, education and leisure. Understanding why will take us inside the most important invention of all time: the computer.

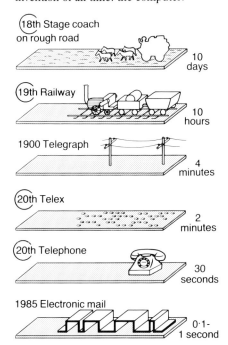

18th Stage coach on rough road — 10 days

19th Railway — 10 hours

1900 Telegraph — 4 minutes

20th Telex — 2 minutes

20th Telephone — 30 seconds

1985 Electronic mail — 0·1-1 second

Figure 21 The time needed to send a short message from Glasgow to London has fallen sharply since the 18th century.

Chapter 3: Inside the computer

Computers come in all shapes and sizes. For ease they are usually divided into three categories: *mainframe, mini* and *micro*, which basically mean big, middling and small. Generally speaking, mainframe computers are expensive, powerful, have large memories and are split into many separate parts. They can be used by lots of people all at the same time, often from a distance. Microcomputers, on the other hand, are cheaper and smaller, and usually have some or all of their different bits packaged together so that the system is easy to carry around. They also have smaller memories and work more slowly than mainframes. Most micros are used by just one person at a time; some micros – often called *personal computers* – belong to someone who keeps it at home or at work and who is its sole user.

Minicomputers come in between micros and mainframes in size, power, memory and price. A typical mini might have between 5 and 50 different users. However, the distinctions between the three types of computer are not sharp, and they are constantly being overtaken by new developments. Some recent mainframes are smaller than minis of the late 1970s; some recent micros have larger memories than typical minicomputers, and so on. A dealer might describe the same machine as a mini or a micro depending on whether he was selling or buying!

Mainframe computers are used for a wide range of purposes, and often by many different people, in large organisations. Mini and microcomputers tend to be used by small businesses, schools and colleges, and home users; micros are sometimes used as personal computers. (See Chapter 4 for some examples of the different systems at work.) Regardless of size, appearance and cost, all computers work on the same lines, as I shall explain in this chapter. The first and very fundamental principle to define is the difference between *hardware* and *software*.

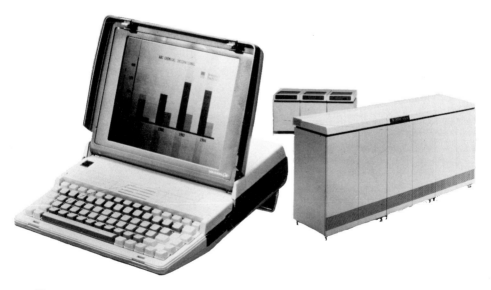

Hardware and software

Hardware is the general name for all the equipment which makes up the computer – the boxes, screens and keyboards. The term software covers the programs and data which make the hardware do what you want it to. It's like a hi-fi system, where the amplifier, loudspeakers, turntable and so on are all hardware, and the music on the records or cassette tapes is the software. What you get out of the hardware depends on the software you choose to put in.

This analogy should not be pushed too far, however: a hi-fi system can only do one thing – namely reproduce sound. A computer, on the other hand, can do any job which can be spelled out in enough detail. The secret of how a computer can be a general-purpose machine lies in the way that one piece of software (*program*) can easily be replaced by another.

A *program* is a list of instructions that the computer can obey, written in a special language. Data here means the words, numbers or pictures which the program processes. The same program can be made to do many different jobs by keeping the data separate from the instructions about how to process it. The same payroll pro-gram can be made to print out wage slips for different companies in different places by treating the rates and employee details as data instead of building them into the program.

Programs are usually prepared in advance, and before you can *run* (ie use) a program, you have to *load* (ie enter) it into the computer. After you have finished with one program, you might decide to feed a different one into the computer, or you might switch it off. The first program will then have been 'forgotten' and cannot be run again without being re-loaded.

Figure 22 Modern computers come in various shapes and sizes. From left to right: a lap-held personal micro; a business mini; an IBM mainframe.

The four-stage model

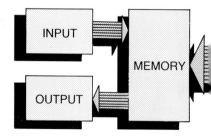

Any information system can be thought of as carrying out four kinds of activity: input, memory, processing and output. These activities may be performed in distinct stages or they may be performed continuously, overlapping each other.

Imagine someone working in an office, receiving input – information about the outside world – in the form of memos, letters, telephone calls or visitors. That input is stored in the person's memory and processed by their brain. The result may be output in the form of writing or typing, a 'phone call, a verbal instruction or an unspoken decision.

Computers are far less flexible than humans about how they handle information. They need *input* devices to turn words and figures into a form which they can handle, ie binary numbers. Once the information has been transferred from the input device into the computer's internal memory, the processor acts on it according to the instructions in the program.

On occasion everyone has to retrieve information from other sources to complete a task. For example, sometimes you might have to look up something in a reference book, or pick up the 'phone and dial Directory Enquiries. Other times, you may have all the information you need in your own head. In computer terms, this corresponds to the difference between *external memory* and *internal memory*.

Programs usually have to be loaded from external memory whenever they are needed, though some very basic or frequently used programs may be permanently fitted to the computer (Chapter 6). Once processing is complete, the results are passed to a special output device, which transforms the data back into figures, drawings and words that humans can understand.

Some people imagine that all computers have huge memories, but this is far from the truth. Their *internal* memories are often surprisingly small, limited and usually *volatile* – ie everything is forgotten when you switch off. So all computers depend heavily on external memory – sometimes called *backing store* – to store almost unlimited amounts of software.

Computers' internal memories vary enormously. Their sizes are usually quoted

Figure 23 The four main stages of computer operation.

in kilobytes (K) or Megabytes (Mb). One kilobyte is just over 1000 bytes and could store around 150 words of text (less than half the words on this page, see page 29). One Megabyte is over a million bytes, and could store this entire book twice over. The smallest micro ever sold had just 1 K of internal memory, though memories of up to 64 K were common among micros of the early 1980s. Business micros seldom have less than 64 K of memory, and the normal capacity by the mid-1980s is from 128 K up to 1024 K (1 Mb). A typical mini-computer might have at least 3 Mb – enough to hold this book six times over. Mainframe computers have larger memories again, anywhere from 5 Mb upward.

Compared with computers, humans have enormous memories. According to a famous psychologist, a 50-year-old person may carry around the equivalent of 10 000 million bits in their head: that's well over 1000 Megabytes. Much of this memory is more akin to computer programs than to data. During each lifetime, a person acquires a lot of 'software' as a result of informal learning, deliberate teaching and their experience of the world; however, most people don't memorise large numbers of facts but prefer to find out where to locate them. By contrast, computers have to be loaded with the correct software for each job. When a person says 'my mind went a blank', they don't mean it literally. But a computer processor's 'mind' does this between each task.

There are lots of other differences between computer processing and human thought, many of them outside the scope of this book. Computers cannot think origi-nally, experience emotions or create jokes. Humans have many advantages even for some mundane jobs that *can* be compu-terised: they don't need to be programmed specially, they are mobile, they can see and hear and they can apply common sense – for example to query anything unusual. However, computers excel at jobs like the routine processing of massive amounts of data, and the repetitive control of mass production. They are incredibly fast and accurate, never bored or forgetful, and don't need tea-breaks or holidays.

Figure 24 The size of internal memory in computers varies widely.

35

Input

Input devices are used to turn programs and data into the binary codes that the processor can deal with. Going back to the comparison with a hi-fi system again, music can be fed into most amplifiers by a record turntable, a cassette deck, a radio tuner or (live) through a microphone. In computer terms, these are all input devices.

At one time input depended on punching holes on paper card or tape: a hole meant '1', no hole represented '0'. A separate machine was needed to read this information into the computer. Old-fashioned telex machines use paper tape in a similar way. Nowadays, input is often made directly to the computer in a wide variety of forms: each requires an appropriate input device.

Keyboard

The most common input device is the keyboard, which looks very like the keyboard of an electric typewriter. Alphanumeric characters are entered by pressing the appropriate keys. The usual arrangement is called QWERTY after the top row of letters. (In some European countries it reads AZERTY instead.) However, even the fastest touch typist cannot hope to keep up with computer processing speeds, so some direct way of feeding in data is needed whenever computers are handling large volumes of data of the same kind. This is not only quicker than typing everything in, it also avoids the main source of mistakes.

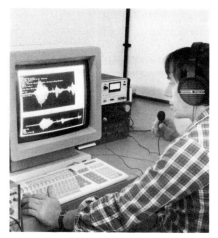

Figure 25 Special software enables a computer to accept input directly from speech.

Figure 26 The QWERTY keyboard is still the most common input device for computers.

MCR and OCR

Banks have to process large numbers of cheques, and it is quicker and better for the information on them to be fed straight into the computer. This is made possible by special symbols printed in magnetic ink on the bottom of each cheque, and the system is called Magnetic ink Character Recognition (MCR). Optical Character Recognition (OCR) depends on printing information in a special typeface so that it can be 'read' by a machine. Other systems allow ordinary typewriting and even hand-writing to be fed in. Some can only deal with capital letters; others require the writer to be trained to make letters in a particular way.

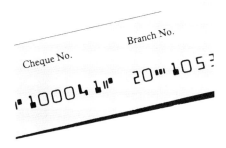

Figure 27 A graphics tablet allows shapes to be fed into a computer by tracing their outline.

Bar codes

Another useful form of computer input is the *bar code*. A bar code appears on the back cover of this book. The information is encoded in the varying thickness and number of the black bars; sometimes the information is also given in letters and numbers for humans to read. A special wand is passed over the bars at a steady speed. This converts the pattern of black and white into a string of binary 0s and 1s. Bar code readers have been common in supermarkets for some time but they are

Figure 28 A bar code reader in use.

also spreading into other areas. For example, in 1984 the computer magazine *Acorn User* offered its readers a bar code reader for £50 and began printing its monthly program listings in bar code format as well as in conventional form. Feeding pro-grams in in this way is quicker than typing. The program supplied with the reader has built-in error detection so that the user hears a bleep if a line is misread, and can feed it in again. *Dot-matrix printers* (see page 44) can print bar codes if controlled by a suitable program.

Speech input

Instead of having to spell out each character, it would be more convenient simply to tell the processor what to do in spoken words. Unfortunately, turning spoken instructions into consistent patterns of binary numbers is *very* complicated. People have widely different accents and dialects; 'voice-prints' are as individual as finger-prints. Furthermore, whenever we speak, we tend to leave many things unsaid, assuming that the listener will guess them from the context. To allow the processor to do this kind of 'filling in' needs a very sophisticated approach to programming. At present, voice recognition units can only respond to a limited number of words and tend to need special training on each voice. But this type of input may become much more important in the future.

Graphics tablets

These allow shapes to be 'traced out' with a *light-pen* and thereby loaded directly into the computer. The tablet turns the analogue movement of the pen into digital pulses that the computer can process. Some light-pens allow you to 'draw'

directly onto the screen; others only allow you to select from pre-defined choices. Input devices like the *mouse* (Figure 42) depend on special screen displays and are covered in the Output section (page 44).

Converters

I have already mentioned that a modem can be used to code telephone signals into the digital form that the processor can handle. *Analogue-to-digital (A-to-D) converter* is the general name for any device that converts analogue data into digital: a D-to-A converter does the reverse. Computers can use these to control robots and production processes.

Sensors

Many robots are equipped with *sensors* to detect touch, temperature, or sounds. The information from a robot sensor can be fed into the computer, and this *feedback* informs the program when an action has been completed successfully (Figure 29).

Figure 29 A three-dimensional input device. The tip of the arm traces the surface of a solid object and the shape is digitised and stored in the computer. It can then be displayed on the screen from any angle.

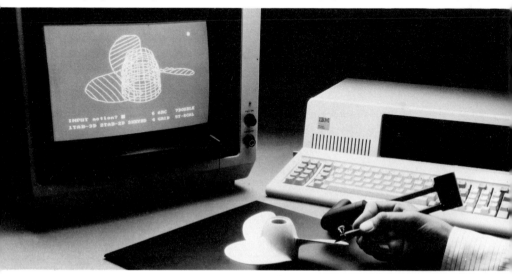

The processor

A *microprocessor* is simply a processor on a single chip of silicon. Modern micro-computers owe their performance, price and compactness to these remarkable chips. Their workings are fascinating but largely irrelevant to this book. Most of the time, computer users can forget about the binary goings-on inside the processor. The other parts of the system – input devices, memory and output devices – have a much more direct impact on them.

Inside the processor, thousands of tiny electrical switches are either 'off' or 'on'. Each 'off' or 'on' represents an atom of information: a binary 0 or 1, or bit. But the processor doesn't deal with bits *individually*, any more than humans read books letter by letter. It groups them into 'words' consisting of one or more bytes. Thus an eight-bit micro processes words one byte at a time. More recent and larger micros can process 16 bits at once; larger computers may have 32- or 64-bit 'words'.

Figure 30 Inside a microcomputer: the processor, RAM and ROM are indicated.

In theory the more bits a processor deals with at once the better. In practice there are many other important limitations on speed. For example, the processor has an internal clock to keep all the operations in step with each other. This pulses at a frequency of millions of times per second. How quickly the processor can move information in and out of memory is also very important. Whether a 16-bit micro-computer will actually deliver results faster than an eight-bit micro also depends a lot on the software which is controlling it. And using the world's fastest mainframe in an inconvenient place may work out slower in practice than having a 'slow' micro on the spot.

You may hear a processor referred to as a *central processing unit* or cpu, and the other parts of the system collectively called *peripherals*. This use of words derives from mainframe computing in which the pro-cessor is usually housed centrally in a computer room and all the *terminals* linked to it are scattered around on the periphery. Even when they are all in the same room, some people still call all the bits that plug into a microcomputer its peripherals.

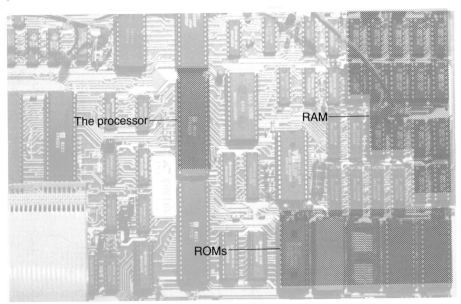

The processor

RAM

ROMs

Memory

We have already seen that computers have two kinds of memory, internal and external (Figure 31). Information can be retrieved (fetched) much faster from internal memory, but it is more expensive to provide than external memory.

Internal memory: RAM and ROM

Internal memory is of two kinds. *Random Access Memory* (RAM) is the computer's short-term working-space and can be used like a scribbling pad or blackboard. During a second of its working life, a computer's RAM may be 'overwritten' with new contents thousands of times. *Read Only Memory* (ROM) can only be 'read from', it cannot be 'written on'. ROM is used to store programs which are needed so often that it would be a nuisance to keep having to load them (Chapter 6). Comparing a computer system with a hi-fi system again, ROM resembles a cassette that can only be played, not used for recording. RAM is more like a blank cassette tape which can be recorded, wiped clean, and re-recorded. The processor can retrieve information from anywhere within either kind of internal memory (RAM and ROM) at random, very quickly. This makes it different from some kinds of external memory which have to be searched through in a particular order.

External memory

Cassettes

The same audio cassette you might play in a music centre can also serve as external memory for a computer. It isn't ideal for the purpose, because it is *serial-access*, not *random-access*: that means to find something at the end of the tape, you have to play it right through. Since the tape travels at its usual speed (under 2 inches per second) this means snail's-pace loading: even a simple program takes minutes to load. However, because cassette recorders are cheap and widespread, many home computer users rely on them for external memory.

Floppy discs

For serious use, random-access storage is essential. *Floppy discs* are rather like very flimsy 45 rpm records enclosed in a paper sleeve. Special *disc drives* locate and read their information while spinning the disc round at high speed. Large amounts of information can be read off or written on in seconds rather than minutes. Unfortunately for the home computer owner, a disc drive is expensive, often costing as much as the microcomputer.

Discs are easily damaged by dust, magnetic fields, or rough treatment, so it

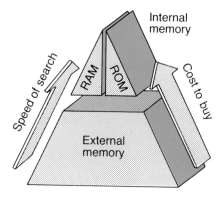

Figure 31 A computer has some internal memory (RAM and ROM) backed up by external memory.

Figure 32 A floppy disc being inserted into a disc drive.

is essential to make copies of important information and programs as *back-up*. It's all too easy to overwrite accidentally something you still need, so discs can be *write-protected* (safeguarded).

Floppy discs have a wide range of different storage capacities, depending on their size (usually 3½, 5¼ or 8 inches in diameter), whether they are single- or double-sided, single- or dual-density. A commonplace 5¼ inch floppy costing US$2–4 would hold at least 100 K (around 50 pages of this book); 8 inch discs have correspondingly greater capacity and could hold the complete text many times over. Surprisingly the tiny modern 3½ inch discs can already hold 500 K per side, and greater densities still will be achieved before long. (See page 196 for details of disc sizes.)

Floppy tape

Floppy tape is like a halfway-house between floppy discs and cassettes, both in price and storage capacity. Miniature cassettes are used (like those in dictation handsets, typically running for 15 minutes per side and holding 50 K or more). Compared with standard cassette players, their motors can be controlled more accurately, information can be packed more tightly and faster storage and retrieval is possible. The compactness of the system is attractive for lap-held microcomputers.

Figure 33 A microchip enlarged (left) and actual size (right). The tiny square in the middle is the actual chip of silicon, the rest is mounting and packaging. The two rows of legs (pins) are for plugging the chip into a circuit. This particular chip has a circular window so that its contents can be altered by exposing it to ultra-violet light.

Enlarged   Actual size

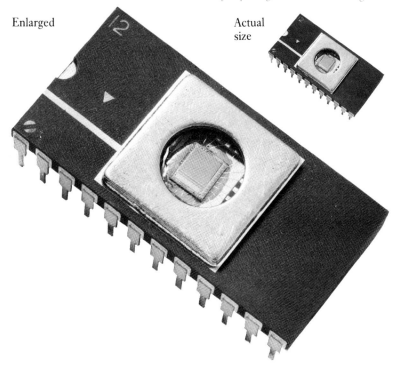

Rigid discs

Minicomputers and mainframes need far greater storage capacity. There are a number of different devices for mass storage, such as *rigid* or *hard discs* and *disc-packs*. These also store information magnetically, but their capacity is much greater than floppy discs: a pack consisting of six discs might hold in excess of 300 Mb (over 300 000 K).

Hard discs are permanent sealed units which rotate many times faster than floppies; storage and retrieval times are correspondingly faster. They also hold vastly more information and are becoming cheaper, smaller and more easily integrated into microcomputer systems. Win-

chesters are a series of hard-disc units which were derived from the mainframe world but have become very popular on smaller machines. Because they are fixed in place, the data must be backed up (copied) regularly in some other way. Recently, removable hard-disc cartridges have become cheaper and more powerful: they hold more than floppy discs without the back-up problems of hard discs.

Bubble memory

Magnetic bubble memory (MBM) chips are more compact than conventional internal memory and more robust than floppy discs. MBM chips can store between 32 K and 4000 K in a small space (less than

Figure 34 Some ways of storing software.

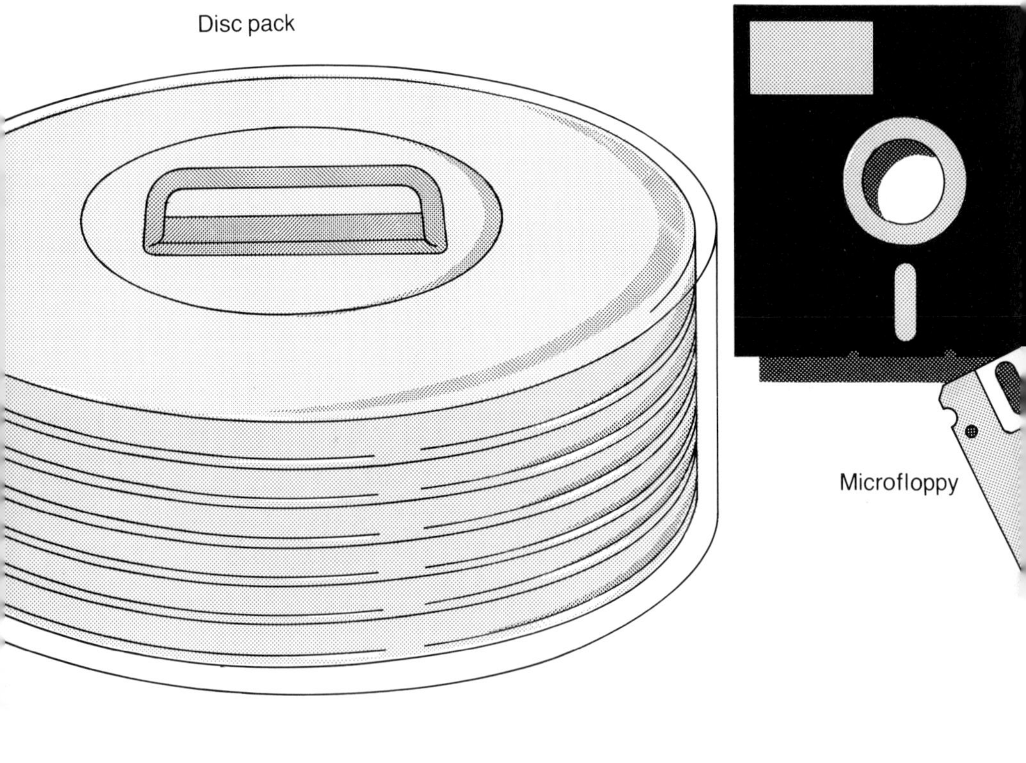

Disc pack

5¼" (mini) floppy

Microfloppy

10 cm × 10 cm), have a low power consumption and retain their data once removed from the system. They can withstand hazards such as shock, magnetic fields and tobacco smoke that can be fatal to floppy discs. MBMs need no maintenance and are very suitable for battery-powered systems. Their main drawback has been expense, but their cost is falling and they have begun to appear in lap-held microcomputer systems.

Videodiscs

Videodiscs have other important applications (discussed in Chapter 8), but viewed just as computer memory, they have immense capacity and are much more robust than floppy discs. A single video-disc could store 30 000 complete books of this length! At present information is pressed onto them permanently at the factory, like a gramophone record. However, optical videodiscs have been developed which will also allow the user to store information on empty sections of the disc. Because the capacity of a videodisc is so huge and its price so low, the fact that this cannot then be erased and re-recorded may not matter.

The technology of mass memory is developing very rapidly: current ideas of price and capacity may soon be out of date.

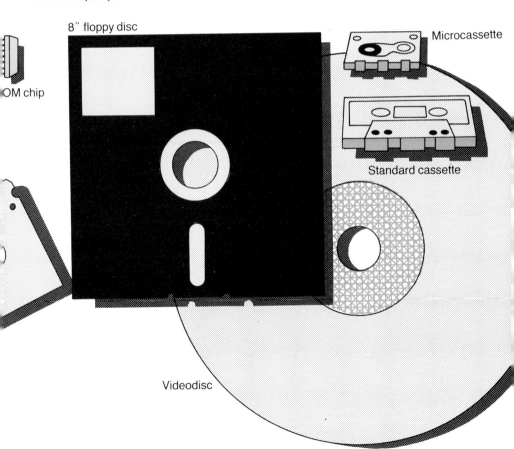

8″ floppy disc

Microcassette

OM chip

Standard cassette

Videodisc

Output

The ultimate value of any computer program depends on how easily humans can interpret its output. Most computers can send information to a number of output devices at once – usually at least to a printer and a screen.

Monitors and television sets

Anyone who is *interacting with* (ie using) a computer needs a *screen* to see what is happening at any moment. Special computer *monitors* give a steadier display than television sets and may allow you to adjust the viewing angle – very important for prolonged use. The ability to display full-colour is useful for modern software.

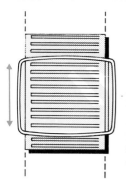

Figure 35 A computer screen can only show a small amount of text at one time. Scrolling is the process of moving the text up and down past the screen, which acts as a window on the document.

Computer printers

A screen is essential for immediate results, but it goes blank when you switch off. If you want a permanent record (*hard-copy*), you will need a printer. Printers vary enormously in cost, quality and speed. Small computers are often used with *dot-matrix printers* (Figure 36), which forms each letter or number from a pattern of dots (see inset). At high speed, you can see the dots quite clearly. Some can produce better-looking results at lower speeds. Different letter sizes, founts (typefaces) and *graphics* can also be printed by using special control codes.

To get the kind of quality produced by a good electric typewriter, a different method is needed. Letters are arranged like petals on a rotating *daisy-wheel*

Figure 36 A dot-matrix printer.

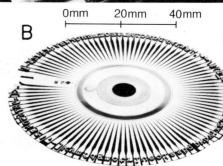

Figure 37 A daisy-wheel.

Figure 38 A plotter can draw shapes and characters in a continuous line using different pens to produce lines of different thicknesses and colours.

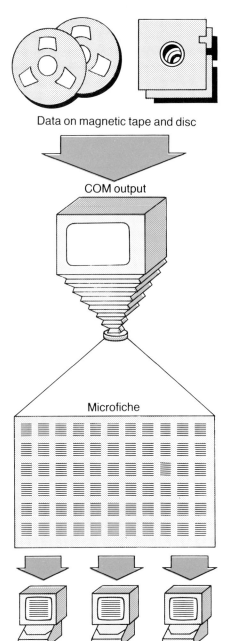

Data on magnetic tape and disc

COM output

Microfiche

Microfiche readers

(Figure 37), which works on the same principle as a typewriter golf-ball. It can be exchanged for a different daisy-wheel when a change of typeface is needed. Daisy-wheel printers tend to be slower than dot-matrix printers and may cost two or three times as much.

Line printers are much faster since they print a complete line of text at one time (from the bottom up). They are not used widely outside large organisations, partly because of their high cost, but also because having a slower printer often makes people think more carefully about what print-out they really need and so can prove economical in more ways than one. *Laser printers* are very fast and high in quality; they can print lots of different typefaces and sizes in a single pass. These are very expensive, but they offer speed, flexibility and superb results, so they may well become more widespread in future.

Most computer printers work on digital principles. Although dot-matrix printers can reproduce diagrams by making a dot-for-dot copy of the graphics on the screen, diagonal and curved lines often have a sort of 'staircase' appearance and the whole picture looks rather 'dotty'. High-quality drawings of the kind that architects and designers need are produced by *plotters* (Figure 38), which work on a different principle. A plotter converts the digital output of the processor into analogue signals that control the movement of one or more pens. Pen-nibs of different types, thicknesses and (sometimes) colours can be fitted as appropriate.

Microform

Microform is a general name for the storage of documents as tiny photographic images on thin sheets of film. It includes *microfilm*, where the film is in a continuous roll, and *microfiche*, where the film is divided into rectangular sheets the size of index cards, which are more convenient to handle. A single microfiche (around 6 × 4 in) can store 60 to 300 A4 pages and might contain 20 000 to 200 000 words of text or an immense number of detailed technical

45

drawings. Microfiches are used, for example, by libraries to store newspapers, and by motor car distributors to store drawings and details of parts. Special machines allow computer data to be output directly on to microform (a process known as COM for short) without first having to print it onto paper and then photograph the paper output (Figure 39). COM is useful for cheap distribution of large banks of information, such as a complete list of books in print to libraries and booksellers; it is also used by large organisations that need to transfer substantial amounts of paperwork from place to place cheaply, and for long-term storage of bulky documents such as company accounts.

Computer sound

Many computers can produce some kind of sound. Beeps and hoots can be useful to attract the user's attention to an error, or to signal the need to load some data. Some computers can also manufacture music and speech, using special synthesizers. Their quality varies enormously: early attempts at synthesized speech sounded very odd because they lacked the usual rise and fall of the human voice. But recently better-quality speech output has become more common, even at the cheap end of the market. It can be very useful for partially sighted users and for people, such as lorry drivers and airline pilots who have to watch many instruments at once.

Movement

Computers can produce and control a variety of movements. This might be the simple raising or lowering of the protective door on a cash card machine, a delicate adjustment of the temperature and gas mixture fed to a furnace, or a complicated series of movements performed in three dimensions by a welding robot (Figure 40). Simple movements are often executed 'blind', ie without feedback; complicated or delicate movements are usually monitored so that feedback on the action becomes feed input to the computer, making a 'closed loop'.

Figure 40 Spot-welding by robots on t Mini Metro assembly line at British Leyland.

46

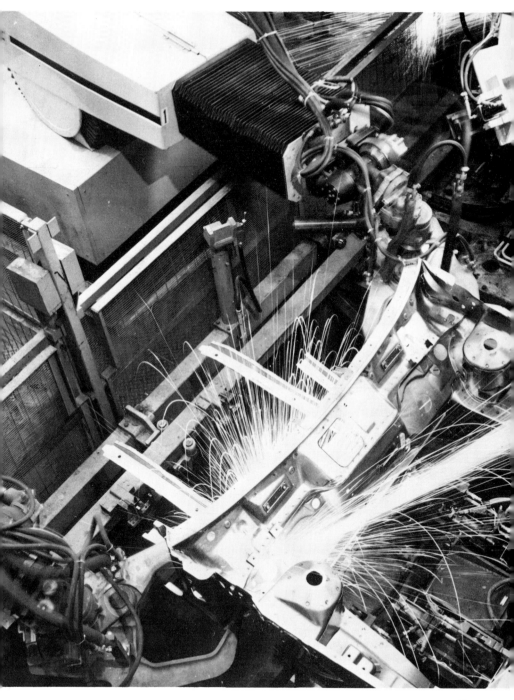

Resolution

Resolution is a measure of the fineness of the lines that can be drawn on the screen. Low resolution graphics divide the screen into about 40 squares across by about 20 down. The squares are called *pixels* (picture cells). You may see a computer's power to produce graphics quoted in pixels, eg 'high resolution graphics (720 × 300)' meaning 720 pixels across by 300 down (Figure 41).

Low resolution is good enough for bar charts and simple diagrams, but curves need medium resolution (about 300 × 200). Accurate maps and drawings need high resolution, which means at least 500 × 500 pixels have to be controlled separately. This uses a lot of processing power and memory – more than most microcomputers can manage. To take full advantage of high-resolution graphics, a good quality monitor is essential.

Graphics

Well designed graphic output allows the computer to display data so that it is clear and easy to digest. Sometimes it can help to make the computer seem more friendly generally. It may even form part of the input system, eg a light-pen or touch-screen can detect each time the user presses different parts of the screen and act accordingly. However, for sustained use constant reaching is tiring on the arms, so a device called a *mouse* can be rolled around on a special desk-top in order to control the movement of a pointer on the screen (Figure 42). Together with special *icons* (symbols) it can act as an input device. For example, by pressing a button on the mouse while it points to a 'filing cabinet' icon, you can *save* some data, whereas pointing to a 'rubbish bin' would delete it.

99 pixels   1584 pixels   23544 pixels   126176 pixels

Animation

Animated graphics are moving images, like cartoon figures. Animated effects can be produced quite easily on many microcomputers and arcade games usually make good use of these. Some microcomputers come with *sprites*, which are ready-made coloured figures designed for easy animation.

However, the control and display of high-quality fast-moving colour images like those used in films and television makes immense demands on processing power and memory, and uses very specialised and expensive software.

Figure 41 The higher the resolution, the finer the detail.

Colour

Most modern computers can produce a colour display, though not all software takes advantage of this fact. Used with discretion, colour can be a helpful addition to any display, text or graphics, and some printers are able to print out in colour too (Figure 44). Most users prefer to view coloured displays if given a choice. Among monochrome monitors, green or amber screens are generally considered more restful than black-and-white.

Figure 42 (*left*) Car body shapes can be designed, redesigned and have their wind resistance tested by computer programs.
Figure 43 (*above*) A robot hand: sensors allow it to grip gently but firmly.
Figure 44 (*below*) Colour print-out from a modestly priced dot-matrix printer.

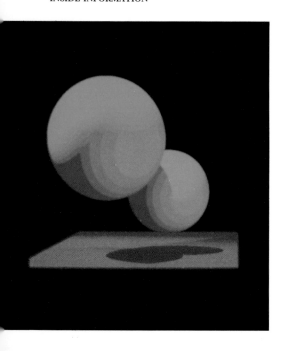

Three-dimensional graphics

The three-dimensional images shown in Figures 45 and 46 were produced using special graphics software. The computer needs a large memory to control the screen display and a lot of processing power to work out what the object would look like from different angles. Programs can also show cut-away views of objects and fill in the hidden parts. These possibilities are very useful to people like architects, engineers and designers.

Figures 45 and 46 Computers can store three-dimensional shapes and display views of them from various angles. To portray solid shapes and directional lighting realistically, the computer needs a large memory and sophisticated software.

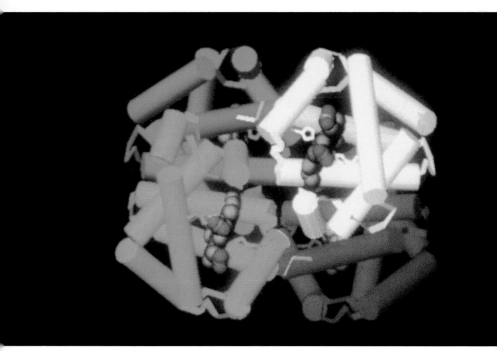

Chapter 4: Some computer systems in action

In the last chapter we looked at the different parts of a computer system (input, processor, memory and output). This chapter examines a few examples of complete systems to see how they operate in practice. First, there are some more bits of jargon to be mastered.

Interfaces

An *interface* is something which may consist of some hardware, some software, or bits of both. It doesn't exactly fit any of the categories we've met so far, yet it profoundly affects whether they can talk to each other and together add up to a useful system.

An interface is where two parts of a system meet. You could say that a beach is the interface between land and sea. If an interface is built into a computer, works well and was included in the price, you

may be blissfully ignorant of its existence – yet you would certainly miss it if it weren't there. For example, a business micro wouldn't be much use without its disc interface (the part that lets the processor swap data between memory and the disc drive). Many personal micros have a cassette interface fitted as standard; some can have a disc interface added as an optional extra – often at considerable cost.

To interface two devices means to do whatever is necessary to make them communicate with each other. If they were produced by different manufacturers and were not designed with this in mind, interfacing them could provide a major research project for the technically qualified entrepreneur! If an interface is supplied as a separate box complete with suitable cables and plugs, getting them to communicate may take a matter of seconds. It all depends.

Figure 47 An interface is needed to allow two systems, or parts of a system, to communicate with each other. It often involves both hardware and software.

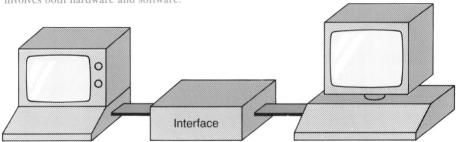

Serial and parallel transmission

Information coded in binary form may be transmitted in two ways: *serial* or *parallel* (Figure 48). Serial transmission means sending the bits down the line one at a time. But if you use eight parallel wires you can send information eight bits (one byte) at a time; with 16 wires you transmit two bytes at once. So parallel transmission is faster.

Over short distances the greater cost of the extra cable needed for parallel transmission is often justified by the extra transmission speed. Over long distances, however, parallel transmission may be out of the question – for example, sending data to a remote printer down a telephone line. Furthermore, bits that *set off* at the same instant do not necessarily travel at exactly the same speed and thus may *arrive* out of step – a problem known as *data skew* (Figure 49). Sorting out which bit belongs with which could be impossible. So before you can transmit data over long distances you must *serialise* it, ie take each byte and read out the bits one at a time at the right speed. Computers with a serial *port* (socket) contain a special unit that does this automatically.

Inside the computer, where distances are small and speed is important, data is transmitted in parallel. The computer's internal communications highway is called a *bus*. Like a household electrical ring main that provides power to whichever socket needs it, different parts send messages to each other by using the bus whenever they need to (Figure 50). Outside the computer, connections to *local* input/output devices (ie ones in the same room) are through parallel or serial interfaces. The broad ribbon cable is a visible indication of parallel communications. You will often see this type of cable linking up disc drives.

Sales literature about microcomputers often boasts of models having both serial and parallel interfaces. Clearly it is useful to keep both options open.

a) Parallel

b) Serial

Figure 48 (a) Parallel transmission. (b) Serial transmission.

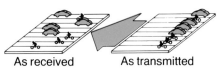

As received   As transmitted

Figure 49 Data transmitted as groups of bits may arrive out of step (skewed).

a)

b)

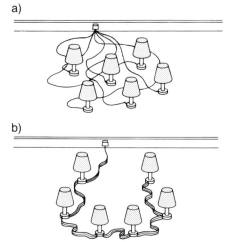

Figure 50 (a) If a number of devices are connected separately to the same power source, the result is a tangle of wires. (b) Linking all the devices to one cable supplying power makes the connections much simpler. The same principle applies to communications inside a computer where a single highway, called a *bus*, connects the different parts.

The configuration

To newcomers, one of the most puzzling features of the computer world is the number of choices to be made. Even cheap micros seem to have a bewildering array of add-ons, or peripherals, available; in practice the cheapest are often unduly limited and lock their owners into non-standard options that turn out more expensive in the end.

In fact, most people are surprised to learn that almost *any* modern processor may be adequate to their needs; for many purposes the choice of processor hardly matters. What *is* important is that the elements of the computer system work harmoniously together and allow room for future expansion or change of purpose. The selection of peripherals, interfaces and software they need to communicate with each other is called the *configuration*. Both technical factors and market forces

affect what configurations are possible for a particular processor. For example, a micro sold as a cheap games-playing machine may be incapable of using disc drives or of communicating with other micros because it lacks the necessary interfaces or because of the way its built-in software works.

Some computer systems at work

A stand-alone micro

A typical home micro is known as a *stand-alone* system because it is complete and self-contained. Suppose you want to run a game program called SNAKE on your home micro, which you bought perhaps on cassette from a high-street store. Once everything has been connected up and switched on, you type in at the keyboard

LOAD"SNAKE"

Figure 51 The user has typed in LOAD "SNAKE." and can begin to play the game.

This is an instruction in the programming language BASIC telling the system that you want to load a program called SNAKE. The program itself might be written in a language like BASIC but in this case it is more likely to be written in the processor's own language of binary 1s and 0s (see Chapter 6). Both the instruction and the system's response ('Searching') will appear on the screen. When you start the cassette recorder playing messages on the screen will show you how the process is going. After a few minutes, a *prompt* shows that loading is complete. But the instructions will not be obeyed until you type **RUN**. (If you are unlucky and loading is imperfect, you may have to repeat the loading process.)

After loading the program, you can rewind the tape and even unplug the cassette player if you want. The original program is still on the cassette: all that happens when the processor 'loads' a program is that it is *copied* from the cassette into the computer's memory. As far as the processor is concerned, the effect is exactly as if you had just made up the program, or typed it out from a book of printed lists of programs – or even read it in using a bar code reader.

If instead of running a pre-recorded program like SNAKE you want to instruct the processor directly, for instance to use it as a calculator, you must interrupt the game by pressing a key called BREAK or RESET, or, if necessary, by switching off. You can then issue instructions that will be obeyed immediately. For example, suppose you want to work out an average examination mark.

PRINT (42+74+61+79+52+58) /6

is a BASIC instruction to calculate the average of six numbers and 'print' the result on the screen. (If you have a printer connected, the result could be printed on paper at the same time.) The result (61) will appear (instantaneously, it seems) underneath the instruction. Here the system is in *command mode* and tries to obey each instruction as soon as it is typed in, as opposed to being in *program mode* where the instructions stored in its memory are obeyed line by line once the RUN command is given.

A local area network

A computer can operate as a stand-alone system or it can form part of a computer network if suitable interfaces and software are available. Organisations such as schools, colleges and small businesses often want to give dozens of people access to computer power simultaneously. But it would be very expensive to give each person a complete system and may be quite unnecessary. Although each user typically needs a screen and keyboard constantly, he or she may make use of a printer, disc drive or modem only occasionally. A *local area network* (LAN) can make it possible for dozens of people to share the same expensive peripherals without having to move away from their seats. If the network is well designed and not overloaded by too many stations or too much traffic, each user may have the illusion of having the peripherals to himself or herself. This is because to a human a tenth of a second is a very short time, barely noticeable as a delay, whereas to a processor it is an era – long enough to complete thousands or millions of instructions.

There are many different designs for LANs. A common one links all the network stations by a single cable that acts like the communications bus inside a computer. Collisions are mostly avoided because each station automatically waits until there is a gap in the traffic before trying to transmit any messages or requests. If by chance two stations try to jump into the same gap at the same time, a special detector 'notices' the collision and makes them wait different lengths of time before trying again.

Suppose a college student is using a LAN for computer studies. After switching on her machine, she must first identify herself by *logging on* to the system. She might have a student number by which she

Figure 52 A local area network – usually installed within a single building or complex – allows dozens of users to communicate with each other and to share expensive resources.

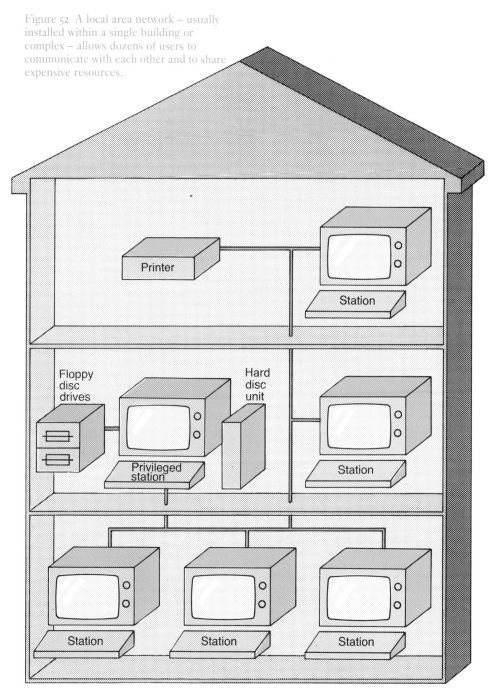

is known to the system, and also a private password that allows her to control access to her own files. Having been accepted as a network user, she will automatically be told when she last used the system, where she left off the last lesson, and perhaps have the lesson loaded from disc automatically.

While she is working at her station, her progress may be followed by the lecturer; if he is working at one of the privileged stations he can 'eavesdrop' on her work by viewing what is on her screen. He can even take over her station completely if he wants, disabling her keyboard like a driving instructor with dual controls, for example to show her the solution to a problem on which she is stuck. (He can also send messages to any or all of the other stations at any time.)

However, the student can also opt out of the lesson. Instead she might load one of her private files from the communal disc drive to work on a half-finished *simulation* program, perhaps. Alternatively, she can use the network to exchange messages with other students working in other parts of the building. To do this, her station sends a short *scout* message to the destination station(s), to see whether they are switched on and ready to listen. If so, the destination station sends a short reply and the main exchange of messages can begin.

Long-distance networks

The special cabling installed for a LAN means keeping the network stations fairly close together – typically within the same building or campus. When distances are greater, the system depends on the existing telephone network. Given suitable agreed protocols, interfaces and software, computers of all shapes and sizes can exchange messages and software by telephone. Such networks are sometimes called *wide area networks* (WANs), as opposed to LANs.

British Telecom's Prestel information service illustrates the use of telephone

links between various combinations of mainframes, minis and micros all over the UK. The whole Prestel database is held on a network of powerful minicomputers; these are located in different parts of the UK so that subscribers can log onto (*access*) Prestel at local call rates. In addition (as we saw in Chapter 1), other companies' mainframe computers (eg an airport's) can be contacted via Prestel through a link called *Gateway*. Many Prestel users access Prestel through personal or business microcomputers in the first place. Through *Closed User Groups* (page 141) and *electronic mail* (page 114) they even have the illusion of direct links micro to micro.

The role of the telephone is not confined to linking complete systems; it can

Figure 53 The telephone can be used to link patients in their homes with a hospital specialist, who can study their symptoms from a distance, using the hospital computer.

Figure 54 (*opposite*) A lap-held micro allows data to be captured and analysed on the spot instead of having to record it and take it back to the office.

connect input and output devices that are scattered miles away from a central processor. Interesting applications occur in preventive medicine, where patients can supply data through a daily telephone call. Signals are picked up by a special input device and transmitted to the hospital where they are monitored by a suitably programmed computer whose output is examined by a specialist. The result is that the patient need attend only if there is cause for concern.

Systems like these mean that the patients enjoy the privacy and freedom of their own homes and families instead of occupying a hospital bed unnecessarily or having to make long daily journeys. The inclusive cost of long-distance monitoring is estimated at around 6% of a hospital bed. Applications include monitoring the heart-beats of foetuses of women with high-risk pregnancies, and helping to diagnose the causes of acute chest pains.

The telephone can act as a simple link between the input device (eg the foetal heart detector) and the processor, transmitting the sounds as raw analogue data. Alternatively, telephone transmission times can be reduced and reliability increased if the data is turned into digital form with built-in redundancy. A duplex link would allow error-checking and could support automatic requests for re-transmission of *corrupted* data (eg because of line noise). Any combination of local and remote processing is possible as long as there is suitable software at each end of the line.

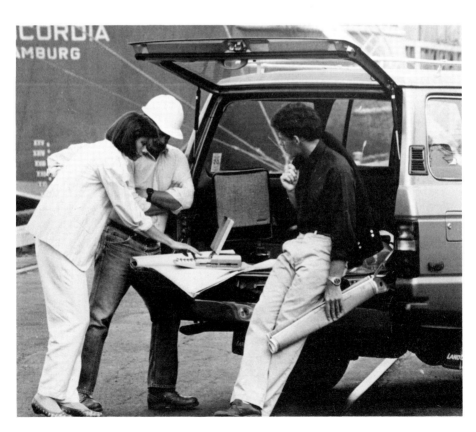

Chapter 5: How programs work

The way programs are loaded and saved has already been mentioned. But whether the program was bought from a shop, typed in from a published book of listings or even read in by a bar code reader, someone had to write it in the first place. This chapter introduces three levels of computer programming, each suited to different tasks. If you are really new to the subject you may not follow all the details, but it will nevertheless give you some idea of how programs are written and adapted, and also show you how accurate and detailed each instruction has to be.

All three of the programs I have used to illustrate the different levels have to do with the exchange of money between different countries. If you travel abroad you will know that remembering and calculating the exchange rates between different currencies can be a nightmare, and that whenever you change money the banks seem to win and you seem to lose. Even if you never travel, varying exchange rates affect you directly through the prices of everyday items which we import from other countries, such as clothes, fuel and electrical goods.

The first section develops a BASIC program for turning pounds sterling into US dollars. The second sets up a *spreadsheet* to carry out conversions between a whole range of currencies. The third section uses an *authoring* language called Microtext to write a tutorial for students on converting currencies.

Programming in BASIC

BASIC is a language designed to help beginners learn programming. It allows you to give instructions using words which are similar to everyday English. For example the command PRINT causes whatever words and numbers follow it to appear on the screen when the program is run (or a blank line if it is used on its own). Arithmetic can be done using ordinary symbols like +, −, =, <, > and ( ). (Multiplication and division look a bit different: * means multiply and / means divide. So 2 * 3/6 in BASIC means 2 times 3 divided by 6.)

Suppose the exchange rate is US$1.22 to the pound and you want to exchange £60. The BASIC command

```
PRINT 60*1.22
```

will produce the result 73.2. So you should receive 73 dollars 20 cents for your £60.

Rather than just displaying a number on the screen by itself, it would be a good idea to say what the number means. To do this we use a PRINT statement. A PRINT statement sends everything inside the quotation marks used to the screen exactly as it stands. So if you type in:

```
PRINT "For £60 you should receive US $"
```

and follow that with 73.2 (the number of dollars), when you run the program you will have a complete sentence. Since we may now want to convert some other amounts into dollars, it would be better to let a *variable* stand for the number of dollars in our program. A variable is just a named 'pigeon-hole' inside the computer's memory where we can store things. We could call this variable D for dollars. In BASIC you assign a value to your variable, ie tell the computer what it is you want to store in this pigeon-hole. In this case we say

```
LET D=60*1.22
```

We just have to add D to the end of the PRINT statement above and the number of dollars will then be printed out. In most cases you also need to insert a semi-colon between the PRINT statement and D. Otherwise the program will automatically insert a space before printing whatever D is and spoil the effect of a seamless join in the statement which is displayed on the screen.

So our BASIC instructions read:

```
LET D=60*1.22
PRINT "For £60 you should receive US $";D
```

Although we've used BASIC words here, this is not a *program* in BASIC because no instructions have been *stored*. So far we have simply used the computer as a pocket calculator, and we would have to repeat the instructions each time we wanted to do a conversion.

All BASIC programs have numbered lines. The line number tells the computer two things:

(1) that it must store the instruction for later, rather than obey it immediately;

(2) in what order to obey the instructions.

No matter what order you use when typing in the lines of program, they will always be obeyed in numerical order. This makes it very easy to change your mind as you go along, and revise bits at the beginning of the program without having to retype any of it. Because it is common to go back and add extra lines, BASIC programs are usually numbered in tens, ie the first four lines might be 10, 20, 30, 40. As we'll be adding to the beginning of this program, I've started my numbers at 100 this time:

```
100 LET D=60*1.22
110 PRINT "For £60 you should receive US $";D
```

These two lines now form a BASIC program. If you type it in on a microcomputer it should work. However, it is good programming practice to begin every program with a line stating its title and to finish with an instruction to stop (END); I've put END at line 200 to leave plenty of space for additions without having to renumber.

For the first line, line 10, we need a REM. REM is short for remark, and it tells the processor to ignore everything that follows on that line. REMs are a convenient way of leaving messages for humans within a program, without upsetting the program's operation. So we can add a title – DOLLAR1 – and a reminder of what it is:

```
10 REM DOLLAR1 (First version of currency program)
```

Here is the complete program so far:

```
DOLLAR1 LISTING

10 REM DOLLAR1 (First version of currency program)
100 LET D=60*1.22
110 PRINT "For £60 you should receive US $";D
200 END
```

If you now type **RUN**, this should produce

```
DOLLAR1 RUN

For £60 you should receive US $73.2
```

Although correct, this hardly makes much use of the computer's ability to store instructions and respond to different data. A better program would let you type in the number of pounds to be converted, and store that for use in the multiplication sum. To do this, we'll use an INPUT command which stores anything typed in at the keyboard in a variable: the program supplies the label for the variable (P, say, for £ sterling), but the contents are not known until the user supplies them. Before a line saying INPUT P we need something to *prompt* the user, ie tell him or her what to do. And we'll have to change line 100 to multiply P (rather than 60) by 1.22 so that D varies according to the current value of P. So lines 80 to 100 now read

```
80 PRINT "Please type in amount in £ Sterling"
90 INPUT P
100 LET D=P*1.22
```

The PRINT statement in line 110 will also have to be modified. It's no good just replacing the 60 by P, or the user would see

```
For £P you should receive US $73.2
```

To get round this we'll have to split the sentence into two parts and use inverted commas again, letting the program supply the values of both P and D at the time of running it. Remember that whatever is *inside* the inverted commas is printed as it stands and what is *outside* is acted upon. To make the final effect look seamless, the trick is again to use semi-colons on either side of the variable so that the space is closed up, and put any spaces you need *inside* the inverted commas – note the space before 'you' here:

```
110 PRINT "For £";P;" you should receive US $";D
```

Finally, it would be helpful to tell the user what rate of exchange is being used, so we'll add another PRINT statement between lines 10 and 80. We can call this improved program DOLLAR2.

```
DOLLAR2 LISTING

10 REM DOLLAR2 (Second version of currency program)
30 PRINT "Converting £ Sterling at US $1.22 to the £"
80 PRINT "Please type in amount in £ Sterling"
90 INPUT P
100 LET D=P*1.22
110 PRINT "For £";P;" you should receive US $";D
200 END
```

The next illustration shows what will appear on the screen at *run-time* (ie when you run the program): the 60 has to be typed in by the user, the rest is supplied by the program.

```
DOLLAR2 RUN

Converting £ Sterling at US $1.22 to the £
Please type in amount in £ Sterling
?60
For £60 you should receive US $73.2
```

This is an improvement over DOLLAR1, but still leaves much to be desired. Firstly, exchange rates vary from time to time, so it would be better to treat the rate in the same way as the amount of dollars, as a variable – called R, say. This means adding an INPUT R statement, preceded by a prompt to tell the user when to type it in (see lines 40 and 50 below). Line 100 will then need modification again, substituting R for 1.22 as the exchange rate. DOLLAR3 is shown below.

```
DOLLAR3 LISTING

10 REM DOLLAR3 (Third version of currency program)
30 PRINT "Converting £ Sterling into US dollars"
40 PRINT "Please type in rate"
50 INPUT R
80 PRINT "Please type in amount in £ Sterling"
90 INPUT P
100 LET D=P*R
110 PRINT "For £";P;" you should receive US $";D
200 END
```

The next illustration shows the new appearance of the screen at run-time. This time the user supplies both the rate (1.22) and the amount (60).

```
DOLLAR3 RUN

Converting £ Sterling into US dollars
Please type in rate
?1.22
Please type in amount in £ Sterling
?60
For £60 you should receive US $73.2
```

This is a more flexible program as you don't have to *edit* (change) the program itself each time the exchange rate fluctuates. But if you wanted to convert a whole list of sums, it would be infuriating to have to keep typing RUN and the rate before doing the next sum. In the next version, I've added a question asking whether the user wants to do another conversion. If the answer is NO, the program continues to the next line (END). If the answer is YES, a GOTO command makes the program jump back to an earlier line (line 80) so

that a new amount is fed in without leaving the program or forgetting the exchange rate. The question appears in line 130, and line 150 stores the reply in A$. A$ is another variable that can store letters or numbers as a string of characters. Line 160 tests whether the string put into the A$ pigeon-hole by the user is YES. If it isn't, the program simply ends. If it is, the program goes back to line 80 to prompt the user for the new amount. The extra PRINT commands at lines 120 and 140 are just to insert blank lines and make the screen easier to read.

```
DOLLAR4 LISTING

10 REM DOLLAR4 (Fourth version of currency program)
30 PRINT "Converting £ Sterling into US dollars"
40 PRINT "Please type in rate"
50 INPUT R
80 PRINT "Please type in amount in £ Sterling"
90 INPUT P
100 LET D=P*R
110 PRINT "For £";P;" you should receive US $";D
120 PRINT
130 PRINT "Another conversion? Type YES or NO"
140 PRINT
150 INPUT A$
160 IF A$="YES" THEN GOTO 80
200 END
```

```
DOLLAR4 RUN

Converting £ Sterling into US dollars
Please type in rate
?1.22
Please type in amount in £ Sterling
?60
For £60 you should receive US $73.2

Another conversion? Type YES or NO

?YES
Please type in amount in £ Sterling
?100
For £100 you should receive US $122

Another conversion? Type YES or NO

?NO
```

This program can still be improved. It would be better to display the exchange rate used in the calculation clearly, especially if you are going to use a printer to print out the results on paper. So we can add another PRINT statement at line 60, and follow it with another blank line (70). Then if we then change the GOTO state-

61

ment at line 160 so that the program jumps back to line 70, instead of line 80, each new sum will follow after a line space.

It is also better to give the user the option of changing the exchange rate after a batch of sums. Rates often vary according to the amount exchanged, or the date on which the transaction occurred, or what bank made the exchange, or whether it is a travellers' cheque, cash or on a credit card. So you might want to do a batch of sums using one rate, and then another batch based on a different rate. Lines 170 to 190 use exactly the same technique as lines 130 to 160. If the answer is YES, control passes to line 40 which puts the question about rate again. If not, the program ends. Below is the listing for the fifth version of the program and the run is shown on page 63.

```
DOLLAR5 LISTING

10 REM DOLLAR5 (Fifth version of currency program)
30 PRINT "Converting £ Sterling into US dollars"
40 PRINT "Please type in rate"
50 INPUT R
60 PRINT "Buying US dollars at ";R
70 PRINT
80 PRINT "Please type in amount in £ Sterling"
90 INPUT P
100 LET D=P*R
110 PRINT "For £";P;" you should receive ";D;" US dollars"
120 PRINT
130 PRINT "Another conversion? Type YES or NO"
140 PRINT
150 INPUT A$
160 IF A$="YES" THEN GOTO 70
170 PRINT "Another rate? Type YES or NO"
180 INPUT A$
190 IF A$="YES" THEN GOTO 40
200 END
```

The process of improving the DOLLAR program could be taken a lot further, but this should be sufficient to get the feel of beginning to program in BASIC. We built up DOLLAR5 gradually so as to deal with the complications one at a time. Figure 55 shows one way of illustrating how it works. For serious programming it is better to *start* by planning out exactly what the program should do before writing any lines. A *flowchart* (as Figure 55 is called) is just one of several aids to planning and understanding how programs work; another is a *structure chart* (see Figure 62).

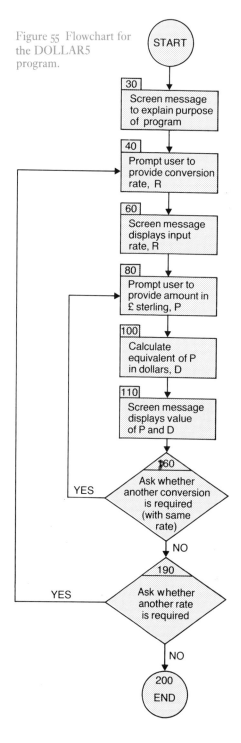

Figure 55 Flowchart for the DOLLAR5 program.

```
DOLLAR5 RUN
Converting £ Sterling into US dollars
Please type in rate
?1.22
Buying US dollars at 1.22
Please type in amount in £ Sterling
?60
For £60 you should receive 73.2 US dollars

Another conversion? Type YES or NO
?YES

Please type in amount in £ Sterling
?100
For £100 you should receive 122 US dollars

Another conversion? Type YES or NO

?NO
Another rate? Type YES or NO
?YES
Please type in rate
?1.20
Buying US dollars at 1.2

Please type in amount in £ Sterling
?60
For £60 you should receive 72 US dollars

Another conversion? Type YES or NO
?YES

Please type in amount in £ Sterling
?100
For £100 you should receive 120 US dollars

Another conversion? Type YES or NO

?NO
Another rate? Type YES or NO
?NU
```

Setting up a spreadsheet

Spreadsheet is the name for a type of program that was designed to help managers with financial forecasting. It takes its name from the idea of spreading out the firm's accounts on a sheet of paper in rows and columns. The rows might show expenditure and income of different kinds, and there could be one column for each month with a total for the year. The manager enters the actual figures into the spreadsheet and also specifies what relationships the different items have to each other. The program then automatically recalculates the rest of the table, showing projected profits for the next year, for example, or the likely effects a different rate of bank interest would have on the company's transactions.

In fact, spreadsheets can be applied to a range of uses from personal budgeting to rotas for sporting fixtures. As far as calculating exchange rates is concerned, a

Figure 56 Screen shot from a spreadsheet program being used to project costings.

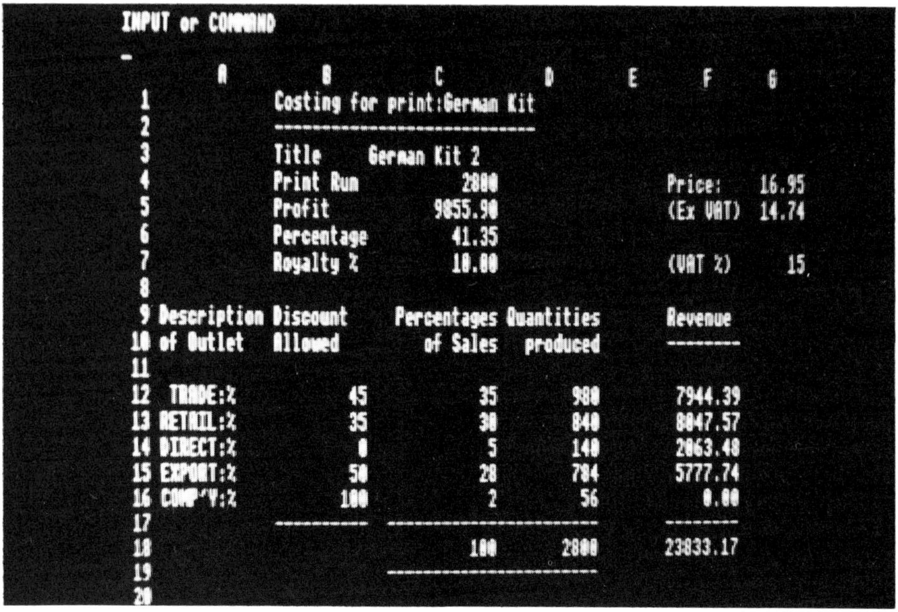

63

spreadsheet provides a neater method of calculating these for a range of currencies than a whole series of BASIC programs like DOLLAR. In what follows I am ignoring the question of how the *program* that produces the spreadsheet is written: it might be in any one of a range of languages. Spreadsheet programs are usually written by professional programmers and sold as a package. What the customer gets is an empty spreadsheet. He or she must learn to fill in each cell with a number or a rule for working out its contents from that of other cells.

We can show the relationship between sterling and other currencies in a simple column. The list below gives the equivalent of £1 in American, then Australian dollars, followed by French francs and Japanese yen.

£	1
$ US	1.19
$ AUS	1.50
FFr	12.00
Yen	300

That's all right if you want to exchange sterling, but if you start out with Australian dollars you will need a different list. Some simple arithmetic is now called for. If there are AUS $ 1.5 to £1, to find out how many £ you would get for AUS $ 1 you would have to divide 1 by 1.5, and you would get the answer 0.667. So AUS $ 1 is 0.667 or two thirds of £1.

Therefore, if two thirds of £1 is equal to AUS $ 1, two thirds of the other three figures given above as being equal to £1 (US $ 1.19, 12 FFr, 300 yen) must also be equal to AUS $ 1. In other words, if you divide all the amounts of currency given above as being equivalent to £1 by 1.5 (the AUS $ value), you will end up with figures which show the value of AUS $ 1 in those currencies.

If you work these sums out you should get the following answers:

	$AUS
£	.667
$ US	.793
$ AUS	1
FFr	8.00
Yen	200

We can now show the relationship of US $, francs and yen to £1 and AUS $ 1 in one go by combining the two columns above like this:

	£	$AUS
£	1	.667
$ US	1.19	.793
$ AUS	1.50	1
FFr	12.00	8.00
Yen	300	200

These will form the first and third columns in our spreadsheet, so let's label them using As for the sterling column and Cs for the Australian dollars (see below).

		A £	B $US	C $AUS	D FFr	E Yen
1	£	A1		C1		
2	$US	A2		C2		
3	$AUS	A3		C3		
4	FFr	A4		C4		
5	Yen	A5		C5		

We've already seen that every figure in column C is two-thirds of the column A figure, ie the column A figure divided by 1.50 (the Australian rate against sterling). Now that we have given labels to the squares, or *cells*, containing the currency values we can express the relationship between the cells more generally in rules, or formulae:

C1=A1/A3 $(.667 = 1/1.50)$

C2=A2/A3 $(.793 = 1.19/1.50)$

C3=A3/A3 $(1 = 1.50/1.50)$

C4=A4/A3 $(8 = 12/1.50)$

C5=A5/A3 $(200 = 300/1.50)$

In addition to helping us to see the pattern, stating the relationships this way makes the spreadsheet more permanent. When the exchange rates vary, only a few figures in column A have to be changed.

Let's insert column B to show the position of US dollars. This time the A column figures have to be divided by 1.19 (the US $ equivalent of £1) instead of 1.50. The numbers aren't as round, but the equations fit the same pattern.

B1=A1/A2

B2=A2/A2

B3=A3/A2

B4=A4/A2

B5=A5/A2

		A £	B $US	C $AUS	
1	£	1	·84	·667	
2	$US	1·19	1	·793	
3	$AUS	1·50	1·26	1	
4	FFr	12·00	10·08	8·00	
5	Yen	300	252·10	200	

Notice that cell B2, like cell C3, is bound to work out to 1: this expresses the fact that any currency can be exchanged for itself 'at par', ie 1 for 1. If you look down the diagonal of the full table of currencies, you can see that this pattern extends to D4 and E5.

To complete the 5 by 5 table, compare the rules for working out the B column cells with those for the C column. You may be able to see the pattern and extend it to the D and E columns. The equations are

D1=A1/A4   E1=A1/A5

D2=A2/A4   E2=A2/A5

D3=A3/A4   E3=A3/A5

D4=A4/A4   E4=A4/A5

D5=A5/A4   E5=A5/A5

The results of the calculations look like this:

		A £	B $US	C $AUS	D FFr	E Yen
1	£	1	·84	·667	·083	·00333
2	$US	1·19	1	·793	·099	·00397
3	$AUS	1·50	1·26	1	·125	·00500
4	FFr	12·00	10·08	8·00	1	·04000
5	Yen	300	252·10	200	25·00	1

In practice this spreadsheet would be quicker to set up than you might think. The only figures to be inserted are A2, A3, A4 and A5. All the rest are calculated from the equations. Normally you would

65

have to type in only one set of equations because the spreadsheet program can be instructed to *replicate*, ie work out corresponding equations for all the other columns for itself. So instead of working out the contents of 25 cells and then having to recalculate them all every time there is a fluctuation in currency rates, the user types in four numbers (in column A), the appropriate equation and the instruction to replicate. Here is how the program stores the information:

	A	B	C	D	E
1	1	$A1/A2$	$A1/A3$	$A1/A4$	$A1/A5$
2	*	1	$A2/A3$	$A2/A4$	$A2/A5$
3	*	$A3/A2$	1	$A3/A4$	$A3/A5$
4	*	$A4/A2$	$A4/A3$	1	$A4/A5$
5	*	$A5/A2$	$A5/A3$	$A5/A4$	1

* Figures typed in by user

Figure 57 The relationships programmed into the currency spreadsheet.

Once a spreadsheet has been set up it can be saved just like a program or data-file. That means that whenever it is needed it can be loaded and used immediately. It is also easy to modify: for example the whole table can be adjusted for a rise in the value of the yen just by changing a single cell (A5). The new E column values will all be recalculated automatically. To change from buying rates to selling ones (as these usually differ) might mean typing in new figures in the A column, thus creating an alternative version of the spreadsheet. Extra rows and columns can easily be added to include other currencies.

The size of a spreadsheet is limited only by its design and the memory of the computer on which it runs: large spreadsheets may have hundreds of rows or columns, but they are constructed on the same principles as this simple example.

In practice, there are various details that differ from one spreadsheet program to another, eg in what order to fill in the cells, or how you type in the equations. The top row and extreme left-hand column would normally be used for labels which the user types in, and it improves the screen appearance if blank lines are left between these and the figures. So a 5 by 5 spreadsheet might actually be stored in cells C3 to C7, D3 to D7, E3 to E7, F3 to F7, G3 to G7. Spreadsheet packages normally include printed documentation explaining all these details.

A Microtext tutorial

The third example of programming is at a higher level still. Microtext is an *authoring* language. It was designed to suit the needs of people in education and training, and those in organisations where the users needed to create questionnaires or present information on computer screens without first learning a programming language.

BASIC programs consist of numbered lines. Microtext programs consist of numbered frames. Each frame presents one screenful of information to the user. The Microtext author types in the contents of the screen exactly as it should appear to the student, with some additional information at the beginning and end of the frame. Each frame has a number, eg *10, *20, *30 etc (like BASIC programs, the numbers usually advance in tens to allow for insertions later). In addition to posing questions in the frames, the author has to define what responses are acceptable to the questions, and has to instruct the program in advance which frame to present in what circumstances. A row of dots at the end of each frame shows that it is complete.

So how could you use Microtext to test and increase someone's knowledge of currency conversion? Figure 60 shows a flowchart of one approach. Frame 10 starts by asking how much the student thinks he knows already. Then he takes a different route according to the answer given.

Figure 61 With suitable software, microcomputers can provide stimulus and
motivation for students to learn subjects
right across the curriculum.

Figure 62 This touch-screen panel can be added to the front of a low-priced colour monitor that is widely used in British schools. It allows the user to respond to the program just by pressing the screen. This is specially useful for those who find mastering a keyboard an obstacle.

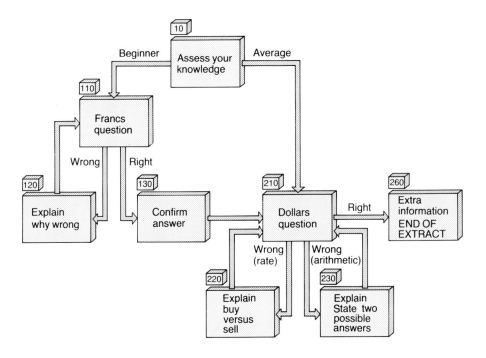

Figure 60 A flowchart showing how a Microtext tutorial on converting currencies was built up.

Beginners will go to frame 110 which puts a simple question about converting francs. If his answer is wrong, frame 120 explains his mistake and he has another go at frame 110. If he answers correctly, frame 130 gives confirmation and sends him straight to frame 210.

Students who rate themselves as being past the beginner stage are routed straight to frame 210 from frame 10. This poses a dollar conversion question, demanding a bit more knowledge than frame 110. If the student makes one particular kind of mistake (mixing up the buying and selling rates), frame 220 reminds him and returns to 210. If he gives any other wrong answer, perhaps because of a mistake in arithmetic or typing, frame 230 restates the two answers to be chosen from. Finally, if he gives the right answer, frame 260 moves on with extra information.

Obviously this tutorial covers only a small part of what might be taught about

currency exchange. Frame 260 could lead on to many more frames. Think of it as an extract from a larger unit, or *module* as it is called in Microtext. A module might cater for three or more different levels of student. An 'expert' branch could easily be added to frame 10, and other frames might be added elsewhere. But this extract gives us enough to work on at present.

Microtext makes it easy to turn this flowchart into a working program. Figure 61 shows what the author types in at the keyboard. The words between the rows of dots are almost exactly what the student sees at run-time, except that none of the control information (shown here in blue) would appear.

69

Figure 61 Microtext tutorial extract.

```
Microtext  tutorial  extract
```

```
*10
     Currency  Exchange

This lesson is about currency exchange. Before
we start, please assess your knowledge of this
subject.
Press a letter:
          B for Beginner
          A for Average


?

B → 110
A → 210
```

```
*110

Banks exchange foreign currency for profit. They
have two rates for each currency: one is for
selling, the other for buying. The difference
between the two is the bank's profit margin.

Suppose you have Sterling and want French
Francs. A notice in a London bank has two
columns. It shows:

          Fr Francs    12.00    11.50

Which rate of exchange will be used?


?

12+ → 120
11.50+ → 130
```

```
*120

You said 12.00 would be the exchange rate. That
is wrong.

If the bank gave you 12 Francs for each £1 it
would make a loss — especially if it then bought
them back at 11.50! It would lose half a Franc
on every £1 it exchanged for you!

Alas, it is the bank, not the customer, that
makes a profit. You get the lower rate when you
buy foreign currency. The "higher" rate only
applies when you sell unwanted Francs back to
the bank.

Press any key when you are ready to try the
question again.


!

→ 110
```

```
*130

You said that the exchange rate would be 11.50.
You are right.

You always get the lower rate when you buy
foreign currency. The "higher" rate of 12.00 FFr
to £1 only applies when you sell your Francs
back to the bank.

Press any key when you are ready to try the
question again.


!

→ 210
```

```
*210

Suppose you have £100 to turn into American
dollars. The London Times shows

               US $ 1.24      1.19

How many dollars should you expect?


?

124+ → 220
119+ → 260
→ 230
```

```
*220

You said you would expect $124. That is wrong.

If the bank gave you $124 for each £100, it
would make a loss — especially if it then bought
Sterling back at $119! It would lose five
dollars on every £100 it exchanged for you!

Remember, you get the lower rate when you buy
foreign currency. The "higher" rate only applies
when you sell unwanted currency back to the
bank.

Press any key when you are ready to try the
question again.


!

→ 210
```

```
*230

You said you would expect $<ANS>. That is wrong.

The rates in the newspaper show how many dollars
you get for each £1. Since you have £100, you
must multiply the rate by 100.

So the answer to the question must be either
$119 or $124, depending whether you think you
will get the 1.19 rate or the 1.24 one.

Press any key when you are ready to try again.


!

→ 210
```

```
*260

You said you would expect $119. You are right.

In practice you may find that the actual rate
varies from bank to bank. Sometimes it changes
from morning to afternoon. The amount you are
exchanging may affect the rate you get and
whether you are charged any extra commission.

The way you pay can also affect it: credit card
companies often charge the rate prevailing at
the time they debit your account, which may be
weeks later.

So the rate given in a newspaper is only a rough
guideline.

*END
```

After each frame number comes the text which sometimes includes a question. After the question, a ? prompts the student to type in his answer. At the bottom of each frame you can see the author's instructions about how various responses should be treated. In frame 10, the bottom two lines mean

If the answer given is B, then go to frame 110
If the answer is A, go to frame 210

(The arrow in Microtext is like the GOTO statement used in our BASIC program.)

Similarly, after frame 110 the student will be routed either to frame 120 or to frame 130 depending on the answer given. "12+" means that all answers that begin with 12, such as 12.0 and 12.000 will be treated alike, and result in a branch to frame 120. There the mistake is explained and the student is asked to press any key when ready to try again. The ! simply means that a single key-press is expected. When *any* key-press is detected, the →110 makes the program return to frame 110. When the correct answer (11.5 or 11.50 or equivalent) is given, the →130 branches the user to frame 130.

Frame 130 confirms the right answer and uses the same ! technique to get the student to signal when ready to progress to the next frame. In frame 210, the answers 124 and 119 are both anticipated by the author and lead to specific frames. Since the student might type in anything at all, a safety-net is needed for other possible answers. The →230 instruction sends the student to a frame which helps him or her to narrow down the possible answers to one of two. <ANS> is a Microtext variable that stores whatever answer the student last typed in. At frame 230 the student would not see <ANS> at all, but $125 or $1.19 or whatever he actually keyed in. This is useful because students don't always type in the answer exactly as they meant to. Unless their response is 'echoed' back to them, they can sometimes get very confused by the way the program reacts.

Microtext allows quite subtle treatment of different kinds of response that stu-

dents may type in. It also allows you to build up a summary of the paths taken by different students and the answers that they gave. Microtext also provides various aids to help authors to develop and test their modules. This short extract can only provide an introduction to some of its simpler features. But it should be enough to give you some idea of how much easier it is to use an authoring system than a programming language for this kind of purpose.

Structured programming

Whatever programming language is used, it is important to avoid any impression that programming can be undertaken in a haphazard way, as the development of DOLLAR5 from DOLLAR1 might suggest! As you may have guessed from the way the lines were numbered, what I actually did was to plan and write DOLLAR5 first. Then I progressively simplified the program into the versions called DOLLAR4, DOLLAR3 etc simply for the purpose of building it back up again. In general it is best to plan programs in a *top-down* fashion: ie start from the task itself, break it down into a number of sub-tasks, and go on breaking each of *those* down until you reach the level of individual instructions.

Returning to the currency exchange problem, you could represent it by a structure chart in which each level shows a breakdown of the one above. Of the four main tasks, only the first has been taken right down to the level of BASIC instructions in Figure 62, but you can probably see how to continue the process for yourself. Unlike flowcharts in which you sometimes have to follow paths going in all directions, structure charts are always read from top to bottom and from left to right. Whether a flowchart or a structure chart is a more helpful method depends partly on the individual, partly on the task, and partly on whether the purpose is to plan the program before writing it or to display it once it is complete.

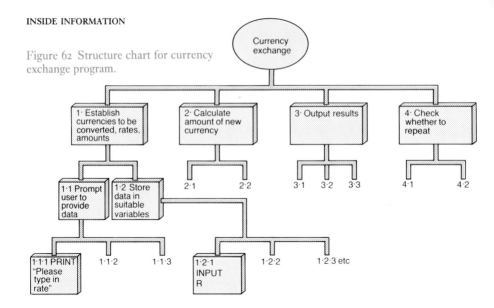

Figure 62 Structure chart for currency exchange program.

Structured programming is a style in which each part of the program is developed as a self-contained mini-program; these units are sometimes called modules, procedures or routines. Think of designing a program as building a ship. Instead of starting at one end of the hull and adding bits until you reach the prow, structured programming means building and testing separately a series of compartments. Only when each is thought to be watertight are they joined together to form the ship. Any leaks are correspondingly easier to trace and mend.

Beyond coding

The three excerpts presented in this chapter can only convey the flavour of the programming languages in which they were written. Statements such as LET D=P*R, Replicate and $END are typical of BASIC, spreadsheets and Microtext respectively. They are examples of lines of *code* – as segments of program are usually called.

However, it is important to realise that coding is only one small part of the process of programming. Whatever language is used, six main stages are normally involved in developing a program:

1 Analyse problem
2 Design program
3 Write the code
4 Translate code
5 Test and debug program
6 Document program

Analysing the problem is often the hardest and most time-consuming stage; not many real problems are as easily solved with a program as the dollar conversion one was. Designing the program is the next stage, often best done with paper and pencil, perhaps using a structure chart or a flowchart. The actual coding is usually straightforward, especially if the program was carefully designed. Translating the code is the process by which instructions in a programming language are turned into binary code statements that the processor can obey. This task is usually done automatically by the computer system, the user may not even be aware of it as a separate stage, but all programs have to be translated into binary 1s and 0s eventually.

The process of testing and *debugging* a program may take far longer than the original coding. Major faults – the kind that make the program *crash* (fail altogether) – are often the easiest to trace. Special care is needed to make a program *crash-proof* for general use where people may type in things that the programmer never expected. Less dramatic mistakes (sometimes called *non-fatal errors*) can cause misleading results, or – worse still – results that may look all right but which actually will be wrong in a particular combination of circumstances. Complicated programs with many possible routes often suffer from these rather elusive *bugs*. Thorough testing means that every conceivable possibility must be tried out, with all kinds of user input – probable and improbable, sensible and silly.

Finally, documenting the program properly is vital if other people are to use it. People who write short programs simply for their own amusement often skip this stage – and are amazed at how difficult it can be to understand their own programs even a few weeks later. Simple techniques such as building in lots of remarks (REMs) in BASIC to explain each section of code can help enormously. Any serious program intended for distribution to other people needs *documentation* for users, for prospective customers, and for other programmers who might want to modify the program. It may even need separate documentation for each of these groups.

For most everyday applications, the time and expense involved in going through all these stages to develop a special program would be out of all proportion to the benefits. Most organisations have so many features in common that a large market has developed in off-the-shelf packages, especially for microcomputers. Buying a standard package may be a more sensible decision than commissioning (or trying to write) a new program from scratch, just as it is often both quicker and cheaper to buy clothes off-the-peg than to have them made to measure, especially if you are a standard shape and size!

If you have the kind of mind that enjoys programming you may relish the challenge

of making a program behave as it should. But in the business world where time is money, it is often better to buy software than to write it. In practice, before embarking on stages 2 to 6 (opposite), the next step after analysing the problem should be to evaluate commercially available packages.

The traditional approach to business packages has been a 'horizontal' one: activities like word processing, accounts, databases and spreadsheets that cut across all businesses are packaged as standard programs. Great interest soon developed in *integrated software*, eg a suite of programs that allows you to take facts out of a database, manipulate them in a spreadsheet, display them using a graphics package and incorporate the diagram into a word-processed letter, without ever having to re-key the information. A further development was the idea of *vertical-markets software*, ie a suite of programs custom-built to meet all the computing needs of people in a particular line of business, such as estate agents or doctors. By 1983 there were thousands of such packages, catering for practically any group you can imagine; for example, there are many rival packages for kitchen designers, pig farmers and theatrical agents.

Whatever the package, it may have some built-in flexibility to allow users to adapt the program to the way that their particular organisations work, or even just to suit the way their stationery is printed. This is a kind of middle way between starting from scratch and forcing the business into the mould imposed by a standard package. It's a bit like getting a shop to make alterations to an off-the-peg garment: how long it takes and how successful the results are depends not only on the skill of the person making the alterations, but also on whether the thing was designed to help or hinder such modifications. Although you may never need to write any serious programs, even a taste of programming should help you to understand what kind of modifications are easy, difficult or even impossible.

Chapter 6: Systems software and applications software

If you had only hardware – no matter how expensive or sophisticated – you would see nothing but a blank screen when you switched on the computer. You wouldn't be able to make the system obey you by typing instructions at the keyboard, nor would you be able to load or run existing programs from cassette or disc. What you would be missing is called *systems software*. This chapter explains what that is, and why it is even more vital than its better-known counterpart, *applications software*.

Applications software means the kind of programs you met in the last chapter: software that applies the computer to some real-world problem such as currency exchange. Educational programs, arcade games and business software are all examples of applications software.

However, it is systems software that determines both what applications software you can run and what sort of programs you can write. You can think of it as the 'behind-the-scenes' software. It

Figure 63 Systems software forms the vital link between hardware and applications software. In many microcomputers, some part of the systems software is built in semi-permanently as *firmware*.

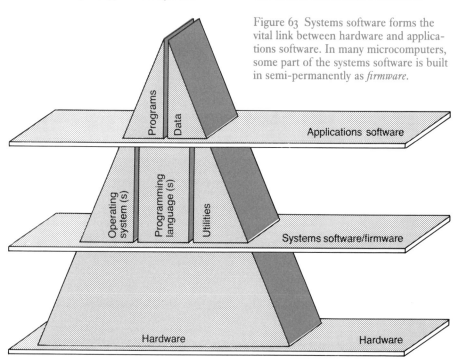

supervises all the operations within the computer, controls communications between the processor and input/output devices and translates programming languages into the binary code it can act on.

Without systems software, the processor is like an obedient but totally inexperienced employee on the first day of a new job in a foreign country who cannot speak a word of the local language. He has capabilities, but no idea what is expected of him and no means of interpreting his instructions. The processor can add and compare binary numbers, but without systems software it cannot translate these into instructions such as the BASIC commands PRINT or INPUT.

There are three kinds of systems software (Figure 63):

1 Programming language(s)

2 Operating system(s)

3 Utilities

Languages for programming

Literally hundreds of different languages have been developed for programming computers; these can be divided into four main categories (see below). What languages are available for any particular computer system strongly influences the software that is produced for it and the problems to which it can be applied.

Computer processors are extremely flexible, and *in principle* can perform any task that can be spelled out in enough detail but whether *in practice* it is worth anyone's while to write a program for a particular task depends on the languages available. Although computer professionals lay great stress on the speed and efficiency of different languages, for most people the more important question is how long it takes to learn and how easy it is to find and correct mistakes.

Figure 64 shows the four main groupings of languages for programming,

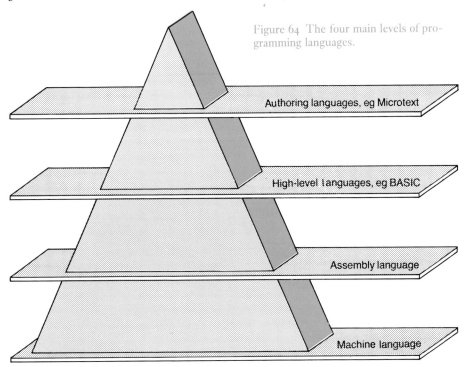

Figure 64 The four main levels of programming languages.

Authoring languages, eg Microtext

High-level languages, eg BASIC

Assembly language

Machine language

75

arranged in a pyramid. From the top down they are:

Authoring languages

'High-level' programming languages

Assembly language

Machine language

You have already met examples of an authoring language (Microtext) and a high-level programming language (BASIC) in Chapter 5. Figure 65 shows corresponding instructions written in Microtext, BASIC, assembly language and machine language.

Machine language

At the base of the pyramid is the processor's own language of binary 1s and 0s: because professionals tend to call the computer 'the machine', this is known as *machine language* or *machine code*. Every instruction has to be turned into the form of long strings of binary codes like 1101101 1101010 before the processor can obey it. In the early days of computing, programmers actually had to write their instructions this way. 'Normal humans' find this kind of language very difficult and time-consuming, both for writing programs and for tracing and correcting mistakes. Machine code programming is not recommended for anyone who has not a special kind of motivation – and the patience of a saint!

Fortunately, it is very seldom necessary to write programs this way nowadays. Early on, computer scientists developed super-programs which could automatically translate instructions written in higher-level languages into machine code. Such super-programs can either be built in by the manufacturer or loaded in by the user. This then allows the user to write instructions like 'LET C=A+B', knowing that the super-program will turn it into the form shown in Figure 65. The two main types of super-program – *compilers* and *interpreters* – are explained later (page 82). The essential point to make here is

that by loading different translation programs, you can make a single processor seem to understand different languages.

High-level languages are preferable to machine language because they allow the programmer to think out and write his or her program in words that resemble ordinary language. This is much easier for people to handle than programs written in binary 1s and 0s, so programs are quicker to write and less prone to error. The only disadvantages are the extra time it takes for the translation to be done, and the fact that the compiler or interpreter program itself occupies some of the computer's memory. Whether this matters or not depends on the nature of the program and the way it is used. The drawbacks can be serious in the case of programs which carry out word-processing where speed and memory space are both important. It also depends on the particular method used for translation: compilers and interpreters do it rather differently.

In practice, situations where the system is held back by waiting for the processor are rarer than you might expect. Three-dimensional graphics (see page 50), recalculating really large spreadsheets and repetitive sorting of large volumes of data are all examples of occasions where programs written in high-level languages would be too slow. Even so, it is not often necessary to resort to machine language. There is a halfway-house called assembly language, which can be used on its own or mixed with other languages.

Assembly language

Assembly language makes use of mnemonics, which are shorthand versions of English words. In Figure 65, LDA 65 is the code for 'Load the Accumulator with the contents of box number 65', ADC 66 stands for 'ADd the Contents of box number 66' and STA 67 is the code for 'STore the Answer' in box number 67. In ASCII, 65 stands for A, 66 for B, 67 for C and so on. Below you will see how the middle of Figure 65 relates to the bottom line.

The advantage of assembly language is that its mnemonics can be translated into machine code very fast. Again this is a job for a translation super-program, called an *assembler*. It looks up the machine code equivalent of each assembly mnemonic in a master table and passes it on to the processor. This is a much faster process than the complicated business of translating instructions in a high-level language into binary code. And although not exactly friendly-looking, mnemonics are certainly easier for humans to handle and check than binary numbers. Figure 66 shows the pros and cons of the four 'levels' of programming languages.

Figure 65 (*right*) Excerpts from the same program written at different levels of programming language.

Figure 66 (*below*) Time taken to write and time taken to run the same program written at different levels of programming language.

Microtext	Suppose that C stands for the sum of A and B
BASIC	LET C=A+B
Assembly language	LDA 65 ADC 66 STA 67
Machine language	1010 0101 0100 0001 0110 1001 0100 0010 1000 0101 0100 0011

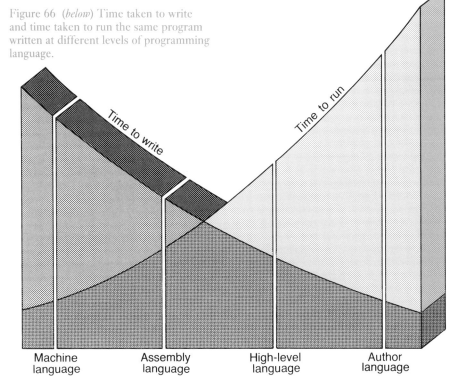

Time to write
Time to run

Machine language Assembly language High-level language Author language

Figure 66 shows that, in general, the higher the level of the language, the quicker it is for humans to write the program. But it also shows that the lower the level, the quicker it is for the processor to *execute* (obey). Machine code needs no translation and is therefore executed as fast as possible.

There is also a tendency for some high-level and author languages to occupy a lot of memory space. They cannot always support the full range of features of which the hardware is capable either. For example, videotape players cannot always be controlled from within an authoring language. On occasions, then, the use of lower-level languages is unavoidable.

High-level languages: BASIC

Programming languages are sometimes called high-level languages because they use words and symbols which are miles 'above' the primitive 1s and 0s in which the computer operates deep-down. Like human languages, programming languages grew up in different places to meet the needs of different groups of people. A universal programming language – a sort of computer Esperanto – might be the ideal, but it hasn't arrived yet and there are unfortunate practical and commercial reasons why it may never happen. Too many people have too many vested interests in sticking with the language they've already adopted.

By far the commonest high-level language is BASIC. BASIC stands for *Beginners' All-purpose Symbolic Instruction Code*. It was developed at an American college in the 1960s to help beginners learn to write computer programs. As Chapter 5 showed, it is a relatively easy first language for newcomers to learn and some form of BASIC is widely available on computers of all sizes. Virtually all microcomputers run BASIC and many have a BASIC interpreter built-in on a ROM chip. Larger computers can run any language for which the appropriate translation program is available, though the nature of their more

complex workload and the high-level training of their programmers mean that BASIC is in less demand. BASIC is a concise and flexible language suitable for a wide range of applications. It can be fitted on a ROM chip so that it doesn't take up precious RAM space. This makes it especially suitable for micros with small memories.

Perhaps the most annoying feature of BASIC from the user's viewpoint is the number of different versions, or *dialects*, which have grown up. Unlike dialects of spoken languages, in which a listener might understand only nine words out of ten but still get the gist of what was being said, programs written in different BASIC dialects may be completely incompatible. Even the most trivial difference between the dialects used by different computers can completely prevent a program written on one machine from being run on another. Sometimes the modifications to the program needed are quite small, but if you are unfamiliar with the two dialects, the barrier can seem insuperable.

Some of the variations arise because different manufacturers were too lazy or too perverse to use the same conventions. Others represent truly worthwhile improvements over the original language. For example, all the Chapter 5 BASIC programs were written and tested on my BBC Micro, which runs an extended dialect called BBC BASIC. This allows you to define *procedures*, which are self-contained mini-programs that you can call up by name from any part of the main program. After a procedure has been carried out, control is returned to the main program until another procedure is needed. Procedures are a valuable aid to structured programming, and my technique of programming in the DOLLAR programs would have been improved by using them. In particular, I could have avoided using the GOTO jump (which most computer experts regard as a sign of bad programming technique). However, I wanted the programs to be capable of running on as many micros as possible in case you wish to try them out. Therefore I avoided using any features of BBC BASIC that are not available in earlier dialects. In general, the need to modify programs written in one dialect of BASIC to make them work in another is the source of a lot of frustration and unnecessary effort.

BASIC has one great advantage over its more recent rivals: most people who can program at all know *some* dialect of BASIC. This means that there are lots of good introductory books to help beginners to learn to program in BASIC and there is a wealth of reasonably priced BASIC software for newcomers to use, study and adapt. Some programs might have been more compact, more professional or faster-running had they been written in a different language – but many might never have been written at all.

Computer experts have tended to look down on BASIC. They have been predicting its downfall for more than 20 years, yet its staying power and flexibility have been remarkable. Its life has been protracted by the arrival of more extended dialects, such as BBC BASIC, and experts disagree over whether that is a good thing. The use of professional programming technique and careful documentation can help to overcome many of BASIC's inherent disadvantages. However, it is important to realise that BASIC has already been used for purposes far beyond the original intentions of its designers. If pushed too far, especially for complicated programs, its weaknesses become very obvious.

High-level languages other than BASIC

There are many high-level programming languages other than BASIC. Traditional languages developed for mainframe computing include FORTRAN (*FORmula TRANslator*) and ALGOL (*ALGOrithmic Language*). These are also commonly used for scientific and mathematical applications on mainframes and minicomputers. COBOL (*COmmon Business Oriented Language*) was introduced in 1960 especially for commercial data processing. It is

specially suited to handling al as opposed to numerical – in COBOL programs tend to be winded and greedy for memo example, because it was believeu uia ̄ commercial programmer would prefer words to mathematical symbols, it uses ADD in place of +! However, trimmed-down versions have been developed for smaller computers.

More recent languages have taken features from the traditional languages and improved on them. *Pascal* was designed in the 1970s to teach good programming style to students. Unlike BASIC, it obliges programmers to *declare* (identify) all their variables (see page 59) at the beginning of a program, and to display the structure of their programs clearly. Line numbers are optional in Pascal, and the errors and confusion that sometimes accompany renumbering of the lines in a BASIC program simply do not arise. Pascal is available on various microcomputers.

PL/1 was developed by IBM with the aim of meeting the needs of both business and science. It uses features from ALGOL, COBOL and FORTRAN, but is in some ways easier to learn because simple programs can be written without a full knowledge of the language. PL/M is the scaled-down version for micros.

Prolog is a language that takes its name from the idea of *logic programming*. It was developed by workers in *artificial intelligence* who believed that traditional programming languages create confusion by mixing statements of knowledge about the problem that the user wishes the computer to tackle with statements about how to solve it. Prolog separates the statements of fact from those of control. In effect, the programmer builds up a database of facts and rules about the problem, while Prolog itself makes the deductions. *MicroProlog* is now widely available on microcomputers, and some people argue that it is a better language for learning programming than BASIC or Pascal.

There are literally hundreds of other contenders for the best 'beginners' lan-

79

.ge'. LOGO, for example, is a simple but powerful language for introducing programming to people of any age. It allows you to define your own building-blocks for programming, and to combine them to produce complicated effects by simple means (Figure 67a). Unlike BASIC, LOGO enables even young children to produce satisfying results quite quickly. It has been closely linked with the graphics produced by *turtles*, which may be remote-controlled floor robots (Figure 67b), or simple representations on the screen of how such a floor robot would move. However, the power of LOGO is by no means confined to its interesting graphics capabilities. It has important applications in the area of *list-processing* too.

So far only three languages have been recognised by ANSI, the American National Standards Institute: FORTRAN, COBOL and (in 1983) ADA. ADA is a *real-time* language developed by the US Defence Department and has been promoted as a possible universal programming language for the 1990s. However, a new language has to be fully standardised, to be learned by a new generation of programmers and to have its software widely distributed. This is a long process, and at present the huge libraries of proven software give the established languages a considerable headstart.

There is no space to describe other important languages such as COMAL and APL and, in any case, a shortlist of programming languages is bound to be controversial: every language has its loyal supporters and its energetic critics. It's difficult for many people to be objective about the merits of programming languages; it takes quite an effort to learn your first language and most people get all too comfortable with whichever one they learn first. Many people who say that *their* language is objectively the best really just can't face learning another. It's important to remember that, with a bit of ingenuity and a lot of hard work, most computers can be made to do most tasks that can be programmed at all in almost *any* language.

LOGO

To make a flower, you start with the command QCIRCLE, which draws a quarter circle.

In fact the QCIRCLE command needs a number after it to set its size, eg 50 units.

If you draw another QCIRCLE at 90° to the first, you can close the shape to make a petal. The LOGO command TO PETAL makes it clear that you are defining a new shape.

```
TO PETAL
  QCIRCLE 50
  RIGHT 90
  QCIRCLE 50
  RIGHT 90
END
```

To form a flower, you repeat the petal shape four times altogether using REPEAT 4. After each PETAL you must turn 90° using RIGHT 90 again.

```
TO FLOWER
  REPEAT 4
  PETAL
  RIGHT 90
END
```

You can make a better flower by using a smaller turning angle and adding more repeats.

```
TO BETTERFLOWER
  REPEAT 10
  PETAL
  RIGHT 36
END
```

Figure 67a (*above*) LOGO is a programming language that allows satisfying pictures to be drawn using simple shapes as building blocks.

Figure 67b (*opposite*) LOGO programs can control a Turtle (a floor robot) connected to the computer. The shapes drawn by the Turtle's pen are called Turtle graphics.

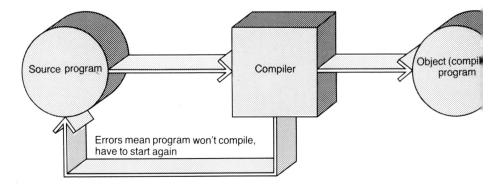

Errors mean program won't compile, have to start again

Authoring languages

Authoring languages form the top layer in the pyramid of Figure 64. They are designed for people without programming experience, and can achieve dramatic reductions in programming time compared with having to learn a language like BASIC. People, usually teachers and lecturers, who use these very high-level languages generally need more support than just the language itself in order to write programs. An authoring system gives a complete service. It provides not only the language, but also help with writing and editing what appears on the screen, and perhaps assistance to develop graphics, to control printers and other devices, and to compile information about students' progress and test results.

Microtext is an authoring language which was developed at the UK National Physical Laboratory, and was a direct offshoot of Edutext, a mainframe authoring system. Two others, PILOT and SuperPILOT, are available on some minicomputers and various microcomputers, and other authoring systems include IIS (available on IBM medium and large mainframes) and TUTOR (which is part of Control Data's PLATO system).

Compilers and interpreters

As explained on page 74 the facility or programming in any language other than the machine's own depends entirely on superprograms which perform the translation automatically. A *compiler* (Figure 68a, top) is like a translation service to whom you might send a book of short stories in French. The service translates the stories you have chosen into the language you

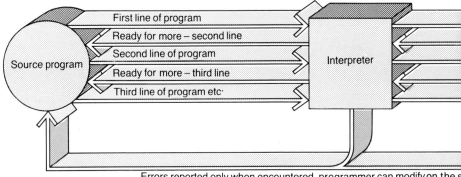

First line of program
Ready for more – second line
Second line of program
Ready for more – third line
Third line of program etc·

Errors reported only when encountered, programmer can modify on the s

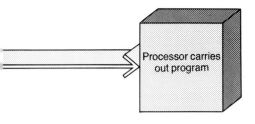

requested – German, say. Only after you get the German text back will you know if the right ones have been done or whether there has been a failure of communication. An *interpreter* (Figure 68, bottom) is more like a simultaneous translator at the United Nations. Each sentence (line of program) is translated (interpreted) as it is heard (read in) and so errors are identified for you as you go along.

The program that the programmer writes is known as the *source* program and the compiled version is called the *object* program. Once the compiler has translated the source program into machine language, this can run without interruption very rapidly and takes up little memory space. And since you need no longer store either the source program or the compiler, large amounts of RAM are available for data. Although a compiler

may take up more RAM space than an interpreter, it need not occupy space at the same time as the object program is run. By contrast, both the interpreter and the program being interpreted have to be held in memory all the time so that the interpreted version can be translated and executed line-by-line.

Not only do interpreters limit the RAM space available, they also make the program run more slowly. Most programs contain instructions to the processor to jump back to some previous line and 'loop the loop'. The interpreter has to re-translate all these lines over again. If the loop is to be repeated 100 or 1000 times, the re-translation must be done 100 or 1000 times. The whole process is very inefficient compared with running a once-and-for-all compiled version of the program. Interpreted programs tend to take around three to five times as long to run as compiled programs, and they leave less usable space inside the computer.

So why would anyone ever have a program interpreted if it could be compiled? The answer is two-fold. First, programmers often spend far longer debugging programs than writing them. With an interpreter, errors are identified as each line is read in and helpful messages are displayed telling the programmer what kind of error has occurred and where. This makes debugging much quicker and easier than with a compiler. Second, although a fully debugged program would run faster and occupy less space if it were compiled, in practice this may not be worth doing because, unless the processor is fully stretched, the program may be quite fast enough already and there may be RAM space to spare in any case. Most microcomputer makers supply a BASIC interpreter on a ROM so that it doesn't compete for RAM space.

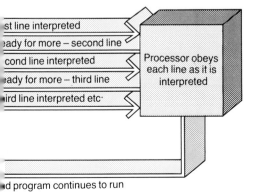

Figure 68 Two methods of translating a program from a high-level language to machine language: compiler (top of page) versus interpreter (bottom).

83

Operating systems

The computer's operating system is the control program that is ready to run all the time. Even when nothing is *apparently* happening, the operating system may be constantly checking the keyboard (or whatever input device is selected at the time) to see if anything is being typed in. When it finds something, it has to evaluate it to see whether it should try to obey a command instruction, forward the instruction to somewhere else (for example to a BASIC interpreter), or wait for more input. The operating system has to supervise input and output activities (for example from the keyboard and to the screen and printer), to decide what jobs the processor should give priority to, and to deal with the computer's external memory, saving and retrieving programs. The operating system is often referred to as OS for short, and the part of the OS that deals with discs is called the DOS (*Disc Operating System*).

The OS is also the computer's 'personality'. It determines whether the user experiences the computer as helpful, giving explanations of what is happening and indicating what input is required (*user-friendly*), or the opposite (*user-hostile*). The former style tends to need a larger OS than the latter (though not all large OSs are friendly!). The size and capabilities of OS programs vary enormously. Systems which have to deal with several users at once (*multi-user systems*) or several programs at once (*multi-tasking*) need more complicated operating systems than single-user, single-task micros (Figure 89). Whenever there are conflicting demands on scarce resources (like access to the processor, or space in RAM), the OS has to sort out the priorities.

Different operating systems are needed for different types of processor: 16-bit processors (see page 39) need different systems from 8-bit ones. 8-bit micros usually have relatively simple operating systems, but unfortunately they are often specific to the processor in use. Even

micros that use the same processor chip often have completely different OSs.

Mainframe OSs and programming languages are more standardised and this makes it easier to transfer software from one machine to another. Operating systems were originally developed to do some of the routine management performed by the mainframe computer's operator – arranging jobs in a sensible sequence in view of their likely running-time and their need for compilers. In the early days of computing, people expected to send jobs off to computer departments, and were willing to wait several days before they expected the results to be returned. The computer room arranged the jobs in batches so as to make efficient use of the CPU (central processing unit); this was known as *batch-processing*. As time went on users came to expect faster results (shorter *turnaround* times) and demand increased for *interactive* computing, where a user had a terminal connected directly to the computer and results could be obtained immediately. Once there was a demand for more interactive computing, operating systems were developed to allow the processor apparently to deal with several tasks simultaneously by dividing its attention among them. This also required the partitioning of memory space to prevent one job from interfering with another. *Time-sharing* (as it is known) allows many users to interact with the processor; unless the system is overstretched, each may have the illusion of having it to themselves.

More sophisticated systems were later developed to let the computer deal with larger volumes of information than would fit in its memory at one time, by exchanging data between internal memory and external storage as and when necessary. Finding the best way of reconciling the demands of conflicting jobs can be quite complicated, especially when several jobs using different programming languages have to be run simultaneously while still giving reasonable response times to people who want to use the computer *on-line* (immediately) for interactive work.

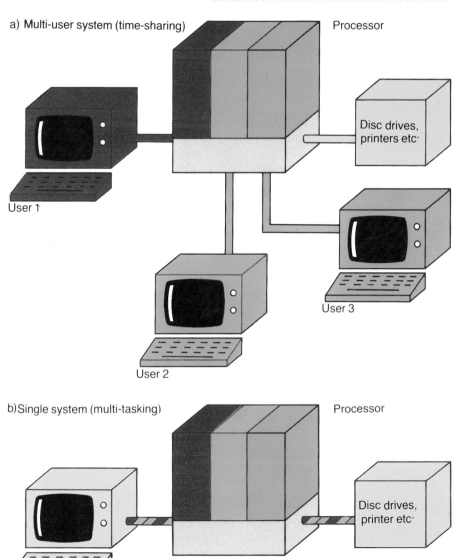

a) Multi-user system (time-sharing)   Processor

Disc drives, printers etc·

User 1

User 3

User 2

b) Single system (multi-tasking)   Processor

Disc drives, printer etc·

Figure 69 (a) In a multi-user system the processor shares out its time between the different users, switching from one task to the next so quickly that each user may have the illusion of having the processor's undivided attention. Mainframes, minis and powerful micros often work this way. (b) The processor of a single micro can also divide its attention, allowing several tasks to be carried out all (apparently) at the same time.

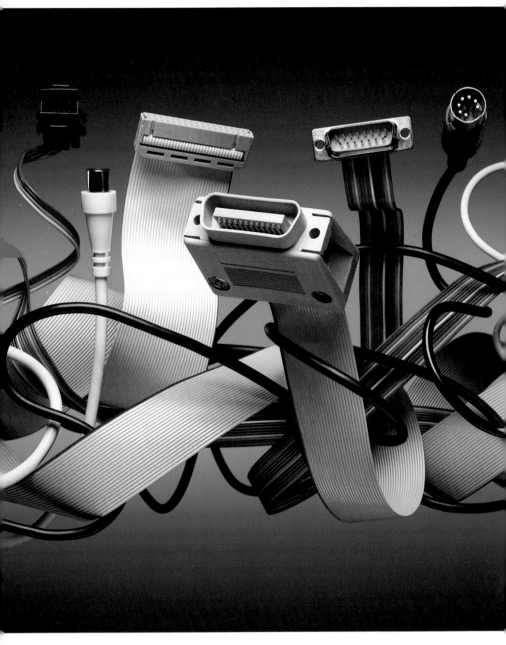

Figure 70 This jungle of plugs and cables suggests some of the problems of connecting computer devices. It is symbolic of deeper kinds of incompatibility in information technology generally.

86

Complicated operating systems exact a price in ease of use. Typically each user has to *log on* (identify themselves to the system), request the facilities they need (eg the BASIC interpreter), give the system enough information for it to allocate disc and memory space, call up any previous programs stored and perhaps make arrangements to retrieve their own printout (which may not be available immediately if there is a major job running on the line printer).

Compared with all this, using a micro is very simple. Often you can just switch on and begin: some systems load part of the operating system in from disc; in others it is *resident* (always available). The fact that micros don't have enough processor power and memory space to make it worth sharing out can be seen as a blessing by the single user. However, some of the new generation of 16-bit microcomputers are being used for multi-user multi-tasking, and their operating systems have to be more flexible. Sometimes they offer a choice of resident operating systems as a step toward overcoming compatibility problems.

Operating systems are important because they affect who feels able to use the system. Inevitably they influence one's attitude to working with the computer. For example, it is easy for a beginner with microcomputers to forget to close the door of the disc drive, or perhaps to try by mistake to save onto a write-protected disc. CP/M, still the most popular OS for 8-bit business micros, will respond to these easily made mistakes with an error message such as

BDOS ERR ON B: BAD SECTOR

This (understandably) causes many beginners to panic! But it could easily have been made to say instead 'Please close the disc drive door' or 'Sorry, can't save onto write-protected disc'.

The OS is more likely to determine what software can be run on a system than is the programming language originally provided. Many micros can run additional

languages just by plugging in additional ROMs or by loading them from disc. Unless the original OS provides for this, however, you may not be able to do so. In particular, the features of the disc operating system (DOS) determine what discs can be read.

There is a general lack of standardisation among microcomputer OSs. The nearest approach to a standard for single-user 8-bit business microcomputers is CP/M (Control Program for Microprocessors). It was devised in the late 1970s to help programmers to develop software. It was taken up by software developers with enthusiasm because it was the first OS to allow a program to be transferred from one microcomputer to another of a different kind. It managed this by separating the basic input/output section (BIOS), which is specific to the processor, from the section which deals with discs (the DOS). This is a bit like providing different shapes and sizes of plugs on a travelling iron so that it will be compatible with sockets in any country. The processor has to be told to read in CP/M off the disc, so part of the program includes a routine to load CP/M automatically. This technique is known as *bootstrapping*: the system 'pulls itself up by its own bootstraps'.

CP/M has become a standard even though it is based on technology which is now out-of-date; the existence of lots of tested CP/M business software guarantees its immediate future. This is not entirely a good thing, since CP/M does nôt use the full power of the processors for which it was designed, nor does it take full advantage of the technology of modern screen displays. The result is that it uses more memory than it should, is slower in retrieving from disc and not as *crash-proof* (fail-safe) as it should be. Nor is CP/M as friendly as it might be – as the error message above shows.

CP/M-86 is a modified version devised for 16-bit microcomputers, but it has not achieved the same monopoly as the original 8-bit CP/M. Its main rival is

87

MS-DOS, the system commissioned by IBM for its Personal Computer (in which it is called PC-DOS). Because IBM is the world's largest computer manufacturer, other 16-bit micro producers soon decided to follow its footsteps. Some manufacturers are hedging their bets by offering both these systems.

MP/M II is a multi-user operating system for micros derived from CP/M but it has not achieved the same popularity as the original CP/M either. A system called Unix has been widely adopted for 16-bit micros doing multi-user multi-tasking.

One interesting development is the rise of *concurrent* operating systems like Xerox's Smalltalk. These allow the user to swap around between different tasks without having to load different programs. It makes switching as quick and easy as changing channels on a television, only unlike a broadcast programme you don't 'lose your place'. With a concurrent OS graphics replace cryptic messages, and the user points to pictures on the screen (Figure 71) using a mobile pointer called a 'mouse' instead of the keyboard (see Chapter 3). By pointing to the calculator, the filing cabinet or the rubbish bin

Figure 71 An Apple Macintosh allows the user to design a training shoe using a table-top mouse to control the pointer which selects options from the pull-down menu. 'Edit' has been selected from the control menu along the top of the screen, so the edit menu has been pulled down, overlapping the main drawings. Other menus offer special effects and different line thicknesses.

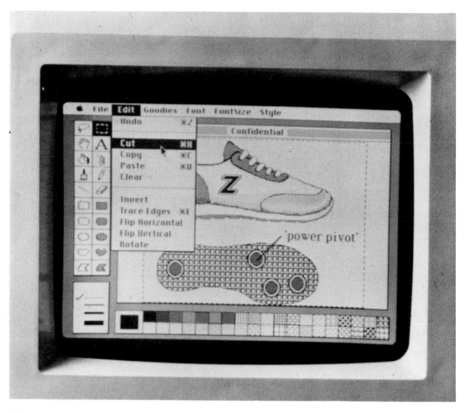

shown, the user can perform calculations, save something or delete it. Although such systems are friendly and flexible to use, they do make heavy demands on the memory and processor, as well as needing special hardware; the Lisa system was expensive when first introduced, but 'Concurrent CP/M' offers some of these features and is much cheaper. It is important to be aware of such developments, as concurrent operating systems designed for users rather than professional programmers represented the first significant advance in operating systems since CP/M.

A second development has been in the home computer field, where the recent arrival of the MSX standard promised fully interchangeable hardware and software for the first time. MSX was the result of co-operation between Microsoft, the

Figure 72 MSX is a new standard intended to bring compatability to microcomputer hardware and software.

American software house and ASCII, a Japanese company; the initials stand for Microsoft Extended Basic. But MSX represents much more than an agreement to standardise on that particular dialect of BASIC. It is also a common operating system that includes an agreed standard for peripherals. That means that any computer with the MSX logo should accept any MSX disc drive (or *joystick*) and that any MSX software should run on any MSX computer.

MSX is too recent for anyone to be sure whether it will become the world standard for 8-bit computers, as has been claimed. Some people believe that the Z80A processor on which MSX is based is already out-of-date: Sir Clive Sinclair commented that it was 'like standardising on a Model T Ford'. But Sinclair Research Ltd's success in selling millions of unconventional, non-standard home computers worldwide makes it hardly surprising that they should resist such attempts at standardisation!

MSX represents the first serious international attempt to solve the problems of incompatibility in home computer hardware and software. Its backing by household names like Hitachi, Philips and Pioneer suggests that some computers may come to be sold alongside normal domestic electronic products. The attractions of plug-in compatibility and a wider choice in software may bring in new kinds of home computer owners, people who previously regarded computers as being solely for hobbyists.

Utilities

Utilities are mundane but vital programs which do jobs like copying discs, telling you how much RAM space remains and preparing output for printing. Some may be supplied with the original computer or disc drive, but there are many useful ones which are marketed independently. For example, you can get utilities to recover the contents of deleted discs and to copy programs from one format or density to another.

89

Chapter 7: The changing telephone

The telephone was invented by Alexander Graham Bell more than a century ago (in 1876). It was accepted more quickly in America than in Britain, partly because of the greater distances to be overcome, and partly because of differences in price and lifestyle between the two countries. In Britain, the cost of a telephone instrument in 1878 was over £10, rather more than a year's wages for a servant. As servants

Figure 73 The spread of telephone ownership in the United Kingdom.

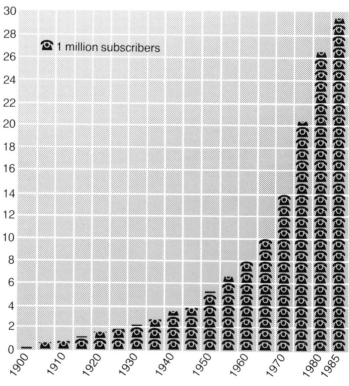

No. of subscribers in millions

 1 million subscribers

were often used to carry messages personally, and as the postal service was excellent, with up to 12 collections and deliver-
ies a day, most people couldn't see the
point of owning a telephone. And unless
enough of the people you know and want
to contact have telephones, there isn't
much value in having one yourself. In any
case, the idea of telephoning friends and
relatives long-distance just to exchange
conversation would have seemed strange
in a world where the middle classes culti-
vated the art of letter-writing and letters
could be exchanged several times within
the day in large cities. So by 1912 there
were only 700,000 telephones in Great
Britain, or one per 55 inhabitants, compared with one for every 18 citizens in
America.

It is only since the Second World War
that the telephone has become a standard
facility in most ordinary homes in
developed countries. Figure 73 illustrates the dramatic increase in popularity
of telephones in Britain, for example. By
1984, around 29 000 000 British telephones had been installed. Most of these
are used to carry conversations – *voice
traffic* as it is known – but an increasing
amount of telephone traffic is of a different kind: photographs and diagrams, for
instance, word-processed documents and
facsimile copies, hi-fi music and television
broadcasts, computer program and data.
Some of these can be transmitted through
the same lines that are used for voice
traffic; others demand so much bandwidth

that they need special circuits. The new
facilities all benefit from the gradual
changeover from analogue to digital
operation. Before examining why and
how this is happening, it would be
useful to see how voice traffic is normally
handled through the Public Switched
Telephone Network (PSTN).

Even the 'ordinary' PSTN is remarkable enough: from virtually any British
telephone you can dial direct to 93% of
the world's telephones. That means you
can have a conversation with someone at
any of 450 000 000 telephones in over 130
different countries – as long as you can
speak the same language and don't mind
phoning in the middle of the night to
reach someone on the other side of the
world! Yet you control this, the world's
largest machine, with a simple dial or set
of push-buttons; you can speak into your
mouthpiece using ordinary English, without having to worry about how your words
are translated into electrical impulses and
back again, or how they are routed
through numerous switches and circuits.
Your only link to this immense network
is probably a pair of thin wires twisted
together. These are enough to connect
you to a vast network of exchanges: over
6600 in Britain alone and thousands more
around the world. An international body
called CCITT co-ordinates the work of
all the Post, Telephone and Telegraph
(PTT) authorities in different countries to
ensure that equipment and networks
remain compatible.

The telephone instrument

Figure 74 shows some examples of how telephones have changed over the last century. The recent flood of new designs gives the *appearance* of great change, but in fact most instruments have the same three basic parts: the handset, the dial and the bell. Some modern telephones offer extra features: an LCD (*liquid crystal display*) is useful to show you what number you have just dialled. Memory telephones store the last number dialled, which is useful for repeat dialling when the line is engaged or there is no reply. These can also be programmed to store 10 or 20 frequently needed numbers so that you only have to press a couple of buttons instead of having to dial nine or more numbers (a facility known as abbreviated dialling). Some cordless telephones can even work from cars or trains by using short-wave radio. However, the essential design of the telephone instrument has changed surprisingly little.

Figure 74 Early telephones had handles that you wound to tell the exchange what number you wanted. Later, rotary dials allowed subscribers to dial local numbers for themselves. Push-button telephones speeded up the dialling process and made it more reliable, and an LCD display (for the number dialled, or the time of day) is a useful addition. Cordless telephones, like the Racal Vodaphone, depend on a network of short-wave radio links.

The handset

The handset normally contains a mouth-piece and an earpiece and rests on a cradle or hook (Figure 75). Lifting the handset releases a switch which acts as a signal that the caller, Miss A, wants the use of a line. The exchange then sends her the dialling tone; she dials the number she wants and, once a connection to Mr B's telephone is made, she first hears a ringing tone, then (if he answers), his voice. (Alternatively if his handset is 'off the hook' she will hear the engaged (busy) signal and will abandon the call.)

These sounds are all sent up the line as electrical signals, which her earpiece turns back into sounds. Similarly, the words Miss A then speaks are turned into electrical signals by her mouthpiece and sent down the line to Mr B's telephone, where his earpiece turns them back into sounds again. When conversation is in progress, there is a continual conversion of sounds into electrical signals and back into sounds again, with traffic in both directions (Figure 76). The mouthpieces act like microphones and the earpieces like loud-speakers in a hi-fi system.

Figure 75 The main components of a telephone instrument.

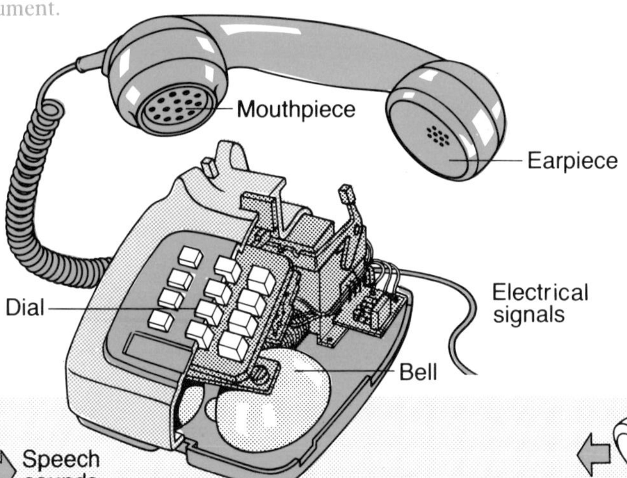

Mouthpiece

Earpiece

Dial

Electrical signals

Bell

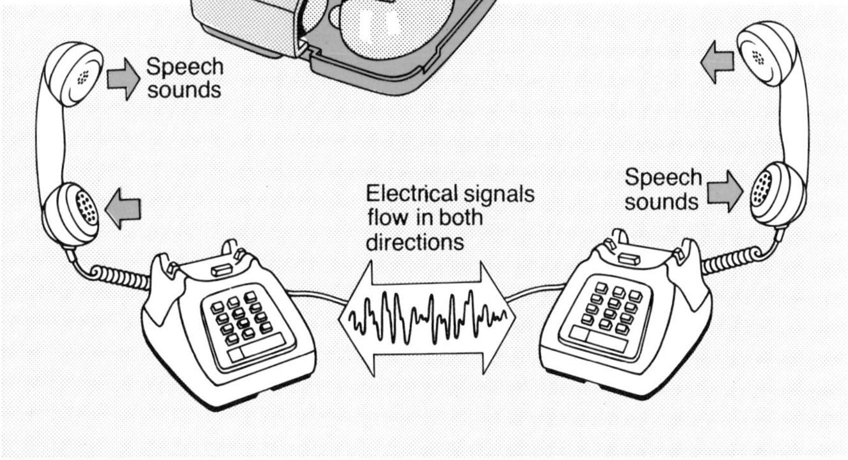

Speech sounds

Electrical signals flow in both directions

Speech sounds

Figure 76 Exchange of signals during a telephone conversation.

It is important to realise that this process is analogue at every stage (see page 25). Sound waves are simply variations in air pressure. The mouthpiece contains carbon granules, which conduct electricity, and these are alternately squeezed up or allowed to spread out by the air pressure variations. Their electrical resistance varies accordingly and varying electrical signals are created. In Figure 77, the top pattern represents the sound waves created when a word of two syllables is spoken. The middle pattern shows the electrical signal made by the mouthpiece. The bottom pattern shows the recreated sound signals produced in the remote earpiece by a converse process. As you can

see, the electrical signal transmitted through the telephone wires is (normally) a close analogue of the sound pattern.

Curiously, the modern mouthpiece is still based on a design patented in 1878 by a Yorkshire curate called Henry Hunnings. The only fundamental changes in recent years have been special arrangements that free the user from the need to hold a handset at all. Conference telephones have microphones that pick up sounds from several metres away and loudspeakers that allow anyone in the office to hear the incoming caller. This provides 'hands-off' telephoning for the individual, and can allow a group of people to take part in a single call.

Figure 77 Analogue transmission of sound waves by telephone.

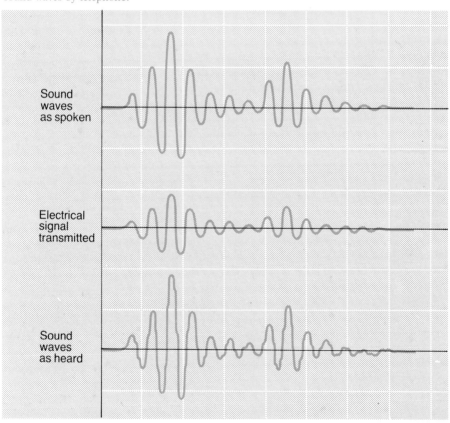

Sound waves as spoken

Electrical signal transmitted

Sound waves as heard

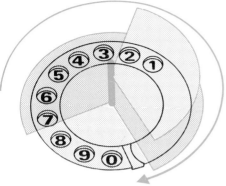

Figure 78 A number is dialled by turning a rotary dial through an angle; the size of the angle depends on the number dialled.

The dial

The first telephones had no dials: all connections were made by human operators. Turning a crank (or, later, lifting the handset) rang a bell at the exchange to alert the operators that someone wanted to place a call. The caller had to tell the operator the number in order for the connection to be made. Once automatic exchanges began to spread, dial telephones allowed subscribers to dial their own connections. To begin with only local calls could be dialled directly. Direct dialling of long-distance calls is comparatively recent: in Britain the first STD exchange (Subscriber Trunk Dialling) opened in 1958, and international subscriber dialling only began in the 1960s.

The traditional rotary dial creates a signal corresponding to each digit of the number being dialled by interrupting an electrical current the appropriate number of times while the dial returns to its resting position (Figure 78). Dialling the digit six creates six interruptions, and so on up to nine, with 0 requiring ten. The distance the rotary dial is turned is an analogue for the size of the number to be transmitted.

Rotary dialling is a slow method of transmitting numbers; modern telephones tend to have push-buttons that the user simply presses in the correct sequence. Although these are digital instruments, it is important to realise that they are often still connected to the same analogue system and their handsets operate on just the same principles as rotary-dial telephones. So the numbers take just as long to be transmitted, but because dialling is faster, the caller's hands are freed for longer. Also, because they are digital it is easier to give push-button telephones other useful facilities like LCD displays and memories.

The bell

Whenever the handset is in its cradle, a telephone is simply a listening instrument: it is constantly monitoring whether anyone in the outside world wants to get in touch. In this way it is like the operating system of a computer, constantly 'listening' to the keyboard to see if anyone has pressed a key. When an incoming call is placed, the telephone gives off a noise: usually a bell rings, though it might be a buzzer, bleep or other sound. This stops only when the instrument detects that its handset has been lifted or that the connection has been broken (eg because the caller has given up trying and replaced his handset). For people with hearing difficulties or who have several telephones on one desk, the signal can be a flashing light as well as, or instead of, a sound.

Lines and exchanges

Automatic exchanges

The first public automatic exchange was based on a design patented in 1891 by Almon B. Strowger in Kansas, USA. Strowger was an undertaker who is said to have blamed his business failure on the exchange operator, who was married to his great rival: he suspected that she diverted business from his prospective clients to her husband. Whether or not this story is true, his automatic switching system was extremely successful, and Strowger exchanges are still in widespread use in many countries including Britain and America.

95

The principle of a Strowger exchange is illustrated in Figure 79. It uses electromagnets and ratchets to move wipers first vertically, then horizontally, against contacts arranged in curved banks of 10 by 10. The movements of the wipers are made in time to the impulses sent by rotary dials – about one digit (up to 10 impulses) per second. That is why a modern-looking push-button telephone often only speeds up the dialling process and not the transmission time; if it is connected to a Strowger exchange, you will still have to wait as long for the connection as if you had used a rotary dial.

By the standards of the 1980s, this mechanical switching is slow, and the moving parts require a lot of maintenance. Furthermore, all the switches required to set up the connection are tied up for the entire duration of the call. The Crossbar exchange was a later design, first operated in Sweden in 1926, which frees the switching apparatus to establish another call once a connection has been made. This is an improvement on the Strowger design, but both are being phased out gradually in favour of modern digital exchanges.

Local and long-distance exchanges

With so many millions of telephone subscribers, it would obviously be impractical to try to connect everyone to everyone else directly: the number of cables needed would be astronomical. This is why the system of a hierarchy of exchanges was evolved. You can think of each trunk (long-distance) exchange as being like a tree: the leaves (telephones) are connected by twigs (twisted pairs of wires) to branches (local exchanges). Small branches sometimes join to form larger branches (tandem exchanges), before joining the main, or trunk exchange (Figure 80). Each country's telephone system can be pictured as a whole forest of trunk exchanges, linked by high-capacity cables. International calls require links to be made between forests, ie through international exchanges. These are often connected by radio waves or underwater cables, or even satellites.

Figure 79 A Strowger switch can route a call to any of 100 subscribers. When a two-figure number is dialled, the wiper moves to connect with the corresponding contact in the bank of 100. To deal with more subscribers, longer numbers are dialled through several Strowger switches in turn.

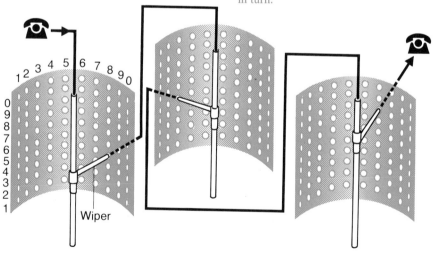

Wiper

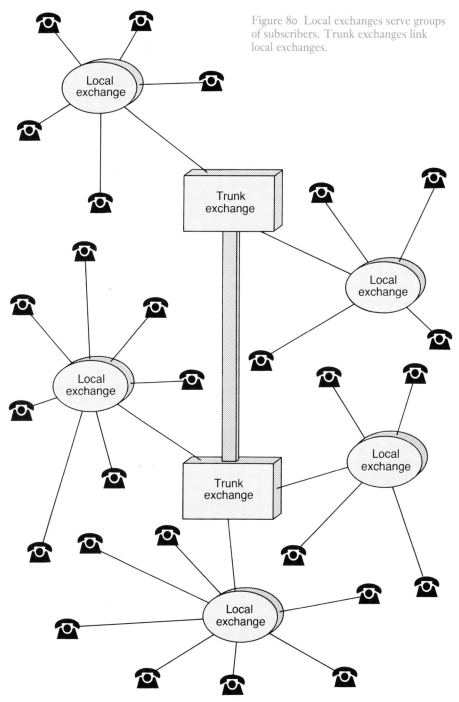

Figure 80 Local exchanges serve groups of subscribers. Trunk exchanges link local exchanges.

How does each exchange 'know' where to route a call? Most countries have a system that gives a unique identification number to each telephone. In the United States, for example, the Direct Distance Dialling (DDD) system assigns 10 digits to each telephone: the first three are an area code that identifies one of 150-odd areas, the next three are a local toll office number, and the last four identify which of 10 000 possible lines is to be selected. Calls within the same area do not require the first three digits to be dialled: the absence of an area code identifies the destination of the call as falling within that area.

Similarly in Britain, each major city has a unique *prefix* (set of numbers at the beginning): numbers with an 01- prefix are all in London, those with an 041- prefix are all in Glasgow. The next three numbers identify an area within the city and the final four select the individual subscriber. An international prefix (in Britain 010) tells the system that a subscriber wants to place an international call, and another set of digits identifies the country, eg 1 calls Canada or the United States, 33 France and 61 Australia. These numbers have been agreed internationally; only the international prefix varies according to where you are starting from. Thus to dial Britain from abroad, you need whatever international prefix is used in the country from which you are calling, followed by 44 (the code that identifies the UK), followed by the number as dialled in the UK (omitting the first 0 which is only used *within* the UK).

Local connections are usually made quite quickly because they just go through the local exchange. However, if you ever dial an international (or even a long-distance call), you may notice a delay of half a minute or more between when you finish dialling and when the connection is made. The reason for this is the number of exchanges through which each call has to be routed. Many exchanges still use mechanical methods of setting up the connections, so each exchange can introduce a delay of several seconds. Once the con-

nection is made, however, the line is exclusive to the two parties and conversation usually proceeds at a normal pace. Indeed you often get a better connection on a long-distance call than on a local one, because it's more likely to have been routed through modern digital exchanges. Transcontinental calls often give unexpectedly good lines for the same reason.

Attenuation and noise

In practice, electrical signals suffer from travelling long distances in two ways: they get fainter (*attenuated*) and they may also become distorted by *noise*. The picture that was presented in Figure 77 is oversimplified in that it does not distinguish between the state of the electrical signal as sent by the caller's mouthpiece and the one received by the distant earpiece.

Attenuation is the weakening of a signal as you get further from its source: a loud shout or a blazing beacon seem faint (attenuated) from a distance. The effects of attenuation are combated in long-distance cables by devices called *repeaters* that boost the signal at regular intervals, often every few kilometres. Repeaters suffer from the basic problem that they magnify the noise as well as the signal (Figure 91).

Across continents

There are various methods of transmitting telephone signals through copper cables over long distances. The cables have different capacities according to their construction (Figure 81): they may be piped underground, strung between telegraph posts, or laid on the sea-bed. The first *submarine* (underwater) telephone cable was laid under the Atlantic in 1956, almost a century after the first transatlantic telegraph cable, and provided 36 voice-grade channels; since then further cables have added tens of thousands of channels.

Submarine cables are expensive to lay and difficult to maintain. One alternative is the use of radio waves. Radio telephony was used in the First World War, and in 1927 a link between Rugby in England and

Rocky Point in New Jersey allowed ordinary subscribers to phone across the Atlantic: the first transatlantic phone calls cost £15 for a three-minute call from the British end. The Rugby transmitter used long wavelength radio, needed vast aerials and had a high power consumption, but the service was reliable.

Shorter wavelengths have various advantages: lower power consumption, higher bandwidth and the ability to be focused into a narrow beam. Microwaves are very short wavelength radio waves; they are used in burglar alarm systems, radar navigation and microwave ovens, as well as in telephone transmission. A microwave transmitter can focus its signals accurately into a dish antenna only a few metres in diameter many miles away, as long as it is in *direct line-of-sight*. Advanced transmitters can carry tens of thousands of telephone conversations simultaneously,

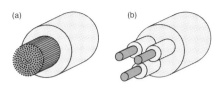

Figure 81 (a) Twisted pairs of wires formed into a cable. (b) An underground coaxial cable. Coaxial cables can carry greater amounts of information within a given diameter than ordinary cables.

Figure 82 Radio waves can overcome the curvature of the earth by simple or multiple reflection off ionised layers in the atmosphere.

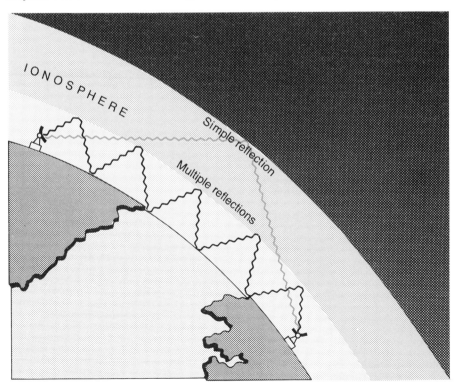

and modern long-distance telephony now depends on networks of microwave transmitters in line-of-sight of each other. In Britain, Telecom Tower in London is the centre of such a network.

Over really long distances, the earth's curvature presents a problem. Short radio waves can be bounced (reflected) off a special layer in the earth's atmosphere called the ionosphere (Figure 82) in order to get them to their destination. *Multiple reflections* allow signals to be bounced over really long distances, but, as you might expect, this leads to considerable attenuation. With the arrival of the space age, communications satellites provide an even better method. If the satellite is launched so as to orbit the earth at the same speed as that at which the earth rotates, it appears to be stationary from earth; this is called a *geostationary orbit.* This means that any transmitter within the satellite's *footprint* (Figure 122, page 140) can bounce signals off it. Early satellites merely reflected the signal passively, but later ones were designed actively to boost the signal before transmitting it back to earth. Thus, in place of the attenuation losses caused by reflection at the ionosphere, satellites can actually *improve* the quality of the signal. One disadvantage in long-distance 'phone calls routed by satellite, however, is that there is often a noticeable delay caused by the time taken for the signals to travel all those thousands of miles. This means that each person must leave a definite gap once they have finished speaking to signal that the other may begin.

Optical fibres

The recent development of fibre optics has profound implications for all kinds of long-distance communication. You may remember (Chapter 2) that the higher the frequency of a wave, the greater the bandwidth, and therefore information capacity, available. The frequency of light is around 100 000 times greater than the highest radio frequency, which means it can pro-

vide immensely larger bandwidth in a much thinner cable. A single fibre of glass, much finer than a human hair, can carry nearly a thousand telephone conversations (Figure 83). The signals are encoded as brief pulses of light at one end and decoded back into signals again at the other: the system is suited to digital transmission. In fact, the 'light' waves used are actually invisible because it was discovered that infra-red waves travel better than visible light inside the glass fibre.

The idea of using ultra-thin strands of glass to carry the light pulses was proposed in 1966 by two scientists at the STC (Standard Telephone and Cables) laboratories in Britain, and progress has been rapid since then. Optical fibres are made from ultra-pure glass so transparent that you could see through a block of it 35 km thick as easily as through a window-panel – light signals would be lost completely within a few metres of ordinary glass. An optical fibre is so thin that it is very flexible and can be bent round corners easily. The light is bounced along it and cannot escape.

By 1977, the world's first optic fibre link was in action between Hitchin and Stevenage in England. It could carry 1920 simultaneous telephone conversations or a mix of telephone, television and data traffic. The overall diameter of the cable was only 7mm and it was laid in existing ducts alongside conventional cables. In 1982, British Telecom (BT) at Martlesham achieved transmission at 140 million bits per second over 102 km of continuous optical fibre without using any kind of boosting. BT laid hundreds of kilometres of optical fibres in the early 1980s and will probably not install *any* new metal coaxial cable after 1985. The first deep-water optical cable was experimentally laid in Loch Fyne, Scotland, in 1980, and a transatlantic optical cable is expected to be in service by 1988. America, Japan and many other countries are going over to fibre optics too.

The light in an optical fibre has to be switched on and off incredibly fast –

thousands of millions of times a second. This requires a special kind of source, usually a *laser* or an LED – *light-emitting diode* (lasers are more powerful, but LEDs last longer). Like electrical signals, light signals get attenuated (weaker) as they travel along. To overcome attenuation, *regenerators* detect, boost and re-transmit the signal, but because the whole operation is carried out on a digital, not an analogue signal, regenerators are not needed at nearly such frequent intervals as repeaters in an analogue system. (Digital pulses are far less prone to noise than analogue ones, see page 24). By 1982, distances of over 100 km had been achieved without regenerators; improvements of up to a thousand kilometres have been forecast.

In addition to their higher transmission capacity, greater compactness, easier installation and reduced regenerator requirements, optical fibres have other advantages over metal cables. They are light-weight to handle, immune to electro-magnetic interference, safe to use in dangerous places such as mines and oil refineries, don't suffer from interference as metal cables do and are more secure because they cannot be 'tapped' in the way that conventional 'phone wires can.

Figure 83 A single optical fibre can carry a thousand telephone conversations, yet several can pass through the eye of a sewing needle.

(a)

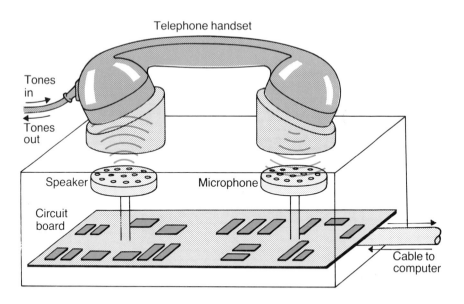

Figure 84 (a) An acoustic coupler converts sound signals from a telephone
handset into digital electric impulses for a
computer to process, and *vice versa*.

(b) A modem connects the computer
directly to the telephone system and converts the analogue electric impulses into
digital form for the computer to process.
(Modems give more reliable results and
permit higher transmission speeds but
they can only be used where a suitable
socket is available.)

(b)

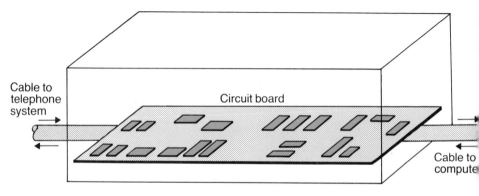

Figure 85 A lap-held computer and
acoustic coupler provide an office in a
briefcase. Messages and instructions can
by typed in and sent to home, to head
office, or to a central computer using any
telephone.

Figure 86 (a) Frequency division multiplexing (FDM): colours represent separate frequencies at which messages are
carried along the same cable.

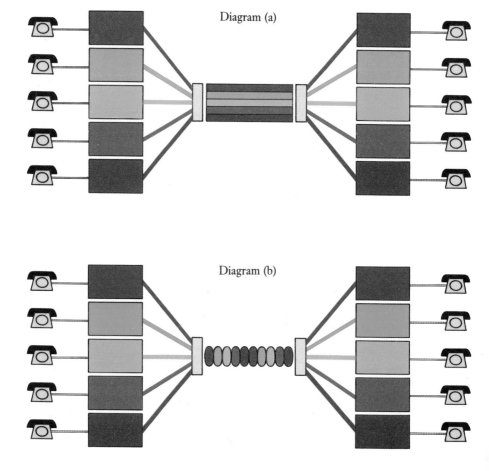

Diagram (a)

Diagram (b)

(b) Time division multiplexing (TDM):
the sources are sampled briefly in turn
and the sample signals sent in succession
along the cable.

Acoustic couplers and modems

The PSTNs that grew up during the first century of telephony were designed for voice traffic. Once computer terminals and microcomputers began to spread, special private circuits were developed for data traffic and other special purposes. In addition, methods were developed to allow computers to transmit and receive data down ordinary (ie voice-grade) telephone lines.

The cheapest method devised was an *acoustic coupler* (Figure 84a). This can be attached wherever there is a telephone handset of traditional design and plugged into any computer with a suitable interface. The coupler transforms the sounds coming out of the earpiece into digital pulses to feed into the computer, and transforms the digital signals from the computer back into sounds whistled into the mouthpiece. It is called *acoustic* because it codes and decodes the signals as sounds; so if the room is noisy or the handset a poor fit, data may easily be corrupted. Its baud rate is normally limited to 300 bits per second in each direction (full duplex). Nevertheless, the acoustic coupler (or *acoustic modem* as it is increasingly known) is portable and cheap: in Britain, such devices are available for £50 or less.

For faster and more reliable transmission, it is necessary to use a modem (Figure 84b), sometimes called a *direct-connect modem* to distinguish it from acoustic devices. *Modem* is short for modulator/demodulator; it converts electronic data into a *modulated* electrical signal directly, without using sound as an intermediary, and *vice versa*. This is a more reliable process, as you would expect, and higher speeds are possible depending on the bandwidth available to the consumer. (High speeds – above about 1200 bits per second – generally require the leasing of a private line from the PTT). CCITT lays down international standards for modems so that computers in different countries using different makes of modem can still communicate by telephone.

Multiplexing

Whatever cabling is used to join two exchanges, it would be quite impractical to provide as many cables as there are subscribers joined to each. Most people's telephones are not in use most of the time. *Multiplexing* is a way of making a single link transmit several signals at once without getting them mixed up. A coaxial cable with repeaters every 1.5 km might have an effective bandwidth of over 60 MHz (60 000 KHz), whereas each telephone conversation needs only a bandwidth of 4 KHz. Multiplexing means that a single cable can carry tens of thousands of calls, reducing the costs and upheaval of telephone cabling without increasing the time that subscribers have to wait for a connection. Telephone engineers allocate circuits on a statistical basis: for example, the target might be that on average no more than 1.5% of long-distance callers have to wait more than three seconds for a line.

There are two important methods of multiplexing: *frequency division multiplexing* and *time division multiplexing*. These names are a bit of a mouthful; most people call them FDM and TDM for short.

Figure 86a shows the FDM principle: each signal is carried on a separate high-frequency carrier wave. The signal is actually coded as variations (called *modulations*) superimposed on the carrier wave. The modulated signals are all transmitted in parallel and the frequencies separated out at the other end. The latter process is like turning the tuning dial on a radio to receive sounds from a station broadcasting at a different frequency. Using FDM, a coaxial cable can carry thousands of conversations at once. For example, a cable consisting of eleven paired coaxial wires can provide 3600 voice channels per circuit; as one pair is usually kept in reserve as a spare, this means 36 000 conversations can be carried per cable.

Going back to the radio-tuning analogy, FDM is like the international agreements that allocate different frequency bands to each broadcasting station so that they can all share the same medium (radio waves) without interfering with each other's broadcasts. No-one else is allowed to use a station's frequency band even when it isn't broadcasting at all: so when it isn't broadcasting those frequencies are in effect 'wasted'. Similarly, FDM wastes channel capacity whenever a channel is not using the bandwidth allocated to it.

TDM is another way of solving the multiplexing problem (Figure 86b). The Baudot Wheel (Figure 87) was an early example of a kind of TDM. The rotary switch allowed several Morse operators to send messages down a single telegraph wire: they all took it in turns to transmit some characters. In general, TDM works on the principle of dividing up the transmission time into tiny slices. Each of the signals to be sent is sampled rapidly in turn and transmitted in quick succession. A special pulse is used to distinguish which sample belongs to which conversation. This method has the advantage that the full bandwith is available to each signal, and that a channel not in use need not take up any of the channel's capacity.

Figure 87 (*below*) The Baudot wheel allowed several Morse operators to take turns in sending signals down the same line – an early example of multiplexing.

Figure 88 (*right*) System X is British Telecom's new generation of digital switching systems. The exchanges use compact and reliable electronics in place of the electromechanical switches and relays in the analogue exchanges that they replace. This makes them easier and cheaper to maintain. System X exchanges take up less space, give higher quality and offer more services.

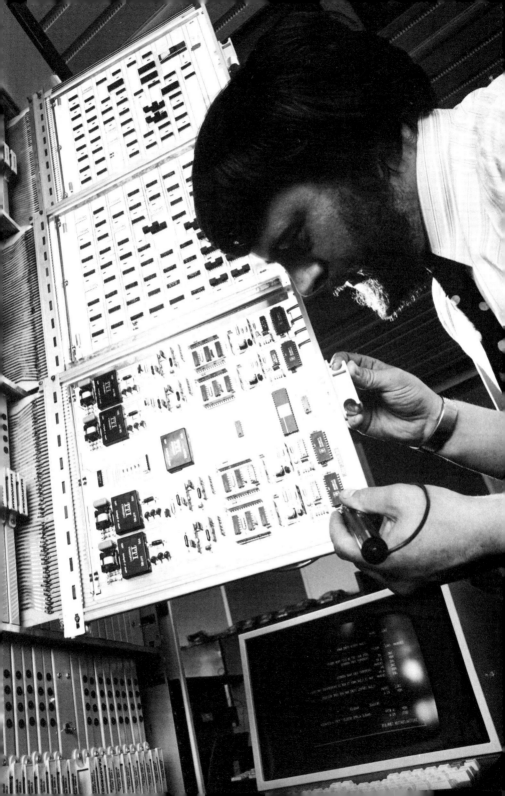

In many telephone systems, both systems of multiplexing are combined. FDM is especially suitable to analogue transmission, and TDM to the digital methods described below.

The digital revolution

The last 50 years have seen a worldwide expansion of the telephone network, but remarkably little change in its fundamental design. PSTNs in most countries are dominated by analogue instruments, slow electromechanical exchange equipment, and lines with bandwidths adequate for human voices but too restricted for high-quality sound, let alone fast exchange of computer data or the transmission of moving pictures.

The key to revolutionising the speed, quality and flexibility of telephone communication is simple: the replacement of analogue means by digital ones. Earlier in this chapter we saw how telephone numbers can be dialled digitally with push button 'phones, how optical fibres can transmit immense numbers of digital pulses rapidly and how TDM allows many sources to make use of the same transmission channel. The next step is both simple and logical: if the telephone sounds are themselves coded as digital pulses, they can be routed and controlled by digital exchanges, transmitted by optical fibres, multiplexed by TDM and processed by any method known to digital computing. *All* telephone traffic, whether voice, data, image, computer programs or whatever, can be encoded, switched, routed and decoded in digital form.

Earlier chapters have made it clear that modern computing is fundamentally the story of electronic digital processing. A modern digital telephone exchange is not hard to understand: it is no more and no less than a computer. Admittedly it looks a little different from computers you may have seen. It has an immense number of inputs and an immense number of outputs. But most of its work is simply concerned with making the right connections.

Usually its job is not so much to process the information as to keep the information intact (though some exceptions are mentioned later). Nevertheless, it works on exactly the same basic principles as any other digital computer. What the telecommunications engineers grandly call Stored Program Control simply means that the exchange computer's behaviour is controlled by a program.

The worldwide move from analogue to digital operation started in America in the 1960s. The British Post Office (as it then was) installed the Empress exchange in 1968, and by 1983 most British Telecom trunk exchanges had been converted to digital operation. Installation of System X (Figure 88), a high-capacity, high-speed integrated digital network began in 1981, and by 1984 already offered a wide range of extra services and improvements in speed and quality. However, any country changing over from analogue to digital telephony has to proceed gradually, so as to maintain full compatibility with the analogue instruments still in people's homes and with the existing analogue network in most of the rest of the world. The full benefits of digital transmission cannot be realised while digital signals still have to be converted back to analogue immediately before entering the exchanges, and, likewise, the value of digital exchanges is restricted without fully digital transmission.

Digital coding of sounds

So how are sounds turned into the digital pulses that the new digital exchanges are designed to deal with? Imagine a buoy bobbing up and down on the waves against a pier at the seaside. If the pier has regular markings showing the height above the low-water mark, a casual observer (with nothing better to do) might take height readings for the buoy every now and then. Working to the nearest centimetre, he or she might record 310, 318, 308, 317, 309, 319, and so on. Each of these readings could be turned into a long binary number (see page 195). The analogue motion of the wave bobbing up and down could in this way be turned into a string of digital pulses (Figure 89).

How faithful the digitised picture is depends on how often the observer took his readings. The 318, 317 and 319 readings might look like the crests of waves and the 310, 308 and 309 ones might look like troughs, but if the observer only took his readings once every couple of minutes they could just be random variations bearing no relation to the actual size of the wave. If the readings were taken twice a second, however, then they would probably be reliable. It all depends on the sampling being more frequent than the oscillation (up and down movement) of the water waves. In practice, it turns out that the sampling frequency for digitising must be at least double the bandwidth of the waves observed.

Figure 89 Digital coding: the more frequently samples are taken of a waveform, the more faithfully it can be reconstructed. To reconstruct digitised sound waves accurately, the sampling frequency must be at least double the bandwidth.

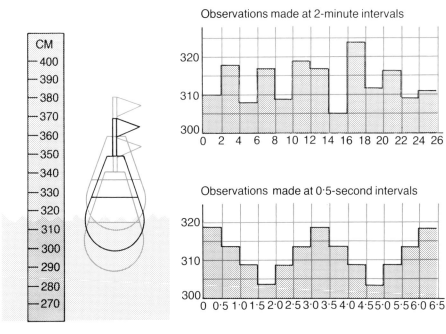

Observations made at 2-minute intervals

Observations made at 0·5-second intervals

In the telephone system this process is called *Pulse Code Modulation* (PCM). The sampling frequency for a telephone bandwidth of 4 KHz must be at least 8 KHz: that is, the sound waves produced by speech must be sampled 8000 times per second. Suppose that the waveform in Figure 90a represents 1/800th of a second (10 samples); it might correspond to a tiny fraction of a spoken word. The vertical lines show the samples taken, and there are seven possible levels (which can be positive or negative) plus zero. The table below is then used to convert the numbers into three-bit binary codes. In practice, an extra bit would be added to show positive or negative (above or below the line). Figure 90b shows the shape of the waveform as reconstructed from the binary codes. It looks 'squared off' and would sound badly distorted. But if 127 different levels are distinguished instead of only eight, each level can be represented by an eight-bit code. This gives good reproduction of telephone speech and requires a transmission speed of 64000 (8000 × 8) bits per second.

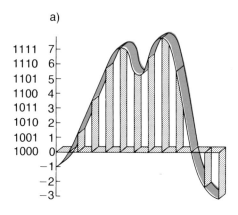

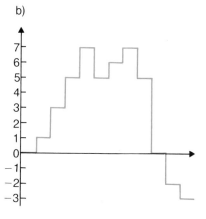

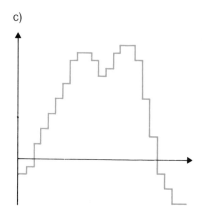

Figure 90 Pulse Code Modulation. Diagram (a) represents a fraction of a sound wave transmitted via a telephone line. Ten samples of its shape are taken and converted into binary code (see table below). Reconstructed, these 10 samples would look like diagram (b) and sound badly distorted. Diagram (c) shows the waveform produced by doubling the number of samples; its similarity to the original has increased markedly.

digital	1	3	5	7	5	6	7	5	0	-2	-3
binary	1001	1011	1101	1111	1101	1110	1111	1101	0000	0010	0011

+(positive)			−(negative)	
1	1	001	0	001
2	1	010	0	010
3	1	011	0	011
4	1	100	0	100
5	1	101	0	101
6	1	110	0	110
7	1	111	0	111

So if you increase the sampling frequency you increase the accuracy or *fidelity* of the digital information. Figure 90c shows the effect of doubling the sampling frequency used. With thousands of samples being needed every second, and TDM allowing thousands of conversations to be multiplexed down a single cable, you can see why optical fibres capable of switching thousands of millions of times a second are required!

PCM signals are above all *robust*. Each binary number is transmitted as a string of pulses, and the difference between on's and off's (1s and 0s) can withstand a great deal of attenuation and noise without becoming blurred (Figure 91). This is

because regenerators can take an attenuated digital signal and recreate the original *exactly*. Their performance is far better than analogue repeaters, which are obliged to amplify the noise along with the signal.

Figure 91 (a) Repeaters amplify both signal and noise. (b) Regenerators ignore the noise and reconstruct the original signal.

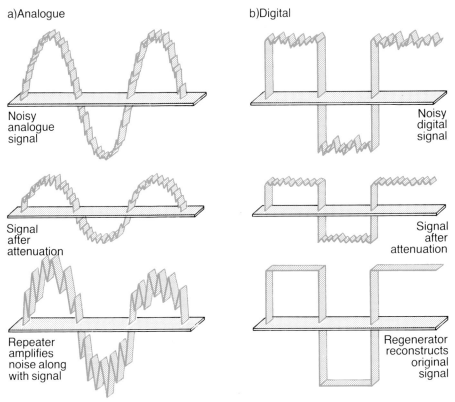

a) Analogue

Noisy analogue signal

Signal after attenuation

Repeater amplifies noise along with signal

b) Digital

Noisy digital signal

Signal after attenuation

Regenerator reconstructs original signal

Private Branch Exchanges

Many firms have Private Branch Exchanges to help internal communications without running up large bills on the PSTN. These may be controlled by a switchboard operator or they may be automatic. The most recent kind are called *call-connect systems* and use digital microelectronics to provide a whole range of facilities. Some, such as abbreviated dialling and repeating and storing the last number dialled, are widespread. Other options include the barring of incoming or outgoing calls and the diversion of calls to a different extension; this can be unconditional or it may be activated conditionally, eg only if the call is unanswered for a certain time, or only if the extension is engaged. 'Hold' buttons and 'call waiting' allow the operator to attend to more than one caller at a time, and the 'three-party' service allows a sort of three-way *conference call.*

Voice store-and-forward systems

Unlike conventional answering machines, voice *store-and-forward systems* allow you to leave a spoken message for any person or group of people, for distribution either immediately or later. A computer digitises the voice message before storing it, which saves memory space; later it reconstructs the message before transmission. The computer program makes it easy for the user to give different priorities and destinations to different messages. Although dictation is faster for the sender than typing out the words of a message, listening is slower than reading for receivers, who may also have to take their own notes. It is not clear how acceptable such systems will be to users.

Figure 92 Call-connect systems are simply modern private branch exchanges. Microelectronics make them smaller and more reliable than the previous generation, and they offer a wide range of services.

Voice Response Systems

Voice Response Systems (VRS) are computer-based information systems that can be used by up to 100 000 people telephoning from anywhere. The user enters data, orders, questions and instructions using the telephone touch-keypad. The computer responds immediately with a natural-sounding voice in whatever language is desired, providing the information, confirmation or messages. This is useful for credit card verification, travel reservations, ordering goods or catalogues and answering account enquiries.

The touch-keypad works by producing a different tone for each key; these are detected by the digital exchange according to a CCITT protocol called Q-23. The VRS unit also detects the tones and turns them into digital form for the computer. In effect, the keypad can act like the keyboard of a microcomputer. VRS units employ advanced multiplexing so that each can handle up to 48 telephone lines at once, or 15 000 calls a day, giving immediate response to each.

Current VRS systems use pre-recorded speech stored on EPROMs (*erasable and programmable* ROM *chips*). Each word or number is stored separately at an *address* known to the central processor, which combines them in response to the input. A vocabulary of a few hundred words covers most applications, with alternative language versions stored separately. Before long, synthesised speech is likely to be of a high enough quality to replace pre-recorded speech, thus making the system much more flexible.

The Packet Switched Service

So far this chapter has concentrated on the familiar PSTN type of service where a connection, once established, is exclusive to the two parties. Throughout the duration of the call, the line is occupied, whether or not anyone is talking, waiting for attention or has put the handset down to go and get some information. The circuit may actually be idle for a considerable proportion of the call. This type of connection is called circuit-switching.

There are many other types of service offered by PTTs. Some are private lines that can be leased semi-permanently, others are made available to subscribers on a different principle. One important group is known as Packet Switched Services. *Packet-switching* is the method generally used for connecting devices like computers. Circuit-switching is not suitable for computer networks for many reasons: telephone noise is usually only a nuisance in a conversation, but it can wreak havoc in an exchange of data between computers. Also it takes a long time (in computer terms) to establish the connection, and the PSTN bandwidth is too narrow for fast data transfer. Furthermore, telephone connections are usually only two-way, whereas computers may need to exchange data with hundreds of terminals at once.

Packet-switching means sending information in little packets of an agreed size and format, each labelled with its source and destination. Imagine a group of people travelling together by railway. Circuit-switching would be like putting them all in a special train hired for the purpose, and closing the railway lines to other traffic between the point of departure and the destination. Packet-switching is more like labelling each person with their source and destination address and letting them mingle with other passengers on normal train services. The group or packet is reassembled at the other end of the journey. In some systems each packet is of a fixed length; on others they may range from a few bytes to several kilobytes.

PSS services make better use of the network and offer much higher transmission speeds than PSTNs; error rates are much lower than on the PSTN too. Also charges are normally based on the length of connection time rather than the distance between sender and receiver. This can cut the cost to the user dramatically. Most PTTs offer packet-switching systems; IPSS is the name of the international PSS which uses satellites and other high-speed links. Virtually all computer manufacturers offer software that allows their machines to communicate using the standard CCITT packet-switching protocol known as X25.

Electronic mail and messaging

Electronic mail allow its users to share access to data and exchange messages without having to coincide in time or place. There are many competing systems: one of the best-established is the *Dialcom* system; it is known in Britain as British Telecom Gold (BTG) and access is via the PSS. BTG subscribers effectively rent private space in a Dialcom computer which stores, receives and forwards messages to anyone else who is a BTG subscriber. You can log on to BTG from anywhere, using a computer, a telex terminal, or a word processor. You log on to receive messages at your own convenience, rather than being interrupted by the telephone ringing. When you log on, you are told if any messages are waiting and can choose whether to read them or just scan them. When you send messages you can choose to force the recipients to acknowledge them, you can copy them to any number of other people, and you can be sure that delivery is almost immediate.

Electronic mail works best when groups of people who need to communicate join a system together. One disadvantage is that unless everyone logs on frequently, urgent messages can sit waiting for a long time on the Dialcom computer. At present you can only find out whether a message is waiting for you by the positive decision to log on. There is no indicator lamp, as on a telephone answering machine, to alert you to your messages. And unless logging on is part of your daily routine, it can seem rather a chore, especially if you don't need to *send* any messages in the same session.

Like the telephone in its early days, electronic mail is caught in a chicken-and-egg problem; until enough people sub-

scribe, there is little point in being a subscriber. At present, it is most beneficial to people who travel a lot and want to communicate with their offices, or people who are based overseas. Any organisation with a large telephone or telex bill might do well to examine the costs and benefits of electronic mail.

Telex and teletex

Telex is the direct descendant of the old telegraph system devised by Samuel Morse. It was originally set up using teleprinters fed by paper tape. Subscribers rent telex lines and rent or buy machines to connect to them. The telex network employs ordinary circuit-switching, just like the PSTN, so that the equipment and line is occupied for the duration of the call. The difference between telex and telephone is that once the circuit is connected, the channel is set up for telegraph operation using a restricted alphabet at 50 baud instead of voice conversation. Thus telex is slow and inflexible compared with electronic mail; its fastest speed is only around 80 words per minute, little faster than a good touch typist. It is restricted to capital letters and a few symbols as defined by an international alphabet called ITA2. This restriction is a by-product of the limited number of combinations possible on five-column punched paper tape.

Nevertheless telex is reliable, standardised and well established. There are over 90 000 telex lines in the UK, and over a million more in over 200 countries all over the world. Half of British telex calls are international, compared with under 1% of telephone calls. Nearly all government departments, press agencies, universities and large firms have telex lines.

To send a telex message you first establish contact with the distant terminal; if the terminal is not occupied, out of order or switched off you will receive a special number called an *answerback*. This is important because it is your proof that contact was established. After the standard information has been given, the message can be sent, terminated by a string of plus signs (+ + + + + +). A final exchange of answerbacks proves that the connection was held throughout the call. Both parties have a printed record of the 'conversation', and delivery is immediate, unlike a letter. What's more, the telex machine can be left unattended, unlike a telephone. This is especially useful when communicating with people in different time zones.

Teletex is the name of a faster and more recent international service gaining popularity in Britain, West Germany, Sweden, France and Canada. It operates at around 300 characters per second (roughly 30 times the speed of telex), and allows subscribers to use their word processors, computers or other equipment to prepare messages. Teletex is fully automatic; unlike telex, each terminal can receive incoming messages while preparing outgoing ones. Repeated attempts to transmit a message can be made automatically and at pre-arranged times, so that advantage can be taken of cheap rates for non-urgent messages.

Figure 93 Old-fashioned telex machines had to be attended by operators. Numbers were dialled on a telephone-style rotary dial, and messages punched out on paper tape. Because the machinery was noisy, it was often placed in a separate telex office.

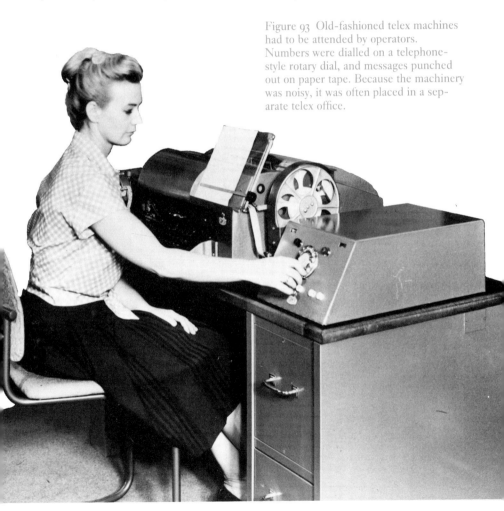

AaÁáÀàÂâÄäÃãÅåĂăĀāÆaeBb
CcĆćĈĉČčĊċÇçDdĎďĐđEeÉ
éÈèÊêËëĔĕĖėĒēĘęFfGgǴĜĝĞ
ğĠġĢģHhĤĥĦħ IiÍíÌìÎîÏïĬĭĪīĮį
ĲĳıJjĴĵKkĶķĸLlĹĺĽľĻļŁłĿŀMmN
nŃńÑñŇňŅņŋηʼnOoÓóÒòÔôÖ
öÕõŐőŌōŒœØøPpQqRrŔŕŘř
ŖŗSsŚśŜŝŠšŞşßTtŤťŦŧŢţPⱣUu
ÚúÙùÛûÜüŨũŬŭŰűŮůŪūŲųVv
WwŴŵXxYyÝýŶŷŸÿZzŹźŽžŻż
1234567890▯¥£$c!¡″″(),[]-.:;/¿?
≪≫²³-x:=±¼½¾#%&*@μΩ°o̲a̲

Figure 94 Characters from the extended alphabet permitted by teletex, the new high-speed automated service that is replacing telex. Telex machines are around 30 times slower and are restricted to the ITA2 alphabet of capital letters and a few symbols.

Figure 95 Modern telex machines are fully electronic and nearly silent in operation. Built-in microprocessors allow message editing, abbreviated dialling and unattended operation.

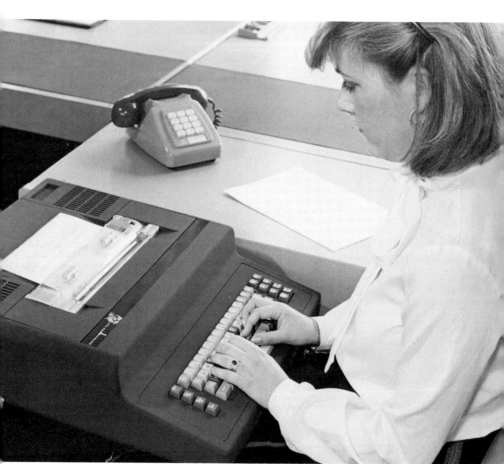

Facsimile transmission

Facsimile transmission (*fax*) is another circuit-switched method of conveying information. Fax uses ordinary voice-grade lines but achieves speeds of up to 9600 bits per second. Fax machines electronically scan the original document, measure the amount of light reflected by each tiny part of its content and transmit the tones of grey as well as the black and white. As a result, an *exact* copy of the original, including letterhead, signature, diagrams or photographs, can be transmitted across the world almost at once. A standard A4 page might take a minute to transmit, or even as little as 15 seconds depending on the amount of information it contains, the quality required and the type of equipment used.

Newspapers have used fax to transmit black-and-white photographs for years, and recent machines can transmit in colour. The first fax machines were analogue, but more recent equipment is digital. The incompatibility and expense of fax equipment (there are three main groups) has limited its popularity outside large companies, news agencies and organisations dealing in languages like Japanese and Chinese, which use very different characters for text.

ISDN

Integrated Services Digital Network (ISDN) is just one example of what is made possible by the new digital systems. Launched in 1985 in Britain, it is aimed mainly at business users and will provide each subscriber with two communication channels: a high-speed link for voice and data traffic at 64 000 bits per second and a second data channel operating at 8000 bits per second. Instead of having to choose between the PSTN, PSS, fax, telex or teletex, or to lease special-purpose private circuits, subscribers to ISDN will ultimately have access to all of these at will. The aim of ISDN is to meet all present and likely future needs in a single network.

ISDN will allow subscribers to call up information from a database and view it on their terminal screens while at the same time discussing it with colleagues hundreds (or thousands) of miles away. They can exchange drawings and documents using the same link. Secretaries might have a single work-station combining a VDU, facsimile equipment and teletex, also connected to a local computer network. The screen could be used for word processing, electronic mail and slow-scan television (for surveillance/security). ISDN is typical of the rapid convergence between telephone, computer and video that is underlined in the next chapter.

Figure 96 Fax machines scan documents and transmit an exact copy at high speed down a telephone line, allowing weather maps, photographs and signatures to be sent round the world in a matter of seconds.

Chapter 8: The video revolution

Only 50 years ago, the idea of sending moving pictures through the air seemed miraculous. Nowadays television is so commonplace that it is difficult to imagine the excitement that greeted the world's first TV broadcast by the British Broadcasting Corporation in 1936. Since then, the television has become a standard piece of living-room equipment in most developed countries, far more prevalent even than the telephone. Many countries have well established television industries, often with several competing broadcast networks, and some have cable TV, which provides an even wider choice of channels.

Nowadays, television is probably the most powerful single influence on how people think, vote, shop, learn and spend their leisure. It has far more impact than radio or newspapers; in many countries TV viewing is by far the most popular leisure activity. In the US, it is estimated that a child of five will already have spent an *average* of over 5000 hours watching television. The social effects of viewing are immense and controversial. In some places, government monitoring of broadcast television is very strict, giving the state close control over what is transmitted, particularly with regard to the news, and strong influence over the beliefs and attitudes of its citizens. Television can make an actor famous overnight, it can help politicians win or lose elections, it can arouse powerful public concern over a disaster or cause, it can stir up violent feelings and behaviour, it can educate, entertain, select, distort – or merely numb the senses. In recent years, television has been

greeted by some as the most important 'open door' to enlightenment ever invented – and held by others to be responsible variously for the decline of live theatre and cinema, the rise of the 'permissive society', and even for the breakdown of family life!

So there can be no doubt about the importance of television in modern society. Yet its most important effects may be still to come. Acting as a receiver to broadcasts is just one among many tasks that a modern television set can already perform (Figure 97). Given the immense progress in telecommunications described in the last chapter, the role of television may undergo profound changes in the near future. The implications of cable and satellite television are only just beginning to be considered.

To understand both the problems and potential of television in information technology, it is essential to understand the origins of the television set as a simple receiver for off-air transmission. Many different ways of building up and encoding TV pictures grew up in different countries, but the picture has now simplified to just three separate sets of technical standards for colour television: PAL, SECAM and NTSC. (These are spelled out in the Glossary, but everyone always calls them by their initials.) PAL is the system that was developed in West Germany and has been adopted in the UK, most of Europe, the Middle East, Africa, Australasia and South America. SECAM originated in France and is used in the USSR and its satellites, and some Middle Eastern and

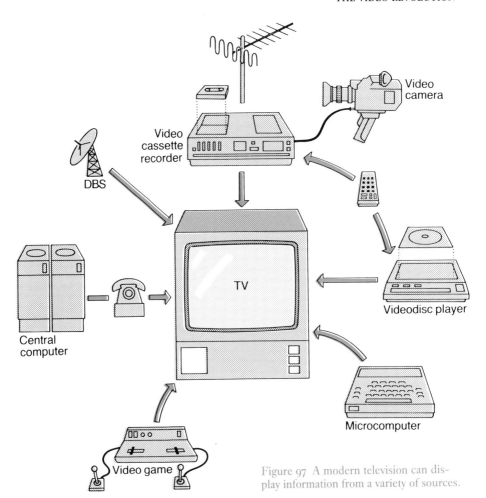

African countries. NTSC, the first practical colour TV broadcasting system, was launched in the USA in 1953 and is now universal in North America, Mexico, the Bahamas, Japan and the Philippines.

Each standard requires different kinds of cameras, recording equipment and television sets. Special equipment and techniques allow some kind of compatibility between them, at least in black and white, because all three systems collect and display information about light and shade separately from information about colour. (Or, to put it more technically, the *lumi-*

nance is handled separately from the *chrominance*.) However, unless you are technically well equipped it is safest to assume that a videotape recorded abroad on a different standard will not play on your domestic equipment, and vice versa.

The historical accidents that produced this chaotic situation have far-reaching effects. Now that television sets are being used for a greater variety of purposes, there is increasing interest in international exchange of broadcasts and videos, computer-processed text and pictures, and computer data and software. Both for the domestic user, and for organisations concerned with education, training and international operation, the consequences of this incompatibility are considerable. It stems from the way in which the picture is built up on the screen.

A modern colour television set is a surprisingly complicated piece of equipment. Indeed, if TVs were not manufactured in huge numbers, they would be impossibly expensive to buy. Fortunately, the details of how they work are important only to people who work with and repair them. We only need to understand the basic principles of how the picture is created and maintained in order to see the implications.

How is a television picture created?

The picture you see on a television screen is really a grand optical illusion. It depends on the inability of the human eye to follow very rapid changes in what it sees. This is called *persistence of vision*. For example, a flashing light will appear steady if it flashes fast enough. If you are reading this by artificial light, you are depending on a useful application of persistence of vision. Unlike a torch battery, which gives a steady direct current (dc), mains electricity is alternating current (ac): this means the light level is constantly rising to a maximum and falling to blackness again. If this happened slowly, the flicker would make reading (or anything else!) impossible. However, our eyes can only detect flicker at speeds of up to 45 cycles per second at most. Since the mains frequency is at least 50 cycles per second, persistence of vision means that we are not even aware of the fluctuations.

In the same way that our eyes are slow to follow these changes in intensity, if we see several similar still images of an object in quick succession we tend to perceive the object as moving; our brains 'fill in' the intermediate positions that we assume the object must have occupied. This is how our eyes seem to see moving images at the cinema when what is projected is a series of still photographs shown in quick suc-

cession. The fact that cart-wheels sometimes appear to rotate backwards in old cowboy films illustrates (Figure 98) how our eyes can sometimes be tricked!

Figure 98 Successive film images of a wheel rotating (a) slowly and (b) fast and how they are perceived. (Only four wheel spokes are shown for simplicity.) (a) If the wheel rotates slowly each image shows a slight advance compared with the one before. Our eyes assume (correctly) that spoke A has moved forward between each frame and that the wheel has advanced a quarter-turn clockwise. (b) If the wheel rotates faster, spoke A travels nearly a quarter-turn *between each frame*, ie in the second frame A has nearly reached the point where B previously was. But our eyes cannot distinguish one identical spoke from another, so we assume A has moved backward in the second frame to the point where D previously was, to C in the 3rd frame and to B in the 4th. So the wheel appears to be rotating slowly anti-clockwise.

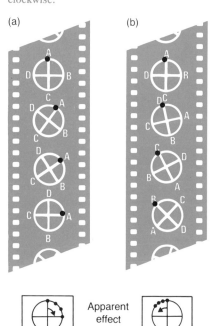

Figure 99 Colour television pictures are made by lighting up phosphor dots of different colours. They are arranged in groups of three called triads. Each triad contains a red, green and blue dot – the three primary colours.

Figure 100 (*above*) A frame grabber captures (grabs) a video picture and digitises the information that it contains. The image can then be stored in a computer and manipulated by it in the same sort of a way that a word processor manipulates text.

Figure 101 (*left*) The keypad of a teletext television allows the user to call up pages of teletext information (text and graphics). The reveal button allows teletext subtitles or news-flashes to be shown on top of the broadcast television picture.

Actually, cinema film is shot at 24 frames per second and the motion would look rather jerky if it were projected at this speed. So in practice each frame is projected twice in quick succession, giving the effect of 48 pictures per second and making the movement appear smooth.

Television pictures create the illusion of motion in a similar way to cine films, but they depend on a further trick to create each picture in the first place. What *seems* to be a still picture on a TV screen is actually built up by the rapid motion of a tiny spot of light which shoots across the screen illuminating a pattern of dots at a speed of around 6 or 7 miles per second (8–10 km/s)! The beam of light moves in turn along hundreds of closely spaced diagonal lines, arranged in a pattern called a *raster* (Figure 102). The beam takes about 50 microseconds to scan from left to right, drawing its pattern as it goes, and another 10 microseconds to fly back without leaving a trace. In PAL and SECAM there are 625 such lines, in NTSC only 525.

The inside of a television screen has a phosphor coating which acts a bit like the human eye: it has a 'persistence' of its own, and goes on glowing for a few thousandths of a second after the beam has moved past. That's why you can sometimes see a spot of light for a while after you switch off. When the screen appears to show a steady image, it is actually being maintained by the beam of light constantly *refreshing* the display before it fades. Thus what you see is the *illusion* of a steady picture, supported by ceaseless frantic electronic activity.

Figure 102 A television picture is built up by a spot of light travelling very fast along a pattern (raster) of slightly diagonal lines. The diagram shows only 10 for simplicity; in practice there would be at least 500.

Scanning lines $\Longrightarrow$ 0·00005 second   Flyback (leaves no trace) $\Longleftarrow$ 0·00001 second

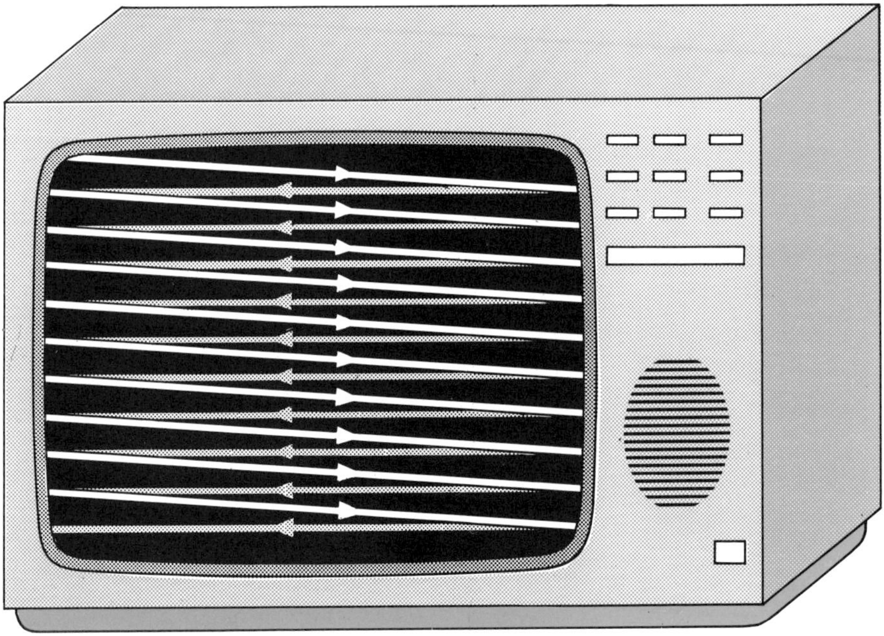

One complete scan of the screen is called a *field*, and it takes ¹⁄₅₀th of a second or less. (In PAL and SECAM countries, the mains voltage is generally 50 Hz which readily provides 50 scans per second; in NTSC countries, the mains frequency is 60 Hz and 60 fields are scanned each second. (In practice, in all systems the first scan only illuminates every other line (Figure 103), with a second scan immediately afterwards filling in the remaining lines. These two fields are woven together (*interlaced*) to produce a complete *frame*. Thus in NTSC, 30 complete frames are shown every second (half the number of scans), whereas in PAL/SECAM, there are only 25 frames per second. Incidentally, the 24 frames per second of cine film is close enough to the PAL/SECAM frequency for broadcasters often to ignore the slight speed difference. (This is why you may have noticed that cine films run slightly faster on television!)

Figure 104 shows how the PAL, SECAM and NTSC standards compare. As you can see, the line and field standards of PAL and SECAM are the same, and in fact you can play a SECAM videotape on a PAL player (and vice versa), but only in black and white. This is because SECAM handles colour information quite differently from PAL, which is in this respect closer to (and a refinement of) the NTSC system. The SECAM system provides more stable colours than the NTSC standard, but it does so in a way that makes the luminance signal harder to extract. Its black-and-white reception is therefore poorer than the other two systems. SECAM videotape is also harder to edit than NTSC or PAL, but SECAM receivers are correspondingly simpler to design and build. Although the technical

Figure 103 The principle of interlace: the first time the beam travels across the screen it scans every alternate field line. Then it flies up to the top and fills in the lines in between. The complete frame of video consists of these two interlaced fields. (Flybacks have been left out for simplicity.)

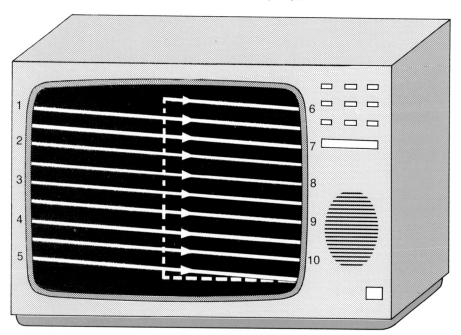

details of these three systems do not matter at present, it is important to realise that they differ fundamentally, as this has important practical effects.

Luminance and chrominance

A black-and-white picture is built up by making the intensity of the spot of light vary as it passes across the screen, creating the effect of black, white or shades of grey. The luminance at each point is controlled by variations in the electrical signal received. This signal carries coded information about the luminance at each spot in the original scene when it was scanned by the broadcasters' television camera. The camera depends on a similar process to the TV receiver, only in reverse, ie the camera turns patterns of light into electrical signals that can either be broadcast immediately or recorded on videotape. The electrical variations provide an analogue for the luminance; the camera turns the visual pattern into electrical variations, the television reconstructs the picture from the electrical signals it receives. If the electrical variations are transmitted accurately, the reconstruction of the original scene will be faithful to the original picture. The whole process is analogue throughout.

Colour information (chrominance) is also stored in analogue form. Like many things to do with television, the technical details are quite complex, but the principles are simple. Any shade of any colour can be represented by a mixture of three primary colours: red, green and blue – pure colours from the beginning, middle and end of the rainbow. For example, a mixture of 30% red, 59% green and 11% blue light makes white. By varying the proportions of the different colour ingredients, any shade or *hue* can be created.

Unlike a black-and-white TV, whose screen is coated with phosphor of a single kind, a colour TV screen consists of about a million tiny dots of three different kinds

Figure 104 Some characteristics of the world's three TV colour standards.

Colour standard	PAL	SECAM	NTSC
Number of lines	625	625	525
Frames per second	25	25	30
Fields per second	50	50	60
Frequency of mains electricity (cycles per second)	50	50	60

of phosphor. Each kind gives out red, green or blue light when activated by the beam that 'draws' the picture. If you look closely at the screen you may be able to distinguish these dots. They are arranged in groups called *triads*, one of each colour (Figure 99). Special masks with holes ensure that each type of phosphor is activated only by the appropriate signal for that colour. The chrominance signal received by the television contains information about the relative proportions of the three colours at each spot on the screen. The TV receiver separates this information into three signals, each corresponding to the level of one of the three primary colours at each part of the screen. If the picture is to show a blue sky, only blue dots will be activated in the upper part of the screen; red poppies in a green meadow would be represented by groups of red dots in among the green below. The effect of mixtures of colours like purple is created by activating dots of different colours, in this case red and blue, side by side. Because the dots are so small, and the whole picture is viewed from a distance, the human eye effectively 'mixes' the colours and sees each area as a single hue. By varying the proportions within each area, the effect of any colour in the rainbow can be created.

Television receivers and computer monitors

It is an accident of history that TV sets and computer monitors look so alike. Because the manufacturers found it convenient to re-use the same basic components, monitor screens are the same shape as televisions, although for many computer applications a different shape altogether might be preferable. For example, for word processing a taller, thinner screen would have resembled a sheet of paper more closely. However, a computer monitor nearly always has the same 4:3 proportions (known as its *aspect ratio*) as a television set: Figure 105 shows how this compares with the cinema screen or photographic slide.

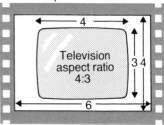

Figure 105 Comparison of the aspect ratios of cinema and television screens.

Monitor screens, whether colour or monochrome, display computer output in the same general way as television screens display broadcast pictures, ie a beam of light scans along a raster of parallel lines, illuminating the screen's phosphor coating in accordance with electronic instructions. What is different is the way in which the monitor receives the instructions. A television signal is a complicated mixture of information bundled together in a way that makes it suitable for broadcasting (ie modulated onto a carrier wave). It has to be unbundled and decoded by the receiving set before the picture can be displayed. But if a computer simply sends the information directly to the screen (ie without encoding it as if for a television), the monitor can simply display it without having to go through the complicated unscrambling process. This gives a clearer and steadier picture than would be seen on a television set.

Nevertheless, cheap microcomputers often can *only* be used with a television set, simply because their manufacturers didn't expect home users to want to buy a special monitor when they doubtless already had a television in the house. Similarly, expensive computers often can *only* be used with proper monitors for marketing reasons: business customers would be unlikely to want to make do with a poorish-quality television display, so it wasn't thought worthwhile providing the extra electronics to allow the computer to connect with an ordinary television. Middle-range computers like the BBC Micro leave the user the choice by providing sockets for both. Indeed if you plug in both at once, you can see the quality difference quite clearly.

In the early days of microcomputers, monitors were more expensive than televisions simply because there was a much smaller demand for them. The economics of mass production meant that a colour television was often much cheaper than a colour monitor even though it is a rather more complicated piece of equipment. As demand for computer monitors grew, however, their prices fell, and recently the trend has been towards making screens that can accept information in either form. Some of these TV/monitors can detect what kind of signal is being fed in and switch themselves automatically to the appropriate mode.

Resolution and memory requirements

People sometimes have the mistaken impression that computer monitors can only display the rather chunky-looking letters and crude graphics that you see in public places. In fact, monitors can show pictures with a resolution at least as great as a television set. The limit is set by the number of dots of phosphor in the screen coating: the pixels (see page 48) cannot be smaller than these. However, there might be at least half a million dots (625 lines down by 800 dots across) which would give high resolution by any standards. The reason that this ability is not often used to the full is because of the large demands it makes on the memory of the computer that is supporting the display.

Some simple arithmetic will confirm this. To treat each dot as a pixel so that it could be switched on or off independently would demand one bit of memory for each pixel, or 500 000 bits of RAM. That would be enough to support only a simple black-and-white display with no colours or shading tones. To control the colour and intensity even crudely, the processor

would have to allocate at least 8 bits (1 byte) of RAM per pixel, or 500 Kilobytes for 500 000 pixels. But 500 K is far more internal memory than a normal 8-bit microcomputer can *address* (have direct access to). One common solution is to divide the screen up into a much smaller number of pixels and to control the contents of each pixel by a single ASCII code which occupies just one byte of memory. *Graphics characters* can represent different shapes within each pixel (Figure 106). By combining different graphics characters, simple graphics can be constructed that make very small memory demands. For example, British teletext (and viewdata) is displayed on a screen divided into 25 rows of 40 columns (1000 cells). At one byte per cell this needs only 1K of memory, yet it gives the same effect as a resolution of 75 down by 80 across. Many 8-bit business micros use a similar principle to achieve reasonable resolution without committing too much RAM – often dividing the screen into 25 rows of 80 columns.

High-resolution screen displays are often impractical even for computers with larger memories, because the user's programs and data must compete for the same precious RAM space. Because of this trade-off between quality of display and the amount of RAM available for the user's programs, some microcomputers offer a choice of display modes so that the user can change the memory allocation according to the application.

Videotape and closed-circuit TV

Videorecorders (VCRs) have become popular both for business use and for leisure. Like sound-only recorders, there is a basic division between open-reel machines that you have to thread by hand and videocassette recorders that can play pre-threaded cassettes. Professionals use open-reel videotape machines of various kinds: there are lots of different widths of videotape (from $\frac{1}{4}$-inch all the way up to 2-inch), different threading systems, playback speeds and (as we have seen) different line, field and colour standards for the picture. (Systems that differ in any one of these respects are generally incompatible with each other.)

Domestic users prefer the cheaper players and easier handling of videocassettes. These also come in various incompatible designs and tape widths. They are bulkier than audiocassettes; videotape has to be wider than audiotape, and must be scanned at a faster speed, because of the much greater rate at which information has to be read from the tape compared with a sound-only recording. A VCR is otherwise broadly similar to an audiocassette recorder, with the important addition of time-clock controls that allow users to record broadcasts while they are out or even away on holiday (Figure 107). By recording their favourite programmes, home VCR users can escape the restrictions of the broadcasting schedules and replay programmes at their own convenience (Figure 108). By joining a video library, they can view a wide range of feature films without the limitations imposed by what happens to be on at the local cinema. They can also exercise control over the presentation by providing 'intermissions' and even slow-motion, repetition or fast-forward skipping. One disadvantage is that although

many people find home videos more convenient than cinema-going, the picture quality from domestic videotape does not approach that of cinema film.

Some home enthusiasts go on to acquire portable cameras and make home video movies of their holidays, children and animals and major events such as weddings and religious ceremonies. In effect, they use videotape in the same way as many amateurs use camera film, and develop programme-making into a hobby. Industrial users also sometimes have video production facilities and use videocassettes for in-house training, for point-of-sale demonstrations of products to customers, or for internal communications,

Figure 106 Graphics characters allow simple pictures to be built up using very little memory space. Putting the four characters shown bottom right side by side makes the legs of a man running. Each cell is divided into 6 squares and each character is made up of a different combination of squares. Only 64 characters are needed to represent all the possibilities ($64 = 2^6 = 2 \times 2 \times 2 \times 2 \times 2 \times 2$). Each character can be controlled by an ASCII code needing only 1 byte of RAM.

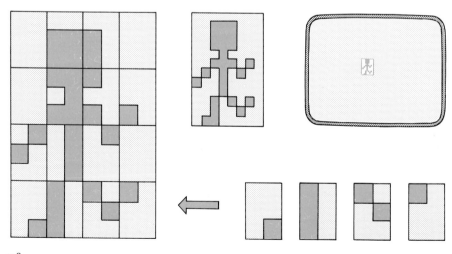

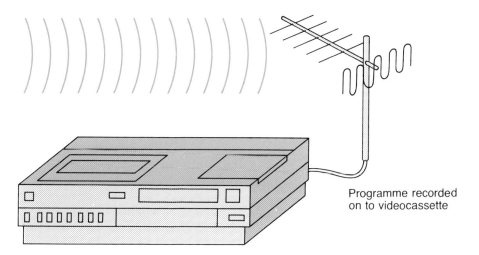

Programme recorded
on to videocassette

Figure 107 (*above*) Off-air recording: the broadcast signal is recorded on magnetic tape inside the videocassette recorder. Most VCRs have automatic operation and there is no need for anyone to watch the broadcast at the time of recording it, or even to switch on the television. Time-clocks mean that programmes can be recorded even while the user is out.

Figure 108 (*below*) Playback of pre-recorded videocassette. Instead of displaying a live picture from one of the broadcast channels, the television set is tuned to the VCR and shows a pre-recorded programme. The cassette may have been bought, hired, recorded off-air or through a video camera (see CCTV, page 130). The viewer controls the presentation by means of controls on the VCR or on a hand-held keypad.

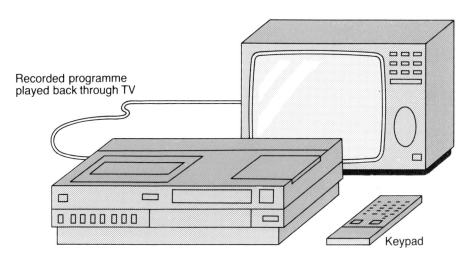

Recorded programme
played back through TV

Keypad

perhaps for a regular company video newsletter.

Closed-circuit television (CCTV) is the general name for a set-up where a video camera sends pictures to one or more screens, but the signal is not actually broadcast (Figure 109). Sometimes it is used simply to relay a lot of different television pictures to a single point – for example, so that a single security guard can monitor all possible entrances to a factory. The pictures might be stored in order to help identify anyone who tried to break in. In other applications, the pictures are recorded on videotape so that they can be viewed and discussed by the participants. This is very useful for training purposes, especially in the areas of communication skills and sports. For example, trainee bank clerks might have to act out how they would deal with difficult customers and watch their performance on videotape before and after training.

Videodisc

For a long time, hi-fi music lovers have had a choice between buying their music pre-recorded on gramophone records (discs) or on audiocassettes (tape). In computer terms, a revolving disc is *random access* (you can move the stylus straight to a particular groove anywhere on one side), whereas a tape is *serial access* (you have to wind it forwards or backwards to find the bit you want). The same choice is now available in video: random-access videodiscs offer an alternative to serial-access videotape (Figure 110).

There are various sizes of videodisc and various systems for coding and decoding information on the disc; virtually all are incompatible with each other. The videodisc spins rapidly inside the player, which reads information from it either by using a laser beam to detect minute pits just below its surface (*optical systems*) or a sensor to detect changes in its electrical properties (*capacitance systems*). Either way, control is electronic, often using a simple

Figure 109 Closed-circuit television does not involve broadcast signals at all. Family events or training materials are recorded on videocassette for subsequent re-play (see Figure 108). The picture can be checked on a TV set at the time of recording if the camera has no built-in monitor.

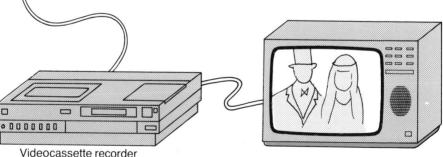

Live pictures from video camera recorded onto cassette

Hand-held video camera

Videocassette recorder

remote-control keypad, and the storage capacity is immense. Figure III gives some facts and figures about two rival videodisc systems operating on PAL colour standards.

Typically, videodiscs are 10 or 12 inches in diameter, each side holding between 36 and 60 minutes playing time of moving video or between 54 000 and 45 000 separate still pictures or any combination of the two. The sound track may be stereo or *dual* (two independent sound tracks): dual sound tracks might be recorded in two different languages, or used to present

Figure 110 Serial-access and random-access in video. (a) A videotape must be wound from one spool to the other to reach a section near the end (shown in colour). (b) A videodisc spins rapidly and the read head can move from the edge to the middle. As a result, it can locate any part very quickly no matter where it starts off.

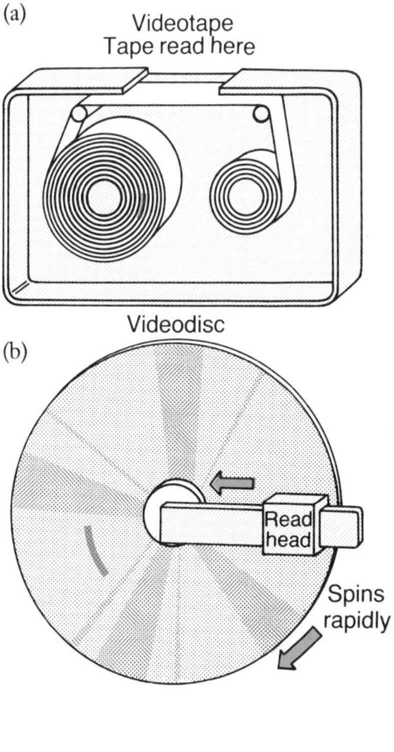

different kinds of information. At present, videodiscs – like gramophone records – can only be pre-recorded. Once the contents have been pressed onto a blank videodisc at the factory, they cannot be changed, and videodiscs cannot be used to record broadcasts off-air by home users nor copied by unauthorised 'pirates'.

Compared with videotape, videodiscs offer better picture and sound quality, with far better control over the presentation: usually there is a wide range of speeds from very slow motion to very fast scan in either direction, with the ability to freeze any frame at random or to step through a sequence one picture at a time. Some videodisc systems allow prolonged viewing of any individual still frame, so that a disc could contain a library of 54 000 colour slides.

Figure III Some comparisons between the rival PAL-standard videodisc systems.

(a)
Videotape
Tape read here

Videodisc
(b)

Read head

Spins rapidly

	Video High Density (VHD)	'Active-play'* Laservision
Diameter of disc (inches)	10	12
Playback time per side** (minutes)	60	36
Number of frames per side	45 000	54 000
Speed of rotation ** (revs/minute)	900	1500
Video frames per revolution	2	1

*Laservision discs can also be played in an extended play mode that gives 60 minutes' playback time, but this is suitable only for entertainment, not for interactive use.
**Note that these figures are for PAL/SECAM only; in NTSC laser discs rotate faster (1800 rpm) and playback time is correspondingly shorter (30 minutes), whereas VHD discs rotate more slowly (750 rpm) and still play for the same amount of time.

So far, the advantages of videodiscs have been appreciated most by business and industrial users, especially in contexts where the video material is shot specially and turned into an active programme which involves the viewer by requiring him or her to respond to questions and make choices. This is *interactive video*, and I mentioned one example of it on page 16; it is explored further on page 148. For home users, the inability to record off-air onto discs has so far proved a major limitation, although several companies are marketing domestic videodisc players as the next step for the affluent consumer who already has a VCR but also wants the option of the higher-quality viewing and listening provided by pre-recorded videodiscs.

Of the two main groups of videodisc systems – optical and capacitance – each has two subdivisions (Figure 112). Optical systems may decode the information in the laser beam as it is reflected from the surface of the disc (*reflective*) or after it has been transmitted through the disc (*transmissive*); the latter has the advantage that both 'sides' of the disc can be played without having to turn the disc over. Capacitance systems may use a stylus to pick up information from grooves, or a sensor that glides over the surface of a grooveless disc. Most systems have to have both discs and players produced in different versions for PAL, SECAM and NTSC, so some players are marketed only in certain countries. Only one (the VHD system) can cope with all three standards in the same player. VHD stands for Video High Density, and the system combines a long video playing time (60 minutes per side) with fast access to any of its 45 000 frames (less than 5 seconds at worst).

Active-play *laservision systems* have some compensating advantages over capacitance systems. Unlike the latter they store just one video frame per revolution. This means that they can hold any of

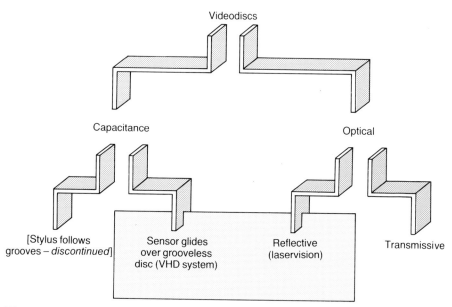

Figure 112 The main groups of videodisc system. Because of the incompatibility of colour video standards, different systems may be available in different countries. For example, in Britain the choice is between VHD and laservision.

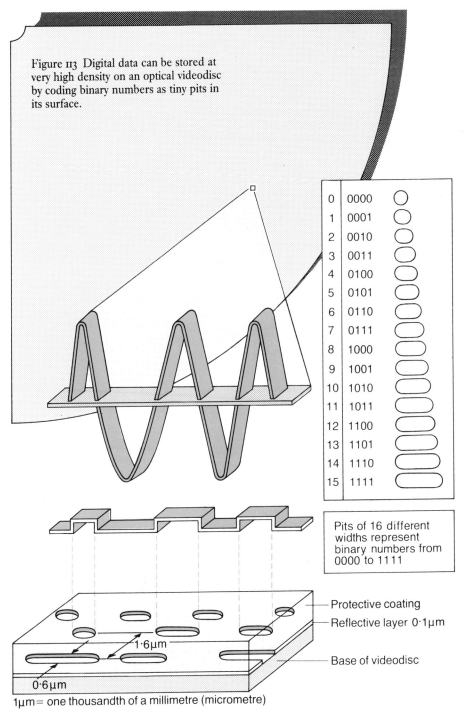

Figure 113 Digital data can be stored at very high density on an optical videodisc by coding binary numbers as tiny pits in its surface.

0	0000
1	0001
2	0010
3	0011
4	0100
5	0101
6	0110
7	0111
8	1000
9	1001
10	1010
11	1011
12	1100
13	1101
14	1110
15	1111

Pits of 16 different widths represent binary numbers from 0000 to 1111

Protective coating

Reflective layer 0·1μm

Base of videodisc

1·6μm

0·6μm

1μm= one thousandth of a millimetre (micrometre)

54 000 frames rock-steady on the screen. (The VHD system stores two frames of video per revolution and the 'jitter' between two not-quite-identical images can be quite noticeable unless the frame was designed to be a still-frame in the first place.) Because laser discs are read with a beam of light, there are no moving parts in contact with the disc and so they are very durable. Indeed, because information is coded in vertical pits *below* the surface of the disc, finger-prints and scratches have little or no effect on picture quality. By contrast, capacitance systems that depend on contact between a stylus and its groove are more liable to wear out, and the surface of the disc needs more protection.

Each system has its advantages for particular purposes, and neither has been established long enough to be certain of the future of these very sophisticated machines. It all depends on what libraries of videodiscs are made available at what prices. This is a field where different technologies are converging very rapidly, and where standardisation would be very much in the consumer's interests. The fact that laservision discs are based on the same technology as the compact disc now used for hi-fi audio recordings could prove to be a significant advantage. In 1984 three Japanese companies introduced players that could play 8-inch or 12-inch laservision discs and standard compact discs. Developments like this promise tremendous scope for flexible presentations. However, it remains to be seen whether the problem of the worldwide incompatibility of colour standards can also be overcome by a laservision player.

Although the commercially available videodisc systems are currently *read-only*, systems have already been demonstrated that can be recorded on by the user, and even re-recorded subsequently. Systems have also been developed to store video and other information in digital form, rather than as analogue variations in the signal (Figure 113). Television pictures, as we have seen, display far more detail than is commonly used for displaying computer text and graphics. If a screenful of such information is stored in analogue form as a television picture, it occupies far more storage space than if its contents are coded and stored digitally. Videodiscs have immense storage capacity for digitised information, and are easier to handle and more durable than floppy discs made of flimsy magnetic material. Some people believe that the videodisc will soon replace the floppy disc as a major form of external memory for microcomputers.

Teletext and viewdata

There are two kinds of electronic information services generally displayed on television screens: *teletext* and *viewdata*. Teletext is the general name for one-way information services transmitted as part of a television signal by broadcast or cable. (It has no connection with either *teletex* or *telex*.) The broadcasting organisations provide teletext as a supplementary service, and it is available free to anyone who has the equipment to receive it.

The teletext signal is carried in a few spare lines at the top of the normal picture; the patterns can sometimes be seen on a badly adjusted television set, but normally they are above the top of the picture and do not disturb it in any way. It is a digital signal, decoded by special circuits built into the special teletext television set and simply ignored by other television receivers (Figure 114). The complete 'magazine' of perhaps a hundred pages is broadcast continuously in an endless cycle, each page taking a fraction of a second to transmit.

Teletext users can choose to see teletext pages in place of broadcast programmes at the touch of a button, usually on a hand-held keypad (Figure 101). Any individual page can be called up by keying its number, but there may be a delay of quite a few seconds before it appears on the screen because if you have just missed the moment in the cycle when it was transmitted, you will have to wait until it comes round again. This delay is known as *cycle time*; in practice it is often hardly notice-able since very popular pages are transmit-ted more than once per cycle. However, the need to keep cycle times acceptably short is the main limitation on the total number of teletext pages. Using the mix button, the user can choose to superim-pose the teletext page onto the normal pic-ture, which is useful for people with im-paired hearing. They can view programme sub-titles from teletext on top of the film or news bulletin to which they relate.

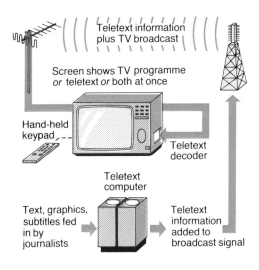

Figure 114 *(top right)* Teletext information is transmitted as part of the normal TV broadcast signal. It is separated by a special decoder, usually built into the TV receiver.

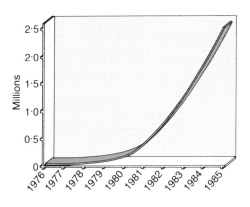

Figure 115 *(right)* The rising number of teletext televisions in use in Britain (1976–1985).

Figure 116 *(below)* Part of a frame from Ceefax, a British teletext service, showing food price information. The columns show popular foods, average price in pen-nies per pound, change or no change (n/c) since yesterday, and likely range over different areas and shops.

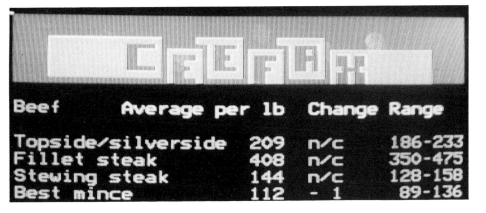

Beef	Average per lb	Change	Range
Topside/silverside	209	n/c	186-233
Fillet steak	408	n/c	350-475
Stewing steak	144	n/c	128-158
Best mince	112	- 1	89-136

By the early 1980s, most European countries and North America had at least experimental teletext services; some of them are identified in Figure 123. Generally teletext spreads fastest in countries like Britain (Figure 115) where significant numbers rent rather than buy their television sets as people can then experiment with the new service by simply changing the set they rent to the special type. For both technical and economic reasons it is not easy to market a separate teletext decoder for existing televisions, and new teletext televisions cost around £50 to £100 more than standard models. (Doubtless this premium would rapidly dwindle to little or nothing if market forces changed.)

In Britain, there are two quite separate teletext services, fortunately fully compatible with each other and using the same 25 by 40 screen display as Prestel. The BBC's service is called Ceefax and Independent Television's is called Oracle. The potential audience for these services jointly is around seven million, and viewers watch for an average of 15 minutes per day. News, sports results and television programme news are the most popular items, followed by weather, travel news and quizzes and competitions. Like broadcast television, the service is one-way; viewers can only select from what the broadcasters choose to provide, they cannot interact with the material on-line. Teletext information is compiled and updated by special teams of journalists and editors, some based at broadcasting headquarters, others perhaps hundreds of miles away. Information is mainly collected from the same sources that feed the television newsrooms, though direct input from other computers is also received. For example, the British Airways computer at Heathrow can 'talk' directly to the Oracle computer to update flight information as changes occur. Ceefax is directly connected to the British Rail computer for

Figure 117 Teletext was originally devised to provide subtitles for television viewers who are hard of hearing. Specially trained caption-writers key in subtitles while watching recordings of the programmes. Some programmes may be subtitled in a choice of languages. However, caption-writing is very time-consuming and only a selection of the more popular programmes are subtitled at all.

information on cancellations, delays and so on. Teletext information is held on a large computer so that each page is always broadcast in its most up-to-date version. Graphic artists draw teletext graphics either straight onto the screen using graphics tablets and light pens, or using paper and pencil and capturing the image electronically using a *frame grabber* (Figure 100). The artist can then add colours and alter details using a light pen (page 38). Specialist subtitle writers produce abbreviated versions of news bulletins and dialogue for selected programmes so that viewers who are hard-of-hearing or non-English-speaking can superimpose subtitles onto their television pictures, with

a choice of normal letters or double-height (Figure 117). Using a direct link to the teletext computer, subtitles can even be keyed in for live broadcasts.

Viewdata is the general name for *two-way* communication systems that allow the user to select from a network of 'pages' of information held on a computer database, and to make choices or give responses to questions using a keypad or keyboard. The network of pages is arranged like a tree, with patterns of branches and twigs (Figure 118). In theory, viewdata systems may be public or private, local or long-distance. In practice, public viewdata systems are always long-distance and generally depend on the telephone to connect

Figure 118 Viewdata pages are arranged like a tree: if the user wants to find out about holidays (page 917), she must make a sequence of choices (2,2,1,2,3) until she reaches the resort and accommodation she wants (page 91722123). This works well if the search is successful but can be very tedious if she has to keep repeating the same series of choices without finding what she is looking for. It is also long-winded if the user's priorities are different from those of the Information Provider. For example, she might be restricted to a low budget but may not mind which country she goes to.

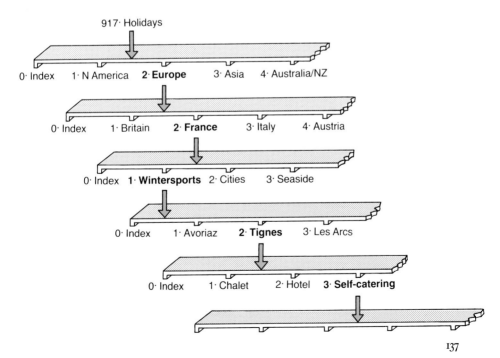

the user with remote viewdata computers (Figure 119). This means that users also need an acoustic coupler or modem and a viewdata terminal or microcomputer. Some viewdata terminals have a built-in modem; others even include a printer. Microcomputers are being produced with built in telephones to suit viewdata and other kinds of computer communications.

Whatever equipment is used, you first have to dial the number of the viewdata computer (for Prestel this is normally a local call). Once contact is established with the Prestel system, you identify yourself with your account number and also with a special password (which you are supposed to change regularly). You then see a welcome screen and index page which offers a menu of categories; if you choose, say, holidays this leads to a further menu from which you can select the continent, country, type of holiday, resort and accommodation that you want. By pressing successive numbers on a simple keypad you arrive (eventually) at your destination. Alternatively, if you know the page number of the frame you want, you can go straight to it.

Prestel was the first example of a public viewdata system, launched in 1978; many countries soon developed rival systems (Figure 123). Like British teletext systems,

Prestel uses a display of 25 lines by 40 characters. This is limited to simple graphics, and up to around 100 words of text per page. Some later systems (eg Telidon and CAPTAIN) have superior resolution and graphics (Figure 121). Unlike teletext, viewdata is not free: in addition to the quarterly subscription, British users have to pay for telephone connection time (in most parts of the UK this is now at local call rates), for time on the Prestel computers (except at weekends and in the evenings) and may also have to pay a small charge per

Figure 120 Software can be sent down telephone lines using viewdata services such as Prestel. Using a home micro, telephone and television, this child can browse through programs held on distant Prestel computers.

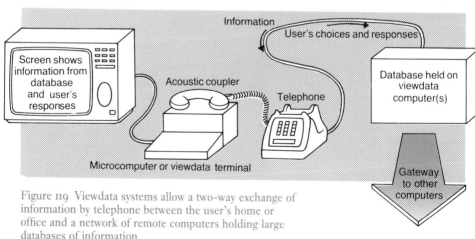

Figure 119 Viewdata systems allow a two-way exchange of information by telephone between the user's home or office and a network of remote computers holding large databases of information.

information providers designate as free. In practice, the majority of pages are free; nevertheless at 1984 prices, the other charges averaged from £0.66 to £15.90 per hour according to the time of day and location of the caller.

By 1984, the Prestel database had about quarter of a million pages, supplied by over 1000 Information Providers. However, in its first five years, the number of subscribers built up was only around 26 000, far below the expectations of its backers. Several reasons have been put forward for Prestel's disappointing uptake: the limitations of the screen display, the need to tie up a telephone line throughout a Prestel session, the cumbersome

sequence of choices sometimes needed to find your way to a particular item of information, the extra equipment needed to get a print-out of a Prestel page, the problem of establishing the right market for a general information service and the three-level system of charges – all have been advanced as possible causes.

A more fundamental problem may be the provision of very general information when business users, who form the majority of Prestel subscribers, tend to have more specialised needs. British Telecom's original policy was simply to act as the common carrier, ie to exercise no control or influence over the information providers, but in response to pressure from

Figure 121 CAPTAIN, the Japanese viewdata service, offers far higher resolution than the UK system, Prestel, is capable of.

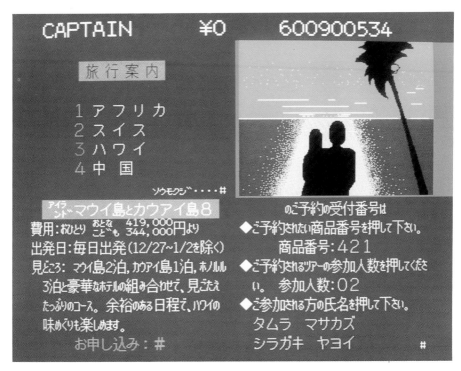

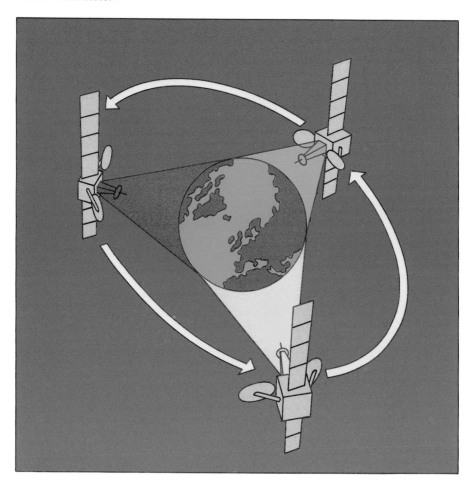

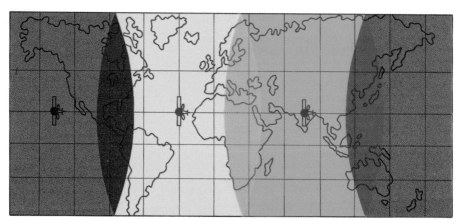

Belongs to top of page 139.

Figure 122 The footprints of three INTELSAT satellites span the globe allowing electronic communications world-wide.

page viewed, except for those pages that the users, there have been significant moves away from that position. One important feature is the growth of Closed User Groups (CUGs), which are organisations or special-interest groups of subscribers who want private and secure electronic communication among themselves in addition to gaining access to Prestel information. Micronet 800 (page 14) is a large and very successful CUG for microcomputer users, who use it to exchange messages, information and to purchase software (see below). In the first six months after its launch, Micronet 800 brought in an extra 5000 subscribers to Prestel, many of them home computer enthusiasts and schools.

Another crucial development was the establishment of *Gateway* links to other computers. Previously, users could talk only to the Prestel computers. Gateway opened up all the possibilities of home banking, *teleshopping* (ordering supermarket groceries from your armchair) and

Figure 123 Some examples of videotex systems developed in different countries.

direct holiday selling by means of direct links between travel agents and the airlines reservation systems. Gateway gives the user potential access to an unlimited long-distance network of computers.

The term *videotex* (sometimes spelled *videotext*) is often used to cover both teletext and viewdata. So *two-way* or *interactive videotex* is just another name for viewdata (and is in commoner usage in North America), and *broadcast* or *one-way videotex* is just teletext. Perhaps when these developments become more widespread their names will be simplified!

Telesoftware

Telesoftware is a new method of transmitting computer software over long distances quickly, accurately and electronically. It was pioneered in Britain in the early 1980s using both teletext and viewdata. Instead of publishing printed listings of programs for people to key in to a computer for themselves, or selling copies on disc or cassette, electronic impulses are broadcast or sent down wires, carrying instructions directly into the memory of the receiving computer. You need suitable software to establish the link and to *download* (receive) the programs. The downloading software translates the program

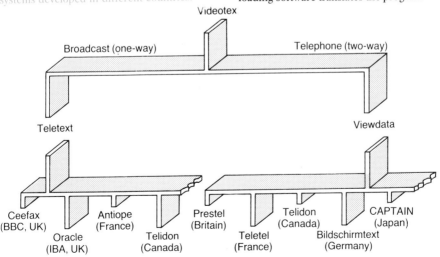

Videotex

Broadcast (one-way)   Telephone (two-way)

Teletext   Viewdata

Ceefax (BBC, UK)   Antiope (France)   Prestel (Britain)   Telidon (Canada)   CAPTAIN (Japan)

Oracle (IBA, UK)   Telidon (Canada)   Teletel (France)   Bildschirmtext (Germany)

from the coded form in which it was transmitted into instructions that can be obeyed by the receiving computer. As with any computer communication, there must be an agreed protocol for the communication link to be established in the first place.

Both teletext and viewdata have been successfully used as a method for transmitting software. Teletext telesoftware sends the programs as a sequence of pages containing the program instructions in a compressed form (Figure 124). The double vertical bars simply marks the end of a line, so that many more program lines can be squeezed onto each page than would be possible if they were displayed in the usual way. A program might occupy a single teletext page or many pages, depending on

Figure 124 Software can be broadcast using teletext pages. This extract is from ELEMNT, an educational program about chemical elements, written in BASIC. It looks strange because the lines have been squeezed up to reduce transmission time.

its length. To download a program, the user has to call up the appropriate pages using the keypad. A separate decoding unit must be plugged into the computer.

Because teletext services are free, telesoftware distributed in this way cannot be charged for. This is a mixed blessing, since the designers of programs then have no way of collecting any reward for their efforts and the result is that the range of software available through teletext tends to be limited. Alternative ways of financing teletext telesoftware may be found if demand is sufficient: for instance, there are ways of *scrambling* a program so that you have to pay for a key to unscramble it again. Another possibility for some arcade games is that advertising space might be sold *within* the program: companies might pay to have their logos or messages displayed on cars, athletes or animals featured in the screen graphics, for example.

Public authorities in several countries have even successfully broadcast programs simply as sound signals within an ordinary radio broadcast for home users to record on audio cassette and then feed into their computers in the normal way. The first radio transmissions of software were broadcast by the Netherlands in 1978. Because this method involves sound waves as an extra intermediate stage, it is not as reliable or convenient as using teletext, but it does avoid the need for special software or teletext decoders. To overcome the problems posed by the different dialects of BASIC used in home microcomputers, radio broadcasters sometimes use the BASICODE system, which allows different makes of micros to decode the same broadcast program.

The collection of payment for viewdata telesoftware is much easier to organise, since viewdata systems have automatic billing facilities and allow Information Providers to attach a price to each page of information. However, no special television set is needed and each page is automatically checked for transmission noise. Any page that contains errors is retransmitted without the user having to take any action, or even be aware that an error has occurred. How long the process takes depends on the efficiency of the decoding software as well as on the speed of the modem. As an indication, in a British experiment in 1981, a program 5 K in length typically took just over 2 minutes to download, and cost £0.15 in telephone time.

Commercial software sold via Micronet 800 is generally cheaper than in retail shops, partly because of the lower packaging and raw material cost, and partly because customers supply the element of labour and handling. Suppliers can be confident that they won't have to deal with customers whose cassettes refuse to load, or whose discs are the wrong format. Many suppliers provide Micronet customers with a scaled-down demonstration version so that they can try out a program free; this allows a form of browsing among programs that is otherwise difficult to arrange because of the problems of software *piracy* (copying programs illegally). However, any program which has inten-

sive or illustrated *documentation* (printed instructions on how to use it) cannot be considered complete until the documentation has been posted to complement the disc or cassette.

Satellite and cable television

Television and radio have traditionally been *broadcast* media: *narrowcasting* is a new word coined to convey the more selective approach to programme-making and distribution made possible by recent developments in satellite and cable television. Subscribers are expected to be prepared to pay extra to receive the channels of their choice from a wide range, some devoted to special interests like sports, music or children's programmes, others to non-stop films, pop videos or news. Cable TV also offers scope for two-way communication, with viewers able to participate in programmes while they are transmitted. For example, they could take part in quizzes and competitions, vote in polls concerning issues of the day, make extended contributions to serious educational programmes, take part in tutorials at a distance and even make use of interactive video (see page 148).

In the past, the restricted bandwidth available for broadcast channels has meant that consumers have been accustomed to a small choice of channels, with most programmes intended to be of fairly wide general interest. Educational programmes, programmes for minority interests and programmes with strong local content have always had great difficulty in securing air-space. Commercial TV stations depend on good viewing figures to attract advertising revenue, and non-commercial channels argue that they cannot afford to fall far behind in mass appeal without endangering public willingness to pay a licence fee. In the past, then, radio and television have been closely identified in our minds with the kind of programmes that the broadcasters believe will appeal to mass audiences. Satellite and cable transmission could change all that.

Satellite TV

Satellites are very expensive to build and launch; lots of things can go wrong, leading to an aborted launch, an inaccurate orbit, or even total loss of the satellite. Once in orbit, their life is uncertain and sometimes short. Communications satellite technology is still a high-cost and high-risk enterprise that demands extensive co-operation between potential users (PTTs and broadcasting companies) and also between different countries. The International Telecommunications Satellite Organisation was formed in 1964 with 11 member nations, and by 1968 three INTELSATs spanned the earth to form a global network of geostationary satellites (Figure 122). (A geostationary satellite is one that always remains in the same position in relation to the earth.) The first real communications satellite – Telstar – had been launched in 1962, but its orbiting height was 10 times too low to be geostationary, so it was only within 'sight' of its receiving stations for 20–30 minutes per revolution of the earth. By 1980, INTELSAT had three much-improved geostationary satellites, and 109 partners who all contribute and receive revenue according to their use of the system.

Progress in satellite communication has been rapid since 1965 when INTELSAT I was launched. This satellite could handle only 240 telephone circuits *or* a single TV channel, but not both at once, and had a life-expectancy of only 18 months. The current INTELSATs can handle up to 12 000 telephone circuits *plus* two TV channels, can transmit all forms of data simultaneously and have a life expectation of at least seven years. INTELSAT VI is due to be launched in 1986 and will handle 33 000 telephone circuits or up to 144 television channels and should last for at least 10 years. By 1984, there were more than 13 satellites and 200 earth stations in active use, some involved with general telephone traffic and ship-to-shore communications, others with television relays.

In some countries, there is great interest in satellite communications simply because distances are so great, or because the land is difficult and expensive to cross by means of a chain of conventional 'line-of-sight' transmitters or telephone cables. In others, satellite TV is important because viewers enjoy receiving live television pictures of sporting and public events as they happen. For example, in 1984 over 500 million people are estimated to have watched the Olympic Games 'live' from the USA, the majority of them by satellite.

When satellite pictures are transmitted back to earth they are normally picked up by a dish aerial before being forwarded to the broadcasting company that transmits them as part of their normal programme offering, alongside live studio work, films and recorded programmes. Used this way, satellite TV simply enriches the diet offered by the broadcasting companies. A more radical development is that of *Direct Broadcast from Satellite* (DBS). As satellites achieved more and more powerful signals, smaller and smaller dish aerials were needed to pick up the signals clearly. Using a dish of less than a metre in diameter – small enough to fit on the roof of a house or to sit in a garden – viewers could make their own choices out of the whole range of programmes carried by the satellite, instead of having them pre-selected by the broadcasting companies.

DBS raises interesting ethical and political problems, as we shall see in Chapter 10. There are also commercial and technical questions still to be answered. In Britain, a DBS project was announced in Parliament in May 1984; the BBC and IBA were to co-operate with five other companies to raise the cost of starting the project – well over £400 million. But in 1985 various members pulled out and the future of the project now looks uncertain. Apart from the considerable costs of special DBS satellites, estimates of the retail price of the dish aerial that consumers will need to receive DBS programmes fall anywhere between £100 and £900, with £200–400 seeming most likely in 1985. However, as with teletext televisions, the size of the

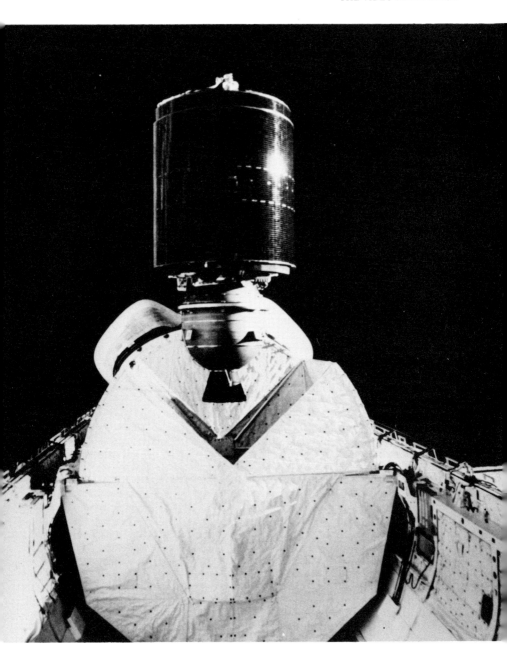

Figure 125 The first launch of a commercial communications satellite from the American Space Shuttle in 1982.

market is probably the biggest factor in determining the selling price and *vice versa*!

Technically, it would have been quite possible for a single satellite to cover the whole of Europe. The implications were discussed at an International Telecommunications Union conference (an agency of the United Nations) in 1977. Governments expressed great concern about the possibility of information and programmes being broadcast across national frontiers, so frequencies and orbits were allocated in a way that tended to restrict the DBS signal to within national boundaries.

Inevitably, however, there is overspill, and technical advances since 1977 have overtaken the assumptions built into the agreement, which covers Europe, Africa and Asia (the USA and other American countries did not sign). In any case, the area covered by a satellite signal depends not only on the strength of the transmission, but also on the size and quality of the aerial used to receive it. Meanwhile, countries like Eire and Luxemburg have been allocated satellite slots that they cannot afford to use, and so they are selling them on the open market. Thus a private-enterprise satellite consortium could buy and broadcast to European viewers in countries which have state-funded official projects of their own. These satellite 'pirates' could threaten the financial basis of the official projects.

There is political disagreement too about the colour standards for DBS. The British Government, with backing from the European Broadcasting Union, argued for an expensive new standard called C-MAC, which gives high resolution but demands a lot of bandwidth. It is, of course, incompatible with existing equipment and could not be carried on some of the older European cable systems, and might need two channels even on the newer ones. The French and West German Governments rejected C-MAC and plan to use the current PAL and SECAM standards. Without a European consensus on standards, the price of receiving equipment is bound to remain high.

Clearly DBS is at the centre of complicated political, technical and commercial controversy. The sums are large and the uncertainties great: for example, the British project is aiming for two million subscribers within five years and anticipates that this will create a market of £800 million for reception equipment and about £800 million for programming; together with the £400 million for the satellite itself this makes a total of £2000 million. These sums should be of concern to viewers as well as to DBS providers: £800 million may sound a lot for programming, but divided between several DBS channels in Britain and spread over five years it comes to a fraction of Channel Four's annual budget – and Channel Four's viewers don't have to pay a subscription. Viewers may not be prepared to pay extra for DBS channels unless far more is spent on providing the kind of programmes they want to see.

Cable TV

Cable TV is sometimes seen as a competitor to satellite, but it may turn out to be complementary to it. Those who have cable TV may not always have to install an extra aerial to receive DBS, since in some countries cable operators will be legally obliged to carry DBS channels. Viewers might simply have the option of paying an extra subscription to receive the DBS channels. Furthermore, some of the entertainment channels carried by cable operators may be beamed to them by satellite direct from the television companies who market them around the world. However, if some advocates of cable TV are right, it is the potential for local and community-based programmes, and the possibilities of making 'broadcast' television truly interactive that will distinguish the future of cable TV.

Cable TV began as a cost-effective way of providing good-quality reception of broadcast programmes, especially in difficult areas. A single expensive roof aerial could distribute a good TV signal to a

(a) Tree and branch

Figure 126 The design of a cable television system affects the purpose it serves.
The switched star system (b) is more
suitable for a high degree of interactivity
than the tree-and-branch system (a).

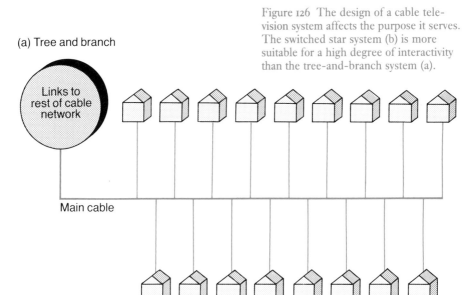

(b) Switched star

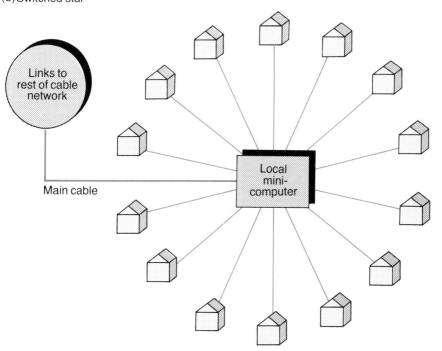

cable block of flats more cheaply (and with less external clutter) than a host of individual aerials. Because of the expense and disruption of linking people's homes by cable, its spread has tended to be linked with new buildings and new towns. Nevertheless its growth, especially in North America, has been spectacular. Given the recent advances in telecommunications (especially videotex), great interest has developed in the idea of providing electronic communication services on subscription as a way of increasing the financial return on the installation of cable to distribute broadcast programmes. For example, there is often enough spare cable capacity for videotex and electronic mail to be provided.

The degree of interactivity offered by cable TV depends on what is technically called its *architecture* – the way the network is constructed. Figure 126 shows two possibilities: the *switched star* system is more suitable for highly interactive services than the *tree-and-branch*. Fibre optic cable provides larger bandwidths within far smaller diameters than traditional coaxial cables, though some cable TV systems will use a mixture of the two. There are four main levels of interactivity possible:

(a) teletext

(b) slow upstream

(c) fast upstream

(d) switched services

Teletext simply means the viewer capturing a 'page' chosen from the ones continuously transmitted down the cable. Teletext isn't truly interactive, of course, since no message is sent back (upstream), but it gives a quite different impression to the user from the passive reception of TV programmes. If a full channel is given to teletext (as opposed to a few spare lines at the top of the broadcast picture), thousands of pages can be sent out without there being an unacceptably long delay in the cycle time (see page 135). *Slow upstream* means that the user could use a

key-pad to send simple messages like YES/NO or BUY/DON'T BUY back to the cable operators; this would allow simple voting during programmes, and limited home shopping, for example. Speeds of one bit per second would suffice for (b). Faster speeds – perhaps 75 bits/second – would be needed for (c) – *fast upstream* – where viewers might need to type at a keyboard for, say, electronic mail, interactive games or home banking. Finally, for full two-way video communication (d), a very fast full-bandwidth upstream line would be needed (switched service). This would allow video-conferencing and would have great possibilities for educational and business applications.

Most cable systems are likely to offer (a) and (b) in the short-term, and some may provide (c) before too long. Whether (d) is commercially viable remains to be seen: around 40% of the network's budget could be taken up by the expense of the switching units themselves. Cable TV demands high investment to install the system, and, like satellite TV, the return on the investment is both uncertain and delayed.

Interactive video

Interactive video (IV) might well feature among the services offered by cable TV. However, it is on free-standing equipment that IV has so far proved itself a powerful medium for distributing information in public places, for providing training in the workplace, and for informing and persuading potential customers at the point-of-sale of the advantages of this or that product.

Interactive video is a new medium created by the fusion of computers with video technology. Presentation of the visual material – whether on videotape or on videodisc – is controlled by microprocessor and may be supplemented by computer-generated text and graphics interposed between video sequences or even superimposed on them. IV can be

(a)

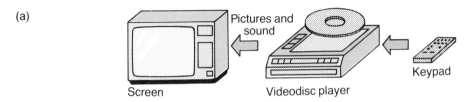

Pictures and sound

Keypad

Screen

Videodisc player

Figure 127 (a) A simple interactive video set-up.

presented on simple-looking equipment where the microprocessor is built into the videodisc player (Figure 127a) or there might be an external microcomputer with a videotape or videodisc player as its peripheral (Figure 127b). Systems like this allow a videodisc showing a shopping catalogue in still and moving pictures to be combined on-screen with up-to-date price information stored on floppy disc. Using a telephone link to a central viewdata computer, prices can even be updated every

night, allowing the videodisc a much-extended lifetime compared with a printed catalogue containing price information.

As in computing, an IV presentation can be tailored to suit each individual: what the user sees depends on the responses given to questions posed by the software. It is also easy for the computer to collect statistics about the use made of the system and the responses given. However, because live sound can be used, and realistic pictures of still and moving

(b)

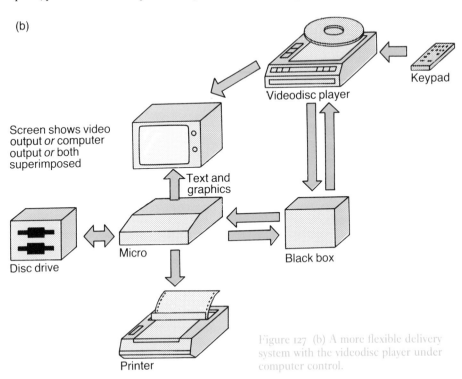

Keypad

Videodisc player

Screen shows video output *or* computer output *or* both superimposed

Text and graphics

Disc drive

Micro

Black box

Printer

Figure 127 (b) A more flexible delivery system with the videodisc player under computer control.

objects shown on video, IV scores over the crude beeps and low-resolution graphics of the computer on its own. Thus IV has many of the advantages of computing without its usual disadvantages. Similarly, compared with traditional video presentations (where a film has to be passively watched in sequence), IV is active rather than passive, places control with the user rather than the programme-maker, and is highly individualised both in pace and content.

IV does not necessarily have to be used with a keypad or keyboard. Touch-screen monitors can sense where the user's finger interrupts a criss-cross grid of infra-red beams, or alternatively they may depend on detecting finger-pressure on the screen surface. Either way, the touch-screen allows the user to express her choice in the most natural manner possible, by pointing to it. Previously confined to expensive special-purpose monitors, cheap touch-screen panels have recently been developed that can be attached to normal TVs, monitors and to switchable TV/monitors. Vandal-proof booths with specially toughened glass containing response panels have been developed so that presentations can be viewed when showrooms and offices are closed.

This kind of equipment has been employed by the Inland Revenue in the UK to provide citizens with income tax information in the anonymity of a public booth. Motor car manufacturers Austin-Rover have also experimented with outdoor booths on a major exhibition site in Birmingham in 1984 (Figure 128). An endless *enticer* loop invited passers-by to press a button, and once 'captured', the user was encouraged to indicate preferences so as to guide him or her towards specific models in the Austin-Rover range. Stills and short video sequences emphasised the cars' selling points. The same videodisc, with different commentary, could be used for staff training. American motor distributors have been using similar approaches since the late 1970s, conscious of the fact that no show-

room can display all combinations of colour, body, trim and accessories, and also that a potential customer may be lost if no human salesman is free straight away. A rather more sinister development is that of car showroom IV presentations with a secret link to the sales office so that sales staff can eavesdrop on a prospective customer's choices made in what the customer thought was privacy. The salesman can then follow up his victim face-to-face, trading on an uncanny familiarity with the prospective customer's preferences and psychology.

The American Sears Roebuck chain stores first used a videodisc (with 5600 still frames and 19 video sequences) in place of their printed mail-order catalogue in 1981 and found it both cheaper and more effective. Several department stores have seen the advantage of an effective video presentation for customer information, especially when the same equipment and sometimes the same videodiscs can also be used for on-the-spot staff training. Travel and tourist information is another area where IV has proved popular: if all possible views of a town have previously been captured on videodisc, the user can 'walk through' any part – perhaps just by pointing at a map – and see what it really looks like. This approach has been applied to attracting tourists to holiday resorts, eg in the town of Biarritz in France.

One example of how IV can provide training and diagnosis when combined with an animated visual encyclopaedia on motor car maintenance has already been described (page 17). IV has also been used successfully to help trainees learn to make appropriate choices for instrument settings by seeing a realistic portrayal of the consequences – for example in train driver education: IV allows the driver to make mistakes without crashing a real train! The educational possibilities of IV are only just beginning to be explored; early results in schools and colleges suggest that it may be a medium of unique power and attractiveness. The fact that IV equipment is designed for use on a one-to-one basis would make it expensive to install in school classrooms, but could be an added attraction when delivered by cable for use in the home.

Converging technologies

A major theme of this book is the way in which technologies that began as quite different and distinct have begun to converge, sometimes quite rapidly. The whole field of television and video monitors, teletext and viewdata, cable and satellite TV and interactive video illustrates this trend strongly. A modern colour television set on public view may be showing broadcast TV with teletext subtitles or viewdata information superimposed on videodisc pictures or simple computer output, or it might alternate between any combination of these possibilities without the viewer being aware of the changing source of the pictures. The user might control the whole complex presentation by the simplest possible means – the touch of a finger-tip. Yet until very recently video monitors and television receivers were totally incompatible, produced in two different price brackets for completely different markets, and touch-screens were confined to systems which cost thousands of pounds.

Figure 128 Interactive video can be used to display information and to promote products in public places and without supervision. Here passers-by are using a videodisc presenting the Austin-Rover motor car range. Specially toughened glass allows users both an unobstructed view of the presentation and the chance to respond by pressing the response panel.

The convergence of technology in laser videodisc, compact audio disc and external computer memory is a further example of the trend. Philips have already announced a compact disc player for cars, and plan to produce a modified version called CARIN (Car Information and Navigation) that will allow the driver to use the system for navigation as well as for entertainment (Figure 131). A CARIN map disc could hold 150 000 pages (enough to cover all major roads in a small country like Britain). The driver would key in the starting-point, destination and preferred route type (fastest, most scenic or least fuel-demanding) and the built-in computer then stores the instructions in RAM, releasing the system to play music. During the journey, the computer would issue directions through speech synthesis, using its built-in navigation system to monitor the car's actual position continuously against its expected progress. By around 1988, an 18-satellite system called Navstar is expected to be in operation and would be linked to CARIN, allowing it to guide the driver around traffic jams, road works or bad weather. This system was only announced in 1985, and it remains to be seen whether it fulfils its promise. However, it is a clear example of the new kinds of integrated systems that are becoming possible.

Interactive cable TV is a further example of the convergence of technologies that previously were separate. Conventional broadcast television, DBS channels, teletext, viewdata, electronic mail, video libraries and interactive video could all be provided and delivered by a single and affordable set of hardware in each home. The potential and problems that these developments present us with – both as employees and as citizens – is the theme of Part Two.

Figure 129 The video juke-box launched in 1985 by Thorn EMI Videodisc and Taitel Electronics.

Figure 130 The VHD videodisc player
can provide interactive training using a
simple keypad (left). The videodisc shown
standing on the player is normally
completely enclosed in a plastic sleeve
(right). It is loaded into the slot at the
front of the player.

Figure 131 Compact audio discs can
already provide high-quality in-car entertainment. Philips' CARIN system pro-
poses to take this a stage further, allowing
the driver to use the system for navigation
as well. The driver loads the appropriate
map videodisc and keys in details of
starting-point, destination and preference
for route. A synthesised speech unit
interrupts the music during the journey to
issue spoken directions at appropriate
moments.

Part

2

Information technology and the employee
Information technology and the citizen

Chapter 9: Information technology and the employee

In Part One we established the basic principles upon which information technology depends, and saw how quickly new developments in computing, in telecommunications and in video seem to be converging. Part Two concentrates on the implications of all this for the individual.

The employment market is of great importance, not only for those who are themselves employers or employees, but also because of its effect on the self-employed, on those in short-term jobs or job-substitutes, on students and trainees, and on all those who are unemployed, whether or not they are actually seeking a job. The world of work strongly influences many who are not actively part of it. This chapter therefore looks at the impact of information technology (IT) on the employee, especially on those who work in offices and places where people and IT systems are side by side and interdependent. (Industrial robots necessarily tend to have a more distant relationship with human workers.) Chapter 10 examines how IT affects us all as citizens.

The effect of IT on the job market is important and controversial. An increasing number of jobs depend on the information sector, as opposed to industry and agriculture (Figure 132). Overall, IT destroys jobs of certain kinds and creates (or preserves) other kinds of jobs. What is not yet clear is whether this balance is positive or negative, either in terms of the quantity or quality of jobs. In any case, the arrival of IT is being accompanied by such important worldwide changes in economic and social patterns that the question may be unanswerable; it is also largely outside the scope of this book. Nevertheless, in thinking about the problems raised in this chapter, no-one can forget the human misery and waste caused by unemployment, nor the despair and need that forces some people to take badly paid jobs in appalling working conditions. How IT can be made to overcome these evils is an economic and political question, not a matter of technology.

Figure 132 Changes in the percentage of people employed in different sectors in the United States over the past century.

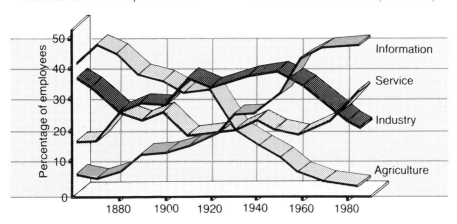

Job content and satisfaction

The introduction of information technology need not *in itself* reduce the amount of satisfaction people find in their jobs. On the contrary, it often increases it. It all depends on the nature of the job, how appropriate the IT system is for the purpose, the way in which its introduction is managed and regarded, the extent of consultation with the workers about the new methods, the initial attitudes, skills and prospects of the workforce and a whole variety of other factors.

This general statement only comes to life when we look at the day-to-day reality of what happens in practice. So I will focus in this section on a modest innovation – the introduction of word processing (wp) to replace typewriters. Similar factors affect job content and satisfaction in other sectors such as manufacturing and service industries.

On the following few pages I have described two real-life instances where word processors were introduced with the aim of improving work efficiency. Before you read them you may find it helpful to look at Figure 133 opposite which illustrates some of the ways in which text can be processed. You may also want to refer to the Glossary for some of the wp terms.

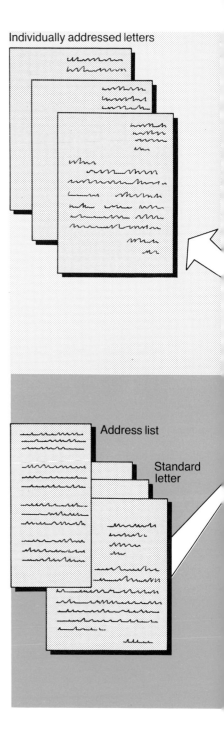

Individually addressed letters

Address list

Standard letter

Figure 133 Some major differences between processed and unprocessed text.

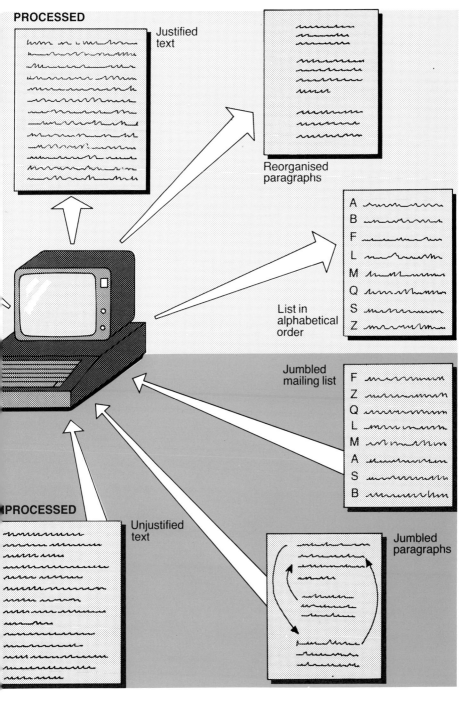

PROCESSED

Justified text

Reorganised paragraphs

List in alphabetical order

Jumbled mailing list

PROCESSED

Unjustified text

Jumbled paragraphs

Case study 1

Typing pool in small firm

Small firm with 30 employees including six secretaries and three clerks. High 'throughput' of typing, especially correspondence. Some secretaries strongly identified with their particular superiors, making travel arrangements and appointments for them as well as typing. Some re-typing of reports etc after revision, but high volume of one-off correspondence.

Decision to purchase word processing equipment

Taken by office manager on his own initiative; no consultation with secretaries, supervisor or other managers. Single supplier engaged for hardware, software and training. No independent consultant used, no statement of requirements, no competitive tender from other firms.

Case study 2

Self-employed journalist

Mother of young children working from home as freelance writer (books and articles). Initially she employed part-time secretary to type material on high-quality electric typewriter. He had other part-time commitments, combined these with half-day visits several times a week. Excellent secretary: arrangement basically satisfactory apart from conflict between typewriter noise and journalist's phone calls, difficulty in writing while study shared, problems for joint work caused by domestic interruptions and general problem of arranging enough sessions to keep up with inflow of work. Journalist professionally interested in computers; decision to buy wp system triggered by departure of secretary for full-time job.

Decision to purchase word processing equipment

Taken after reading widely and consulting colleagues. Journalist was reluctant touch

System installed

Small minicomputer with hard disc unit connected through a local area network to five VDUs, fast daisy-wheel printer for finished copy and two dot-matrix printers for drafts.

Word processing software standard off-the-shelf package on 5¼-inch disc, not customised to printers nor to firm's stationery or filing system. Five-day training course for all secretaries together when system first installed: level of proficiency achieved very variable. No follow-up: none achieved confident mastery within first three months. Software manuals immense and highly technical, seldom consulted.

Effect on job content

Copy typing almost eliminated (some necessary at first because of incompatibility with previous system). Revising and editing

vastly increased: some typed drafts habitually returned four or five times. Many fresh print-outs needed to correct minute errors previously disregarded (or hand-corrected).

Network increased specialisation. Text of different kinds entered at various VDUs for another operator to print out elsewhere, perhaps much later when appropriate stationery loaded into right printer. Link between keying-in and end-product on paper thus weakened, undermining secretaries' pride in efforts and reducing feedback on effects of different wp commands.

Secretaries disliked monotony of constant keyboarding, unrelieved by filing, photocopying and other assorted activities previously involving legwork.

Effect on turnaround

Previous average using memory typewriters one to two days, markedly increased

---

typist with only moderate speed. Not confident of decision, so high-cost system not considered, but decent keyboard essential.

System installed

Initially, one small micro (BBC Micro) with disc drive, green-screen monitor and dot-matrix printer, total purchase price around £1200. (See last section for hardware added later.)

Word processing software fitted semi-permanently on a ROM chip supplied with short manual and touch typing tutor. Word processing self-taught on-the-job using manual and trial-and-error. First results within an hour using only simplest wp features, gradual but steady progression to more advanced features after a few months. Total time spent on achieving mastery of wp system perhaps 20 hours spread over four months. Another five hours or so invested in improving touch-typing skill and accuracy using typing tutor program.

Effect on job content

Profound: in conventional terms, journalist now does 'low-grade' work (typing) previously sub-contracted. In practice, composing, entering and editing text all merged into single process: working at the keyboard replaced writing text in longhand for subsequent typing, checking and editing.

Effect on turnaround

Previously depended on days when typist came in: usually between two and five days. Using wp, replies to letters generally sent by return of post or next day; articles and books no different (faster production of draft offset by greater tendency to revise).

Effect on quality of finished work

First results not as good as typewriter output: poorly laid-out but letter-perfect on standard fanfold paper, often after several reject drafts had been printed out. Consistent control soon achieved of printer by wp system: initially from five to eight days, reducing to three to six days once staff gained experience. For documents that went back and forward between author and secretary four or more times (especially common at first), ten days or more not unusual.

Effect on quality of finished work

Reduced: electric golf-ball typewriters had had proportional spacing plus attractive range of typefaces. Wp software was based on fixed-spacing characters (Figure 136), because of the difficulty of justifying text with proportional spacing. Much of dot-matrix print-out is draft quality, on fanfold paper that demands edge-trimming by guillotine to fit filing system. Daisy-wheel printer for top copy incapable of printing £ sign as supplied, hence £s written in by hand at first. Separate typing of envelopes on manual typewriter meant extra work to link up with relevant letter from batch of print-out.

Reaction of users

System universally disliked.

Secretaries:
* found operating wp equipment tiring and boring compared with typewriters
* felt less involved with end-product
* were less satisfied with appearance of work
* resented extra work, eg repeated print-outs
* some complained of eyestrain etc from VDUs.

Managers:
* dissatisfied with the slower turnaround
* disliked poorer quality
* complained that secretaries had less time for non-typing work.

---

effects: underlining, accurate page layout, centring and alignment of letters produced on pre-printed fanfold. Slow daisy-wheel printer added later for occasional use where appearance important. Far fewer draft print-outs, but still more than in typewriter days. Bulk of work produced as double-spaced copy for editors to amend prior to typesetting, so finished appearance not as important as in prestige letters.

After first year's almost-daily use, commissioned for rush-job: 60-page booklet to be written and printed inside two weeks. Looked up simple codes for effects such as larger type for headings and changes of typeface in booklet supplied by typesetter, and embedded them into text at the same time as writing it. Disc posted straight to typesetter: result letter-perfect professional typesetting by return of post, no need to proof-read.

Reaction of user

Delighted with system, unable to imagine working without it. Easier to produce fast turnaround when necessary because no longer dependent on typist. However, now does much more revising and rearranging than previously, so composing articles not actually quicker overall than writing long-hand plus checking typing – but fond belief that quality improved! For specially important or difficult work, now more likely to circulate drafts to colleagues, then revise again as a result of comments – not done in typewriter days. Much easier to hit length targets than previously.

Main disadvantage: lack of help with jobs previously done by typist (eg filing, photocopying, mailing) because not worth employing someone for these more occasional tasks alone.

Cost-effectiveness of system

Disastrous: system performed badly, reduced productivity, was unpopular and costly. Displaced electric typewriters were five years old so resale value very low. Initial cost £80 000 plus commitment to further £330 000 over next five years to cover lease and maintenance of hardware and software.

Further uses of system

Nil to date. System installed incompatible with existing company computer and so unpopular that other possibilities not explored.

Cost-effectiveness of system

Purchase price recovered inside first year in wages not paid to typist. Running costs comparable with typewriter: less spent on ribbons, more on paper than before. Around 50 discs are in use at any time; disc replacement costs are insignificant since most things can be deleted once published and photocopied for the cuttings file.

Further uses of system

Same hardware also used for running business and educational software and firmware (mainly for newspaper and magazine articles, also for family). Illustrations for books and articles produced directly on dot-matrix printer. Modem added: electronic mail and Prestel both used for trial periods (couple of months each). System also linked to videodisc player for experimental work on interactive video. Second BBC Micro, colour monitor and twin disc drive added for back-up and flexibility in performing different tasks at same time.

These two examples are closely modelled on real life; details of the first case have been changed to protect the innocent! The second case, if you haven't already guessed, is my own. The two were chosen to draw a sharp contrast and to emphasise that whether a system works well in practice depends as much on how its introduction is managed as on its technical capability or price. I would not argue that wp will suit *all* freelance journalists, and I certainly don't mean to imply that wp won't work in small firms! Quite a number have introduced wp both successfully and economically, but they have gone about it very differently – and many found it harder to introduce than they expected.

One of the commonest failings of management when introducing information technology is to undervalue the workers' knowledge of day-to-day routines and the details of how a job is done. To neglect to consult the people who will be most directly affected is to invite disaster. Without active co-operation from the workforce, the most sophisticated systems can be an expensive flop. But by enlisting workers' active support and involving them in the choice of hardware and software, management can expect not only better attitudes but also a more suitable system.

Both cases illustrate clearly how the introduction of IT often affects job *content* and changes the definition of what is and what is not within the worker's role – in other words the age-old question of demarcation. In the first case it led to the separation of roles that were previously combined; in the second, it led to the fusion of a greater variety of roles. Since most people who enjoy their jobs like a variety of tasks and tend to like to see a thing through from start to finish, it follows that where IT leads to splitting jobs up into lots of specialised and repetitive tasks, its effect on job satisfaction may be damaging. Where IT enhances the ability of a single worker to produce a satisfying end-product alone or in a socially rewarding group, it is likely to increase job satisfaction.

Another important by-product of the

introduction of IT at work is the Trojan Horse effect: a microcomputer may at first be seen as a typewriter-substitute if it is dedicated to word processing, but the same micro can later serve an immense range of other purposes. For example, it can communicate with other mainframes; act as a videotex terminal; give access to electronic mail, telex and teletex; download telesoftware and question remote databases. As a free-standing microcomputer it can run programs such as spreadsheets, graphics packages, database systems – in fact an unlimited range of programs in whatever programming language(s) the micro can handle.

Even straightforward word processing can pose a considerable challenge for conventionally trained executives and secretaries. Executives (traditionally male) often have no familiarity with the layout of a keyboard and may be wholly dependent on their secretaries to operate the new equipment, landing them in great difficulties if they need a vital document when she is not around. Secretaries (traditionally female) may have no previous experience of computing, often lack confidence in dealing with equipment they regard as technical, and may be reluctant to trust invisible electronic memories. Unless both sides clearly understand the strengths and limitations of the new system, it will be a recipe for friction.

Furthermore, once an office begins to increase the different uses to which it puts a microcomputer, far-reaching questions about job content and boundaries are raised. A secretary who may have been willing enough to learn wordprocessing may feel that operating spreadsheets and graphics packages demands a further level of computer literacy and competence which – if achieved – should be rewarded by extra payment or even re-grading of the job. An executive who was content to depend on his secretary to operate word-processing equipment may feel the need for a terminal of his own once others in the organisation start to share an electronic diary and communicate by electronic mail.

Since the early 1980s there has been a trend towards *integrated software*, especially for business users. This usually means a suite of closely related programs which are presented and interlinked so as to make it very easy for the user to switch between them and feed the results from one program directly into another without having to re-key them. For example, a communications program, database, spreadsheet and graphics package might all link up with each other and with the word processing software. The user can retrieve sales figures from the database, manipulate them in the spreadsheet, select a column of figures to illustrate a trend as a bar chart, incorporate the illustration into a word-processed sales forecast and transmit the whole report electronically down the telephone using the communications package – all without ever having to re-key text or data.

But who is the user? This style of software directly challenges traditional job definitions where the manager (executive or professional) analyses figures (perhaps using a calculator) and dictates or hand-writes text, whereas the secretary types and lays out the report and is responsible for mailing it. Either the secretary will have to learn skills of running programs and analysing their results – skills that take her miles beyond her original training and job description, or the executive will have to do his own keyboard input – which may or may not be a sensible use of his time. Alternatively the two will have to learn new methods of collaborating on the task in a way that is acceptable to both.

Many claims have been made about the amount of time saved by information technology, but it is important to ask 'Time saved for what?'. Unless an employee's working hours are actually reduced while salary is maintained – and I know of no instances of this – the employee's reaction to IT will depend on whether the new activities are more interesting, more satisfying, and less stressful than the old. A secretary who actually *enjoys* copy typing can be expected to resist word processing. Simi-

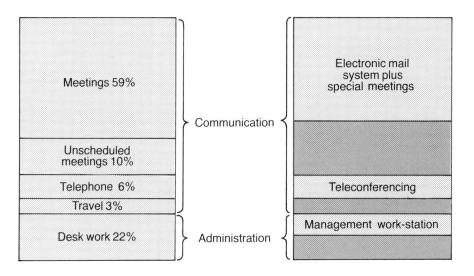

larly a manager who enjoys travelling and meetings can be expected to resist electronic mail, however attractive it may seem on paper (Figure 134).

Figure 134 Possible effects of information technology on a manager's 8-hour working day. (Shaded areas indicate possible time saved.)

Working environment

It is difficult to generalise about the effects of IT on the working environment, but some examples will suggest areas of potential concern to employees. Considerable research attention has focused on comfort, health and safety aspects of VDUs, and as an increasing number of people are using VDUs regularly at work and at home, this is where I will concentrate here.

Ergonomics is the study of the relationship between the design of equipment and the comfort and productivity of the people who use it. VDUs need different lighting conditions and furniture arrangements from typewriters. If an employee is expected to operate a VDU at a desk designed for a typewriter, he or she may well suffer from backache, eyestrain, headaches or other discomforts. This does not mean that VDUs are themselves unhealthy, simply that it is important to recognise that adjustments must be made to the working environment. Prolonged sessions at a VDU can be very tiring, partly because the operator tends to adopt a fixed posture because of the fixed position of the screen, keyboard and copy. Adjustable work-station equipment is therefore very important, especially when different operators may use the same equipment from time to time (Figure 135).

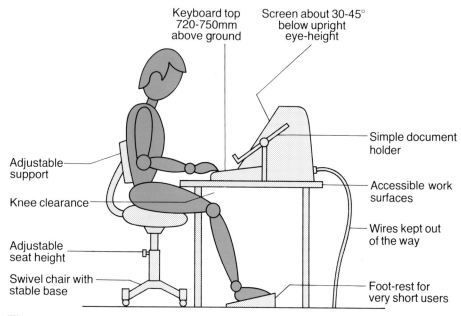

Keyboard top
720-750mm
above ground

Screen about 30-45°
below upright
eye-height

Simple document
holder

Adjustable
support

Accessible work
surfaces

Knee clearance

Wires kept out
of the way

Adjustable
seat height

Swivel chair with
stable base

Foot-rest for
very short users

The amount and type of light around the work-station is crucial: windows that were a source of pleasantly bright light when it was falling on typewriter paper may cause annoying reflections on a smooth VDU screen. Suitable blinds, artificial lighting or changes in the furniture arrangement may help with this problem.

The characteristics of the screen display are also very important. To confirm this, compare the appearance of text on the screen when a microcomputer is connected to a colour TV receiver (flickery white letters, sometimes with coloured fringes, on a black background) with that on a good monochrome monitor (rock-steady light green or amber letters on a dark green or amber background). No-one who is making daily use of a computer screen should be expected to put up with excessive contrast and glare when suitable monitors are so cheap. More recent hardware sometimes produces the black-on-white (or dark-on-light) type of display that is usually preferred (because it resembles type on paper).

Some monitors even display characters with proportional spacing (Figure 136),

Figure 135 Some important features of a well-designed VDU work-station.

Fixed spacing

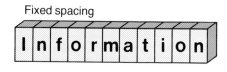

Proportional spacing

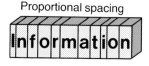

Figure 136 Proportionally spaced lettering is more compact and easier to read than fixed-space lettering.

Figure 137 (*opposite*) The difference between the displays on a well adjusted video monitor (left) and a poorly adjusted television (right) can be enormous. Not only is the left-hand display easier to read, it is also far less tiring to work with.

making them more attractive and easier to read than fixed-space letters. Other things being equal, the higher the resolution of the display, the easier it is to provide an attractive and legible style of lettering (Figure 137). A monitor shaped like A4 paper has the added advantage that it reduces the need for vertical scrolling during word processing. Unfortunately, these features tend to make greater demands on memory and hence to cost more; the normal microcomputer method of producing screen characters tends to result in fixed spacing (page 124). This does not necessarily mean that employees should press their employers for high-resolution screen displays, however, as these tend to require very high-cost equipment. The extra money might be better spent on really good chairs or detachable keyboards, since proper adjustment and good working conditions can make even the cheapest monitor perfectly comfortable to use for long periods.

One feature of the VDU screen that *is* crucial is that the display should be free of flicker. Displays that are supported by continually refreshing the image (see page 123) may be noticeably unsteady, depending on the refresh rate, the persistence of the phosphor coating, and the way in which the system controls the VDU. Although standards for the *technical* aspects of VDU displays have been published, many are unhelpful since the appearance to the human user depends on a complicated interaction between the processor, the software and the VDU. The standards giving recommended minimum size and

spacing between letters are also unsatisfactory since, if taken literally, they can rule out proportional spacing. The International Standards Organisation is studying VDUs and trying to develop standards defined by their effects on people in actual use, rather than by laboratory performance of the equipment.

There has been considerable concern about the effects of prolonged VDU operation on eyesight: symptoms reported have included headaches, red stinging eyes, fatigue and disturbed vision. One study, by the Association of Optical Practitioners, found that many of these symptoms were caused by inadequate operator training, poor siting and lighting, and psychological factors. The more interesting and varied the workers found their tasks, the less likely they were to complain of physical symptoms. It also found that VDU operation more often *revealed*, rather than *caused*, defects of vision. For example, older employees often have difficulty in switching between focusing on documents close at hand and the screen, which is further away. It is therefore in the interests of both employers and employees that operators should have routine eye tests *before* VDUs are installed, as well as regularly afterwards. The AOP investigated and dismissed the idea that radiation from VDU screens could affect the operator's health: research in several countries has found that the levels of both infra-red and ultra-violet radiation were well below safety limits, though some VDUs of an older design were criticised.

Many countries now have laws and regu-

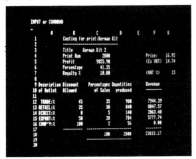

lations about aspects of VDU design and use. In some cases, maximum periods of continuous use are laid down. For example, in 1982 the Norwegian Labour Inspectorate introduced legislation covering several health aspects of VDUs and set an upper limit of four hours for continuous VDU operation. Various trade union organisations have suggested lower limits (usually in the range of two to three hours) and also have recommended regular breaks – for example, of 20 minutes every two hours. How readily these fit the demands of the task and the needs of the employees obviously varies from one workplace to another.

One great benefit of VDUs is that their operation is almost silent. However, the introduction of IT does not always reduce noise levels. Some kinds of high-speed computer printers are far noisier than type-writers, although acoustic hoods can reduce the problem. Improved models provide a better solution. Merely separating the noisy printer from the silent VDUs may be an undesirable move, with far-reaching consequences for the division of labour.

In general, though IT hardware tends to be cleaner and quieter than the electro-mechanical devices it replaces. Compare, for example, the noise levels in an old-fashioned newspaper typesetting room – clattering machinery, metal typefaces and tin trays echoing off a stone floor – with the clean carpeted silence of the VDU room. Whether this is recognised or welcomed will probably reflect how the workforce expects it to affect their work and whether they see it as a threat to their jobs.

Industrial relations

Good industrial relations tend to exist where management and workforce share the same goals and there is some consensus about how they are to be achieved. Whether IT is welcomed, accepted or fiercely resisted depends on individual circumstances. Where a firm is producing IT-

related goods or services, there tends to be little resistance to the use of IT as a means of providing them. Labour is not often strongly organised in IT industries for a variety of reasons, and there may be little or no trade union activity. This may be helpful to management in introducing new equipment and perhaps in increasing profitability, but it also means that the workforce need to be vigilant about any hazards to health or effects on working conditions and job satisfaction.

At the other end of the spectrum, there has been the unrest in, for example, the British national newspaper industry as a direct result of attempts to introduce IT. Here, improvements in working conditions have been regarded as unimportant compared with the perceived threat to job security in an industry beset by financial difficulties. The new technology has been strongly resisted as an attempt by management to reduce manning levels and increase profits. Because the workers both in the composing room (where the copy is keyed) and in the printing rooms are strongly unionised, their resistance has been backed firmly by industrial action. Some papers have ceased publication for weeks or months; others have folded altogether.

Again, I am not implying that IT is *in itself* likely to threaten jobs or worsen industrial relations in the newspaper industry. There are happier examples than Fleet Street: after the *New York Times* went over to a fully electronic system for news-gathering, writing and editing of copy and phototypesetting, the total number of its employees was unchanged, and they were better paid for more skilled work. The paper's circulation increased, it ran more regional editions and attracted more advertising, had more pages and was thought (at least by the journalists) to contain better-researched and more up-to-date stories. Figure 138 illustrates how radically electronic methods can simplify and speed up newspaper production. Although the *New York Times* experienced difficulties during the transition period, this example demon-

Figure 138 The impact of computer technology on the process of producing a newspaper.

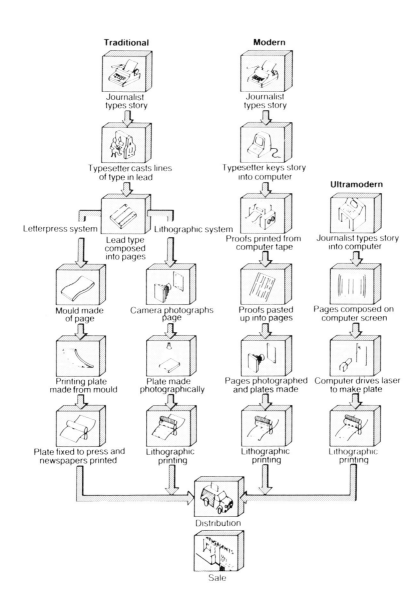

strates that skilled management and patient negotiation can overcome the difficulties if the will exists on both sides.

The facilities built into whatever software is used can be highly sensitive. One of the most controversial features is that of electronic 'monitoring' (or 'snooping', depending on your attitude) of employees' performance. Workers may be understandably suspicious of the collection of such statistics as the average rate of keystroking (number of keys pressed), length of breaks, number of telephone calls accepted, and so on. Much depends on the use that management makes of the figures – and on how the workforce imagines or fears that they may be used. Employees who are aware of the capability of electronic systems to record people's performance secretly will be understandably concerned to know whether and how it will be applied. Management may be called on to justify its practices and give assurances about who will have access to such figures and for what purposes.

Supermarket workers have been considerably affected by the introduction of IT, though in Britain at least there has been less industrial unrest than in the newspaper industry, partly because this group is less highly unionised. Electronic cash tills are superseding electro-mechanical ones, and the spread of bar codes on groceries is paving the way for the next stage in which laser scanners at the check-out read the product and price information encoded into the pattern of lines printed on the item (Figure 139). A speech synthesiser built into the check-out device can even confirm the prices and total in spoken words. By linking the system to a computer which holds information on stocks, orders to re-stock the shelves can be triggered automatically when the till devices indicate that supplies of particular products have run low.

Such a system will be resisted by sales staff if it is perceived as downgrading the skill and dexterity needed for their job, and may be welcomed if it makes their work less pressurised and leaves them more time to give attention to the customers. It all

depends on how management presents the change, and whether it is accompanied by attempts to shed jobs or pay existing workers less. There may be other side-effects of introducing a more automated system: for example, it eliminates accidental over- or under-charging by the till operator (who no longer keys in manually the price that the customer is charged), and with it various possibilities for dishonesty by staff *and* customers. This may also affect how it is received by employees.

Sometimes an electronic system may be acceptable to the workforce only when ultimate control is left in human hands. The British television station Channel Four has used IT as an integral part of its strategy for mounting a full channel's output with regional advertising on a low budget and with surprisingly few employees. Computer systems are used extensively in the commissioning and scheduling of transmissions. Its logo and many of its captions and title sequences depend heavily on computer graphics and animation. Digital devices are used to cut, mix, wipe, zoom and flip the picture. Its news output relies on the database, word-processing and *teleprompting* facilities of the Independent Television newsroom. These are all rapidly becoming common in modern television stations.

Channel Four's most notable innovation is their method for controlling the presentation: live and pre-recorded programmes have to be cued in and inter-cut with trailers and other presentation links. This requires split-second timing: the pauses for commercial breaks must be accurately controlled so that if the regional television companies haven't sold all the time available, music or promotional material can be used to fill in. The result is that although viewers in different parts of Britain are seeing different advertisements and fillers, they are completely unaware of the transition between these and the national programme output. This control is achieved by a special teletext signal carried on a spare line not needed for either the programme nor for Oracle, the public teletext service.

This signal contains coded information about schedule changes and commercial breaks, together with a split-second countdown of the time until the next break (Figure 140).

What is truly remarkable about this system is that it is fully capable of feeding its control signals to videotape recorders in the regions directly, ie without human intervention. In theory, Channel Four's head office in London could beam the TV signal direct to virtually unmanned regional centres: videotape recorders

Figure 139 Laser scanners at supermarket check-outs read bar codes automatically, decoding product and price information. Systems like these affect job content for supermarket workers as well as the receipts and queues experienced by shoppers.

Figure 140 Channel Four is a British television station with an unusually automated system of programme control. Using a special (private) teletext signal, split-second information about the timing of programmes, fillers and commercials is transmitted to engineers in the regions. The figures on the left show the transmission time and the figures on the right, the duration of the item. The central column shows the items coming up, eg COMMS – commercials.

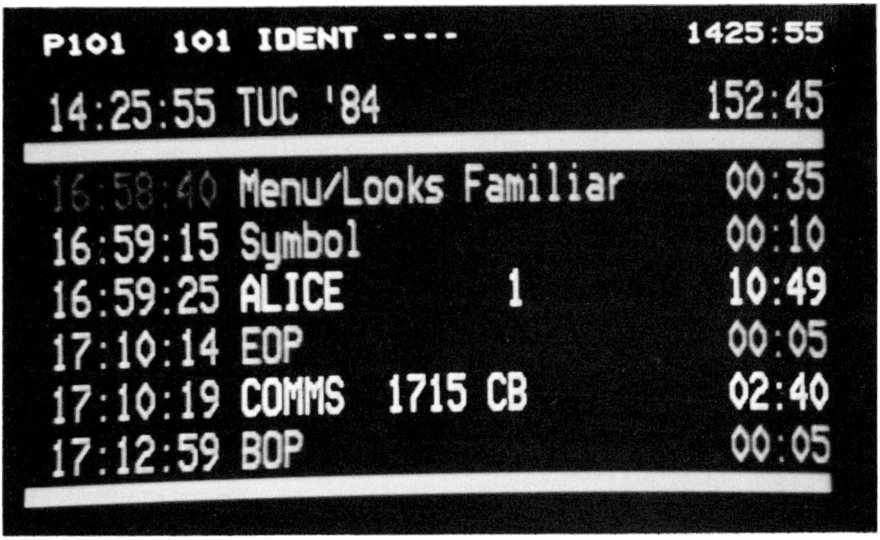

```
P101   101  IDENT ----              1425:55
14:25:55 TUC '84                    152:45

16:58:40 Menu/Looks Familiar        00:35
16:59:15 Symbol                     00:10
16:59:25 ALICE        1             10:49
17:10:14 EOP                        00:05
17:10:19 COMMS  1715 CB             02:40
17:12:59 BOP                        00:05
```

would stop and start under the control of the teletext signal, automatically switching back to the main transmission at the end of the regional input. In practice, part of the price of introducing this technologically advanced system was the agreement that the engineers in the regional offices would personally press the button on cue from the machine. This allows the engineers to retain their option of blacking out specific programmes or even the entire service as a form of industrial action.

Job location and market

IT provides immense opportunities for people to work even when they are at a distance from their normal workplace – for example, while at a remote office or public place, while actually travelling, or even from home. This may encourage a firm using IT to decentralise its operation using electronic links between smaller and more widespread offices, or to encourage its workers to do some or all of their work from home.

Many firms are based in larger cities where employees have serious problems with commuter traffic and affordable housing, and the firm has expensive offices situated in a prime city-centre site. At first sight, decentralisation using IT might have obvious attractions. After the *New York Times* introduced a comprehensive electronic system for news-gathering, word processing and typesetting, the economics correspondent was able to exchange the sticky heat of overcrowded Manhatten for the cool peace of his beach house in Maine for most of each summer. Figure 141 shows how a journalist might use a personal computer for research, drafting and editing across long distances.

For *potential* employees – notably for people, usually women, who are housebound by young children or tied by school hours – work from home might be their only chance of participating in the labour market. One successful international software publishing firm depends almost entirely on home-working by women programmers and systems analysts, and their work enjoys a high reputation. For many groups – the disabled, the chronically sick – those in prisons, hospitals and ships, IT offers new opportunities to do the same work as conventional employees, often for the first time. Distance need no longer present any object, and being physically confined to a home, institution or wheelchair need not prevent a person from working. The fact that IT allows new groups to compete for work – groups who for various reasons may be willing and even grateful to work at below the going rate – can cause resentment among existing employees. It may also lead to the creation of small enterprises and permit self-employment for many who would otherwise be unemployed.

In some cases, decentralisation and home-working through IT may be unwelcome. Some houses do not contain suitable working space for one person (let alone for two or more). Even if the employer provides all the necessary hardware, job opportunities for home-workers discriminate in favour of those who have large, quiet houses and good telephone facilities. In effect, home-working largely transfers the cost of office accommodation from the

Figure 141 One way in which a radio programme might be put together using a long-distance computer network. A radio journalist receives information from a researcher in London and prepares a draft script. He makes use of a database in Edinburgh to check some facts and figures, then sends the script to the series producer who is recording material in Spain. The producer makes changes and sends these back to the journalist, who updates the script. As a final check the producer sends the revised draft to a consultant in Amsterdam who sends comments back. The producer agrees any further changes with the journalist who sends the final version to the BBC in London. All this is carried out via computers and telephone lines.

Database
in Edinburgh

Radio presenter
in East Anglia

Consultant
in Amsterdam

Researcher
in London

Radio producer
in Madrid

employer to the employee. Because of the lack of supervision, payment is often for results rather than for hours spent, thus transferring responsibility for progress wholly onto the employee. Home-workers may be vulnerable to interruptions from domestic causes, workmen, door-to-door salesmen, children and animals. Working conditions may be far below the standard required in offices, not only for heating and lighting but also for equipment and furniture. Neighbours may discover and resent the change from purely residential use, and rating authorities and planning controls may present further problems. Above all, perhaps, many people simply don't *want* to work at home: they miss the social contact of office life and feel isolated.

Training

The rapid advance of IT poses serious questions about the purposes and methods of training, regardless of who provides it – whether colleges, private agencies or employers. Indeed, IT raises important questions about the aims of basic general education and the traditional assumption that education must be 'delivered' face-to-face in schools and colleges.

From the employee's viewpoint, the main questions to be asked of training in IT are about its effectiveness, whether it will demand out-of-hours time and energy, whether the skills will be of lasting value and are widely appreciated, and – perhaps most important – who pays for it, whether in the form of fees, expenses or hidden costs.

The introduction of IT often has a double-edged effect: it usually creates not only immense *needs* for training and retraining, but also great *opportunities*, opening up fresh chances for new groups of people using new methods.

Above all, IT offers enormous flexibility in training methods: it is no longer necessary to recruit or locate dozens of trainees at the same stage needing the same course and gather them all in one place face-to-face with an expert instructor. Self-

contained training materials can be spread into people's workplaces and homes – whether computer-based, audio, video, or simply printed. Using these materials, supported by any hardware needed (eg microcomputers, television screens or cassette recorders), individuals and small groups can be trained conveniently and cheaply. Interactive video, above all other media perhaps, seems to provide a uniquely powerful and effective method of training, and one that may become available in people's homes through cable technology.

No matter how sophisticated the training materials and media, they cannot substitute for a human instructor: a helping hand on-the-spot is often essential, especially for practical skills. However, it is usually much easier to arrange a local tutor for an individual than to bring in an expert instructor and assemble enough other trainees to justify the expense of the sessions. Telephone tutoring and teleconferencing can provide links with experts at a distance and also can put isolated learners in contact with each other.

In considering the role of training, it's important to distinguish between training aimed at the understanding of general principles, and training in specific procedures for operating certain equipment. Knowing the basic concepts and principles upon which computers, telephones and video systems work is likely to be valuable to most employees at some time in their working lives, and may even make all the difference in getting a job or a promotion. (It is also nowadays an indispensable part of the general education of every citizen, and the whole *Inside Information* project (page 222) is dedicated to sharing this knowledge more widely.) By contrast, specific practical training in how to work a particular switchboard, computer or videodisc player is unlikely to transfer readily to different models, and may in any case be overtaken within a few years by progress in design.

This distinction is not hard-and-fast, of course: anyone who has *used* a word processor or spreadsheet is more likely to understand how they work than someone

Figure 142 A videoconference is a long-distance conference in which participants can see, as well as hear, each other. To exchange normal-quality television pictures as they happen, an expensive broadband connection is needed, using cable or satellite, and participants may have to travel to a special studio. For many purposes, however, lower-quality pictures are adequate, in which case slow-scan television, displaying a frame every few seconds, can be used and this needs far less bandwidth to transmit.

Figure 143 *The Videodisc Manual of Motor Car Maintenance* being used in a British school.

who has only read about them in books. But that experience may only be a slight help (and can occasionally prove an actual hindrance) when it comes to mastering a quite different piece of software. In the early days of motor cars, gear positions were not standardised and motorists changing from one car to another were often caught out! In the same sort of way, a key that means 'copy' on one word-processing program might turn out to mean 'delete' on another – with disastrous results.

Employers frequently bear the costs of specific practical training in IT devices. 'Visible' fees and expenses may be less significant than the hidden costs – in particular the loss of productive work while training is in progress or workers are still inexperienced. The true cost of training is often underestimated. From a strictly economic viewpoint, IT has to reduce costs or increase production quite significantly before it justifies all the time and effort invested in its introduction by the management and workforce.

Whether the workers are willing to contribute any of their own time to such training is an interesting indicator of their attitudes, of the climate of industrial relations and of the way in which the technology is presented. A number of large firms have smoothed the introduction of new technology and raised the general level of staff computer literacy by lending their employees microcomputers to take home with them. Where workers (or their families) actually want to spend their leisure increasing their level of computer familiarity, this kind of scheme has been welcomed; on occasion it has been resented as an intrusion or an attempt to provide training on the cheap.

It is important for those who are doing the training to be sensitive to how particular skills are valued by the workforce. Television journalists' attitudes to electronic news handling has varied widely. Some have seen it as a splendid opportunity to acquire skills such as word processing and database interrogation at their manage-

ment's expense. Others view the new technology as an attempt to 'de-humanise' the newsroom and make them do their own typing instead of using secretaries. The same group (journalists) may regard training in the same task (keyboarding) as either enhancing or downgrading their jobs, according to how it is introduced.

It might be thought that the proper time for building up the groundwork in basic concepts of IT is at school. Indeed many school systems, notably in Britain, are making strong efforts to include IT, or at least the computing aspects of IT, as part of their mainstream curriculum. But the school system adapts slowly and IT moves on relentlessly. Even if the schoolchildren of the 1990s are better-equipped than the school-leavers of the 1970s and 1980s, there are several generations of adults today who had never heard of computers when they were at school, let alone had hands-on experience of using one. Closing this gap will require a major effort both by employers and by individuals. The employers' incentive is that investment in training should increase the quality and flexibility of the workforce; the employees' incentive may be that it increases their ability to get a job, to get promotion or to move to a better job with more pay, better working conditions or better prospects.

Chapter 10: Information technology and the citizen

Information technology already affects us all as individuals and citizens. Although we may not know it, information about each of us is stored on a number of computerised databases. As bank users or travellers we are obliged to be computer users, directly or indirectly. As consumers, we receive computer-produced bills for telephone, gas, electricity and rates. Our letter-boxes contain mounting quantities of junk mail containing word-processed offers 'personalised' to everyone on a mailing list. We shop at supermarkets where computerised tills produce bills that can be difficult to check. Our homes contain televisions and telephones – potential terminals to giant databases that offer great scope and unusual dangers. And we live in countries whose national security is defended, and perhaps threatened, by computers that watch the skies and listen to the signals – computers that are vulnerable to human error and sabotage.

The mixture of benefits and dangers for the individual that accompanies the arrival of IT is the subject of this chapter.

Data protection

It is generally believed that everybody has the right to know what data is held about them by organisations, that they should have the opportunity to challenge and correct such data, and that access by other people and organisations to personal data should be restricted. In short, individuals are entitled to expect both *privacy* and *security* for their personal data, wherever it is stored.

These rights have not generally been safeguarded by law until recently, when general concern about the use made of computerised databases has led to legislation in many countries. For example, in 1981 member countries of the Council of Europe signed a Convention on Data Protection. This led directly (and rather belatedly) to the passing of the Data Protection Act 1984 in the UK. Since other European countries already had data protection legislation, it was essential for the UK to conform. Otherwise European countries might have had to restrict the flow of information to the UK for fear that it would become a *data haven* – a place where illicit data processing and exchange could make nonsense of the protective laws of the other countries.

In the jargon of data protection laws, we are all *data subjects*. Many different organisations hold information about us in various places. Some of these *data users* are public bodies, others private companies. Increasingly, such information is held in computer databases. Frequently it consists of *personal data*, ie information about living people who are identified or identifiable. 'Information' here can include statements of opinion, rumour and misinformation!

The UK Act sets up a Data Protection Register run by a government-appointed Registrar. Data users must register their databases and stick to the eight principles laid down by the Act (Figure 144). Number 7 is perhaps the most important: we are all entitled to be told what data is held on us if we ask, and we should be able to get it corrected or deleted if it is incorrect. Data users must supply the Registrar with a description of the data they hold and the purpose(s) for which it is collected and processed. They must also explain where it came from, who has access to it and which countries, if any, it may be transferred to,

Figure 144 The UK Data Protection Act.

The eight principles

1 Data must be obtained and processed 'fairly'. It must only be taken from those who are entitled to have it in the first place, or from those who are required to supply it by law or international obligation. Data users must not mislead data suppliers about their reasons for wanting information.

2 Data must only be held for specific purposes, which must be the ones for which the data user has registered. For example, if a ticket agency registers that it collects personal data to supply theatre tickets by mail order, it cannot also collect data for market research. Each purpose must be separately registered.

3 Data must only be used for the purpose for which it has been registered.

4 Personal data must be adequate, relevant and 'not excessive' for the purpose registered. For example, information about the salaries of its customers would be considered irrelevant and excessive for the ticket agency.

5 Data must be accurate and, where necessary, kept up-to-date. If individuals are harmed by inaccurate or out-of-date information, they can claim for damages against the data user.

6 Data must not be kept for longer than necessary.

7 Data must be made available, on request, to data subjects in a form which they can understand, within a reasonable period of time and at reasonable cost. Individuals are entitled to have data corrected or erased where appropriate.

8 Data must be protected against unauthorised access or alteration, and also against accidental loss or deliberate destruction.

The main exceptions

1 All records held in the cause of national security.

2 Personal data held *only* for accounting and payroll purposes.

3 Personal data collected and processed on a word processor, and any data used *only* for text production. (Mailing lists containing *only* names and addresses are exempt, so the amount of junk mail will be unaffected by the Act.)

4 Membership data held by clubs provided that the members agree to their details being stored on the computer and that the club is small. It must observe the principles about disclosure, however: personal data must not be revealed to anyone other than the data subject.

5 Data held *solely* for domestic and leisure purposes, eg on a home computer.

6 Information relating to judicial appointments, stored by agencies offering financial services to clients and research data and statistics in which individuals are not identified.

7 Data need not be revealed if it is held for the purposes of preventing or detecting crime, catching or prosecuting criminals, assessing or collecting taxes or duties, or controlling immigration. (The effects of this section are controversial: some people fear that it may give the police, tax and immigration authorities immunity from the Act because it makes it easy for them to resist *all* individual requests for access to data.)

8 All data held in 'manual' form, eg handwritten or typewritten on cards or paper. (Although some of the greatest dangers to privacy arise from the computerised databases, this failure of the Act to control other forms of data may lead to loop-holes being found.)

giving an address to which data subjects should write if they want access to their own data.

Complaints against data users are made directly to the Registrar. He can ensure that data is erased if any of the eight principles has been broken – for example, if it is inaccurate, has been stored for too long, or was collected unfairly or for a different purpose. The Registrar can also prevent data users from transferring data abroad other than to countries identified at the time of registration. Movement of data to countries not adhering to the Council of Europe Convention or to its principles would not normally be approved. As a final sanction the Registrar can serve a Deregistration Notice so that the data user can no longer legally process data by computer.

There are many exceptions to the Act (Figure 144) and some critics have suggested that it may not go far enough even to satisfy the Council of Europe Convention. It has been said that individual freedoms have been undermined without giving protection for privacy: government departments and other public sector bodies cannot be sued for failure to comply with the Act. This is in contrast with countries like the US and Canada where the legislation applies *only* to the public sector. Other European countries like France and West Germany have laws that apply to both public and private sector. Some countries have laws that give protection to companies as well as to individuals, and others extend protection to data held in 'manual' form as well as to computer-based data.

Legislation – however comprehensive – can only provide part of the solution to the problem of how to protect personal data. Only some of the risks to privacy and security are posed by companies that will change their policies and practices if they are known to be illegal. Other risks are presented by *hackers*: computer enthusiasts who regard the security of public databases as a challenge to their ingenuity, and who have developed the skills of breaking into them to an advanced level. Most hackers work alone and from home, using micro-

computers and modems to make contact with databases miles away or even in other countries. Some also exchange messages and 'trade secrets' through *bulletin boards* with others of like mind. There are obvious difficulties in detecting and tracing hackers' activities, and it is not always clear what offence(s) may have been committed.

Having found out the necessary password(s) to get into a database, hackers sometimes simply inspect the contents – reading people's electronic mail, for example. Sometimes they change or add entries, leaving jokes or messages to show that they have broken in (an electronic counterpart to carving 'Kilroy was here' on a school desk or mountain top). Subtler and more mischievous variants of this include sending bogus messages or changing existing information without revealing that a hacker was responsible. A minority, indignantly disowned by most of the hacking community, use their skills to move money from one account to another – perhaps their own or an associate's. Thus the effects of hacking range from a simple violation of privacy to a mischievous confusion of messages or information to deliberate and criminal acts of fraud and theft. The film *War Games* about a schoolboy hacker who started a nuclear world war by breaking into a US Defense Department computer portrayed the ultimate danger of failure to take hacking seriously. Its plausibility was confirmed when a 21-year-old hacker took just three minutes to break into a key defence database in Washington at the opening of a London computer show in 1984. Using a BBC Micro and a standard modem, he made telephone contact with a network of British computers before crossing the Atlantic and penetrating the Washington computer via Vancouver.

Hackers' activities have often been beyond the reach of the law, both because few countries yet have laws which take account of computer systems, and because of the difficulties of tracing and detecting skilful hacking. Nevertheless the UK Interception of Communications Bill was debated by Parliament in 1985 and covers *all* public telecommunications including links with systems abroad. Although designed to control phone-tapping, it also provides penalties of up to two years in jail and £2000 in fines for hackers who break into databases like Prestel and British Telecom Gold. Not all hackers are alike: as we've seen, some do it for sport, others for mischief, others for criminal or near-criminal reasons, others again to draw attention to poor security and sloppy working practice. The purpose of the London computer show demonstration was to warn the US authorities of the dangers to their sensitive data. It was said that the hacker's face was hooded because he works for major companies, plugging gaps in their security systems. Another British hacker hit the headlines during 1984 by breaking into the Duke of Edinburgh's electronic mailbox. The hacker subsequently appeared on BBC Television to explain his methods, and criticised the lack of elementary security precautions in the system. Asked about his motivation, he replied that his life savings were committed to the Prestel on-line home-banking system and he wanted to see its security improved.

Hackers' successful break-ins may benefit the rest of us because of the tightening up of security that takes place as a result. Unfortunately for this argument, each increase in security simply seems to encourage more ingenious and persistent hackers to rise to the challenge! Another problem is that it requires ingenuity to design systems that are both secure and user-friendly. If electronic mail is to be used daily, it must be convenient; lengthy logging-on sequences and constant changing of passwords are inconvenient. Voice recognition systems are not yet sufficiently developed for large-scale general use. As long as user identification depends on simple digital information (eg a string of letters and numbers) it is all too easy for hackers to apply their own computers to producing different combinations automatically. Once a correct password has been identified, the hacker can log on as some-one else and may go on deceiving the system for months if he is careful to cover his traces.

High-street cash dispensers combine a reasonable degree of security and user-friendliness with their two-stage system. Neither the cash card nor the Personal Identification Number on their own give access; only in combination do they unlock the system. Since the dispenser retains the card if the right number is not entered within the first three tries, there is little chance that someone who steals or finds a cash card will get the PIN right by trial and error. Databases that are dialled up by telephone, however, lack the physical barrier provided by the cash machine, and are thus many times more vulnerable than this two-stage system. Yet most have been left wide open to hackers who use programs that churn out passwords by a process of trial and error.

Public authorities' innocence about these problems is not confined to Britain. In California, the land of the silicon chip where the microcomputer was born, a trusted inmate broke into the prison's computer system in 1984 and advanced his own release date by four weeks. Having watched prison staff calling up prisoner's files and revising their details, it took him only moments when a warder was out of the room to log on and get himself home in time for Christmas. He was discovered only because he was overheard boasting to another inmate about how easy it was: only the discrepancy between the computer and the old-style paper records revealed that a change had been made. Although no action was taken against the prisoner, the fact that prison records for the entire state of California are held in such a vulnerable form suggests larger-scale and far more sinister possibilities. The number of such incidents reported in the press is doubly worrying as it undoubtedly represents only the tip of a large iceberg: for each hacking incident reported, one suspects that many others – perhaps more serious – go unreported, having been hushed up by embarrassed authorities and firms.

Freedom of electronic information

Information technology is opening up world-wide communications to more people, and at lower cost, than ever before. We saw in Chapter 7 how the telephone allows us to speak to any of 450 million people in 130 countries around the world; with suitable equipment we can also exchange data with them and in some cases transmit pictures too. We can already telephone from cars, trains and even aeroplanes. The Japanese firm NEC has announced progress towards a translation telephone that will enable callers to converse with people who speak a different language. (Their demonstration system has only a 150-word vocabulary and works only between Japanese, Spanish and English, but by the end of the century they predict a large-vocabulary version for the main business language markets.)

Telephone lines also allow computer users to communicate with databases in other countries, exchanging electronic mail, computer software and private information across national frontiers. Satellites bounce television pictures across the world in seconds for mass viewing; developments in DBS (Chapter 8) will offer individual viewers more choice from an international range of programmes and teletext can provide translated subtitles. These developments offer a range of powerful methods of breaking down barriers of distance and language, and could promote international understanding.

These spectacular advances toward what has been called the 'global village' bring acute political and legal problems in their wake. We have already seen how the different national standards on data protection could create data havens for those who wish to evade their national laws. *Trans-border data flow* is the jargon phrase for the whole subject of controlling the movement of information between countries. Governments are concerned that satellites outside their control which broadcast programmes across national frontiers will undermine their sovereignty.

Most countries have detailed Codes of Practice governing the transmission of radio and television programmes and advertising. Material that is acceptable in one country may give offence or break laws in another. The Soviet Union has already publicly warned that it reserves the right to shoot down any satellite broadcasting into its airspace. The European Commission's paper *Television without Frontiers* sanctions the idea of governments jamming unwelcome signals with signals of their own, though whether a Western government would actually do to this is another matter.

Apart from the acceptability of programme content, international communications also pose many unsolved problems concerning copyright and artists' performance rights. Agreements over fees and royalties with a broadcasting authority may not have taken into account the possibilities of vast satellite audiences or selective cable subscribers. Royalties paid to software designers often relate to the numbers sold over the counter; the designer may get little reward for copies distributed through telesoftware. Authors certainly get no return on the many illegal copies swapped and sold by software pirates. Bulletin boards and international networks greatly increase the likelihood of unofficial copies being transmitted – a practice that cheats program designers of their incentives.

Interesting legal difficulties are raised by electronic information services: at the moment they lack agreed codes of practice governing their management and subscribers' activities, and it is unclear who is legally responsible for their contents. For example, Compunet is a subscription-based electronic information service run by a company of the same name. Compunet believes that it is not responsible for legal problems arising from any information provided by subscribers (Figure 145). It claims to be no more accountable for what appears in the sections contributed by subscribers than is British Telecom for what people say on the telephone. However, it is arguable that Compunet should be compared instead to a magazine

'The subscriber may not upload or permit to be uploaded any material which is offensive, defamatory, obscene or of an illegal nature and the subscriber takes full responsibility for any claims or criminal charges which may result from any such material being uploaded under the subscriber's user number and the subscriber shall indemnify Compunet against all costs, charges, claims, demands or other liabilities resulting from any such claim or criminal charge.'

Figure 145 Compunet's conditions of registration and use suggest that the subscriber is legally responsible for information placed on the system.

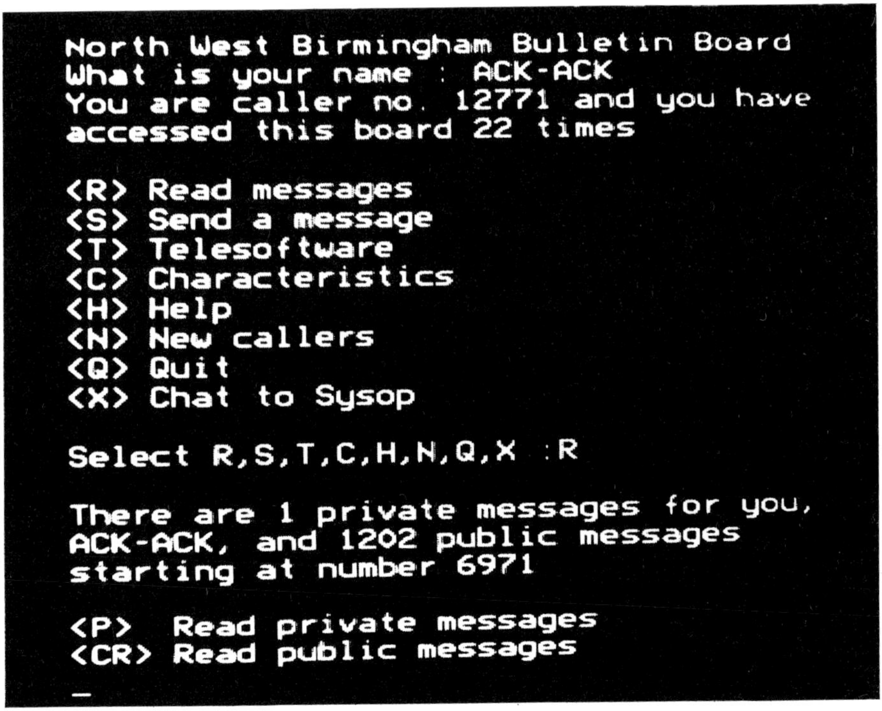

Figure 146 Bulletin boards are popular with home micro owners. But is the system operator (called Sysop here) legally or morally responsible for the messages exchanged?

which prints readers' letters and classified advertisements, in which case normal publishing laws hold the publisher responsible for any and all material he publishes, no matter who supplies it. This kind of issue can only be tested in the courts.

An American bulletin board operator has been prosecuted because someone publicised the number of a stolen credit card through his bulletin board, thus breaking the credit card company's conditions and assisting fraud. If the bulletin board, rather than the individual, is held to be responsible, this case could have far-reaching implications if it is taken as a precedent.

There is similar confusion in Britain about the status of information on Prestel. British Telecom began by imposing a total ban on politics and religion on its 'open' pages (the ones available to Prestel subscribers who do not also belong to any particular Closed User Group). This led to considerable controversy in late 1984 when the Labour Party launched a CUG for

```
North West Birmingham Bulletin Board
What is your name : ACK-ACK
You are caller no. 12771 and you have
accessed this board 22 times

<R> Read messages
<S> Send a message
<T> Telesoftware
<C> Characteristics
<H> Help
<N> New callers
<Q> Quit
<X> Chat to Sysop

Select R,S,T,C,H,N,Q,X :R

There are 1 private messages for you,
ACK-ACK, and 1202 public messages
starting at number 6971

<P>  Read private messages
<CR> Read public messages
_
```

party activists and also provided a number of open pages for the public part of the database. During the disagreement that followed, the Labour Party's service was suspended. Its Technology Spokesman, Jeremy Bray, complained that the ban had 'created a presumption in favour of censorship which is disturbing in a free society'. Eventually the government made it clear that it wanted the viewdata industry to draw up its own guidelines and the dispute was resolved.

Later there was a major dispute between Prestel and one of its main Information Providers, Timefame International. On one of its Prestel pages, Timefame alleged that a 'mole' inside Prestel was leaking users' personal passwords to hackers. Prestel contested these allegations, and when Timefame refused to withdraw them from its Prestel pages, Prestel closed down Timefame's service. There were protests from users, action in the High Court and retaliation by some hackers. The dispute was resolved after Timefame withdrew their allegations and Prestel restored the pages. Nevertheless, whether viewdata systems like Prestel are entitled to censor the information provided on their public pages remains highly controversial. If viewdata is to act as a common carrier of information like the telephone system, there is no precedent for censorship and only very special circumstances can justify 'phone-tapping'. The control of electronic information is highly centralised. This makes monitoring and censorship alarmingly easy. The price of electronic communication is too high if it does not allow subscribers to express views with which the authorities disagree.

Consumer issues

Computers and information technology reinforce the need for consumer protection and education. In a world of automatic charging and computer-generated bills, it can be extremely difficult for the shopper to check whether and when he is being overcharged. Goods with prices marked in barcode format may be convenient for the laser scanner at the supermarket checkout, but it is important for humans that the price is boldly and legibly marked in conventional form as well.

We tend to accept computer-generated bank statements and bills for fuel and telephone services without question, and overall they probably *are* more reliable than ones written out and added up by hand. But computer output can only be as accurate as the input allows, and human error must be expected and catered for. Operators faced with having to key in large quantities of meaningless data are unlikely, and perhaps unable, to exercise much commonsense in vetting the input. Various simple checks can be made on the consistency of data at the input stage, but real responsibility for ensuring that extraordinary bills are queried before they are sent out rests with the software designer. Where gas is supplied to a regular customer, there is no excuse for failing to apply the mainframe computer's large memory and lightning calculation speed to the simple matter of checking that consumption is within the normal bounds of seasonal variation and querying the bill if it is not. Yet sadly the stories of persistent computer-generated Final Demands for £0.00 are *not* legends: recently I received an equally daft piece of computer output from a publisher – a disappointingly detailed royalty statement for £0.00 for a book that hadn't even been published!

Consumers need to have a clear idea of what can and cannot be expected of information technology and of the humans that design and operate the new systems. Otherwise we cannot combat the increasingly common and pathetic attempts to shift blame for all shortcomings onto 'the computer', when most result from incompetence and poor management on the part of human beings. Consumers must also be vigilant about the subtler dangers of some applications of the new technology.

Few people are by now deceived by the phoney personalisation of word-processed junk mail: the typed-looking letter that uses your name and district repeatedly to announce that you have been specially selected from all the inhabitants in your area to receive details of some privileged offer, free trinket or prize draw. The purpose is usually to persuade you to order goods or to send for a catalogue, and the firm presumably believes that you will be impressed by receiving an apparently personal letter. The reality is that these mail-shots are printed by the thousand on fast line printers linked to computers containing mailing lists of names and addresses by the hundred thousand. These mailing lists are routinely traded between, for example, mail order and credit card companies.

Junk mail may be a nuisance, but until recently it has at least been fairly transparent. More sinister developments may be on the way, despite recent moves in data protection legislation. For example, in early 1985 one Rome-based firm that specialises in computerised information was openly offering to sell confidential information about voters to candidates in the Italian local elections. Thus candidates could aim their campaigning (and trim their policies) towards specific groups – for example, female doctors aged between 50 and 60 with outdoor interests, or unemployed males between 20 and 35 – sending a differently worded election communication to each group. In addition to details of family status, job, type of housing, hobbies, clubs and political friendships, this firm's information sheet contained a suspicious 'other information' category.

One of the most worrying aspects of IT is the way in which it makes electronic snooping all too easy. How are members of the public to know whether the computer keyboard they tap their responses into is as private and anonymous as it seems? The software may have been programmed to record their responses automatically, or the terminal may be being monitored continuously from a distance. In Chapter 8 we saw how car salesmen can use secret links to their advantage in interactive video presentations in the showroom which are connected to the office by a concealed cable. Even free-standing self-contained

computer systems are not safe: equipment in a discreetly parked van can display a legible copy of text as it is keyed into an office word processor several hundred feet away, as BBC Television's *Tomorrow's World* demonstrated in 1985. The equipment depends on a good antenna, and works by decoding the radio interference caused by the video signal that the processor sends to the screen. Eavesdropping equipment can be assembled for as little as £100; a great deal of it may already be in active use, invading our privacy and monitoring our use of computers.

There are various ways in which responsible computer users can protect themselves and their data subjects from radio eavesdropping. Most involve shielding the system by completely enclosing it in a *Faraday Cage* – a casing of highly conductive metal. Some systems use metal casings for equipment and cables together with a fine metal mesh over the VDU screen. Others build metal-cladding into the floors, walls and ceiling of the computer room and require double metal doors. Although an amateur eavesdropper might be discouraged by relatively simple shielding, very expensive and sophisticated methods are needed to foil a determined professional. The North Atlantic Treaty Organisation (NATO) has a standard for shielding called Tempest (information about its details is highly classified). But it would be far too expensive for most business users to invest in Tempest-standard protection, and in any case data protection laws do not specify the level of 'appropriate security measures' that data users must take. As we are all data subjects, we are all at risk.

In addition, then, to the possibility that firms may deliberately employ electronic methods to erode consumer rights, they may also unwittingly supply details about their customers (or would-be customers) to electronic spies in the course of routine computer use. The problem of computer fraud is also two-edged: it affects both companies and consumers. Even if the customers are unaware that computers are involved, ultimately it is they who bear the cost since fraud contributes to higher prices for goods and services. For this reason alone computer fraud ought to be a matter for general concern, not merely for the firms who suffer from it.

In many countries, computer fraud is not as commonly reported as, for example, in the United States where it is an everyday event. The rest of the world has no grounds for complacency: the managements of organisations that have fallen victim to computer fraud are often far too reluctant to prosecute the offender – even in the small minority of cases where the fraud is discovered and the culprit detected. Banks and private companies understandably feel that public confidence in their services could be undermined, and government departments often fear political consequences and pressure from civil liberties groups. So a conspiracy of silence surrounds computer crime, and the *lack* of reports is in some ways more worrying than the ones that do hit the headlines. In America firms are obliged to notify computer fraud and there is therefore a somewhat higher level of general awareness of the problem.

One final point is worth noting from the consumer's viewpoint: the IT industry is itself a prime example of poor consumer treatment. Computer manufacturers have constantly changed specifications and discontinued models without regard for their customers' investment in existing equipment and software; sales staff have been ill-informed both about their own products and those of competitors, and have frequently misled customers who have lacked the knowledge and confidence to challenge what they said. Telephone authorities have suppressed competition and been slow to liberalise their services and to modernise their equipment. The video industry is hampered by conflicting standards and incompatible hardware. The pace of change within information technology has given problems to the industry as well as to the general public.

The only real safeguard against many of the problems presented here is a better-informed and more vigilant general public. The short history of information technology demonstrates clearly how sorely needed is a well-informed consumer lobby.

Minority groups

So far this chapter has dwelt on the problems and dangers of the new technologies. However, it is important to take a balanced view of the overall impact of information technology on all sorts of people. IT can have immense practical advantages, and its ability to liberate people from disability and disadvantage should not be underestimated. IT can increase the dignity and independence of those with physical or mental handicaps, giving them greater self-reliance, fresh educational opportunities and, for some, the chance to communicate normally for the first time in their lives. IT has also made some handicapped people employable on equal terms for the first time. The technology has already been developed to overcome virtually every kind of handicap. If society has the economic and political will to make it so, IT could become a major force in reducing disadvantage.

Let's look at some examples in support of this bold claim. A British government-backed project called Visicom recently evaluated different ways for deaf people to communicate using the telephone. The Telecom Gold electronic mail service was found to be the most popular method, and 60% of the participants retained their mailboxes even after the end of the Department of Industry funding which they had been receiving ended. The *Chat* facility allows a continuing exchange of messages as long as both parties are on the line – the typewritten equivalent of a 'phone conversation. For many deaf people this was their first experience of any kind of conversation with anyone at a distance, and many clocked up hours of use.

We have already seen (page 137) how teletext gives viewers the option of adding subtitles to TV pictures as they are transmitted. This service has been widely appreciated by the deaf and hard-of-hearing as it allows them 'normal' television viewing, at least on a selection of programmes. Cable services could greatly increase this type of specialised provision by giving teletext a full channel instead of a few spare lines in the normal picture.

Interactive cable services could also provide the elderly and housebound with an easy method of signalling distress, as well as helping to overcome isolation through bulletin boards and electronic mail. Within a local community linked by interactive cable services it would be simple enough to build up a database to match potential sources of help with specific needs. For example, people who want occasional odd jobs done or who need baby-sitters could be put in touch with people nearby who want spare-time earnings – without anyone having to leave home to place advertisements in shop windows.

The blind and partially-sighted form another major group that can benefit from IT. MEL, the Japanese government-backed Mechanical Engineering Laboratory, has developed Meldog, a robot guide dog for the blind. It has wheels in place of legs, sensors instead of eyes, and a map-reading computer in place of a memory. The blind person feeds a map of the route to be taken into the control box and the computer navigates Meldog using landmarks from the map and ultrasonic waves picked up by the sensor. If produced in sufficient quantity this device could be cheaper than a fully trained animal guide dog, and would certainly be cheaper to run! Blind people who are dog-lovers may well prefer warm-blooded four-legged companions, but guide dogs have to be trained individually and are in short supply. In Japan, for example, there are 340 000 blind people but only 300 trained guide dogs. In any case, not all blind people are able and willing to care for a dog.

Apart from robot dogs, IT has been applied to the needs of the blind in a number of ways. Voice synthesis – in place of screen output – has become relatively cheap and allows a blind person to use a computer almost normally for word processing, programming and running any applications software that does not depend on graphics. More expensive devices using miniature cameras can turn normally printed or typewritten text into Braille symbols, variable tingles sensed by the fingers and other forms which the blind can, with practice, learn to 'read'. Programmed telephones with automatic redial can make everyday telephoning much easier for the blind, and the new generation of electronic switchboard apparatus makes the blind telephonist's job much easier.

IT systems can also provide new hope and independence for the physically handicapped. No matter how seriously disabled people are, as long as they still have some controlled movement in some part of their body and are able to detect its results, they can become computer users if they are able and willing to invest the time and effort. One wheelchair-bound Open University student whose limbs were completely paralysed learned to use a normal keyboard by means of a rod strapped to his head. Having mastered word processing, he was able for the first time to write his own letters and type his own assignments, including eventually his post-graduate thesis. He also taught himself to program and wrote simple software that allowed him to switch on and off the lights, radio, television and bells in his home, again using his head to press the keys. A personal micro-computer thus gave him greater independence than ever before, as well as the means of communicating in writing and thus access to the highest levels of intellectual achievement.

This example demonstrates how profoundly computers can change the life of the handicapped person. Computers can be of immense value to people of below-average intelligence as well, including those with severe mental handicaps. Special input devices such as touch-screens and *Concept* keyboards are of special importance in overcoming the initial barrier presented by the full keyboard. By giving a means of communication to people with severe speech and language handicaps, computers have also been known to produce great educational and social progress and demonstrate that the person's intellect had previously been underestimated. The same effect has been noted with deaf children, who are often treated as if they lack intelligence: the computer provides them with the means and the motivation to express themselves.

Many of these innovations are still in early stages of development, and costs are in some cases quite high. Mass production could transform the picture, as the astonishing tumble of microcomputer prices demonstrates. Indeed the personal micro is at the heart of most self-contained and flexible help systems for the handicapped. What is needed is a range of special input or output devices that can be adapted to suit individual needs at reasonable cost. The question of who pays for such devices is clearly a political one, and outside the scope of this book. However, it is worth weighing the social costs of keeping a person dependent and unemployable against the costs of helping them to become self-reliant and economically active.

Wider political questions surround the impact of IT on society. It appears that certain sections of society are, or see themselves as being, at a disadvantage in relation to IT products and services. For example, older people are widely assumed to be more resistant to IT, although there is ample evidence that adults retain the ability to master new bodies of knowledge and new practical skills well into old age. (The fact that mathematicians are unlikely to do their most original work after the age of 30 is about as relevant to most people's lives as the observation that women are less likely than men to win a Nobel prize for physics.) The general view that IT belongs to the young may have developed from the fact that older people are more likely to think of themselves as settled in their jobs or to have formed strong habits that account for their leisure time: they may simply lack the motivation to become involved in IT.

Similarly, although females are often

assumed to lack competence with computers, this may reflect a lack of confidence or opportunity, rather than a genuine sex difference. Indeed there is considerable evidence that in suitable circumstances women can out-perform men on a variety of IT-related skills from keyboarding to software design and systems analysis. The important obstacles to women's progress are the social pressures that may prevent them from giving IT a try. In addition, as I noted in Chapter 9, because of the speed of change within IT, it is an unusually difficult field in which to work part-time or to return to after a break of several years in full-time working. However, if the technology is adapted to home-working, distance is no longer such a problem. Once the initial obstacles are overcome, then, IT can be well-suited even to the circumstances of a housebound woman with young children.

And for the majority of women, who do not fit this stereotype, IT is too important in the modern world to be left to men.

The crucial question underlying all this is whether IT acts divisively by reinforcing inequality or whether it can be harnessed to combat disadvantage. This is a matter for conscious choice by educational and social services, by politicians, and ultimately by all of us as voters and citizens.

Patterns of everyday life

In recent years, many people have started to question traditional assumptions about the pattern of our lives. IT reinforces these doubts and raises further questions. For example, people who advocate lifelong education have pointed out that adolescence is not the only, or even necessarily the best, time in our lives for education. The pace of change in IT makes lifelong learning a necessity: anyone who wants to keep up with IT must accept the permanent status of student! IT also offers powerful means for pursuing both formal and informal education, for example using computing, telephone links and interactive video, without necessarily having to leave home. It can liberate would-be students from the inflexibility of application dates, the tyranny of timetables, the need to travel to lectures at fixed times and places, and a variety of other obstacles to adult learning.

In an age of mass long-term unemployment, we are also beginning to question our assumptions about the length of the working day, week, year and life. By the standards of the last century, the 40-hour week is part-time, and as workforces move gradually toward the 35-hour week or even less, expectations of paid annual leaves are constantly rising and the age of retiring is getting lower. The result is that employers are getting fewer and fewer productive hours of work from each employee on their payroll, and are having to carry an increasing burden of government-imposed employee costs, retirement pensions and the like. More and more people are trying self-employment and contract work, or are even setting up small enterprises in their spare time, in their early retirement, or instead of being unemployed.

Information technology has given birth to a large number of such enterprises, from the legendary growth of Apple Computers Inc. from its garage workshop origins to the rising generation of schoolboy games programmers. In addition to the possibilities of electronic cottage industries, there is a special value in IT training for those involved in a mid-career change of direction, whether it is voluntary or forced by redundancy. Most people with an eye on the future perceive that IT skills will stand them in good stead.

IT also has an impact on the quality of family life. In an early survey in California, researchers found that the arrival of a home computer caused television watching to fall sharply, and that less time was spent with other members of the family, on other hobbies and even in sleeping. The sharpest decline in TV watching was in families with children, perhaps because the only or main TV set was tied up with computer games. Time spent on homework and study also increased in 25% of the families. Interestingly, the most common actual use of the system was for word processing although that was normally low among the reasons given for buying the computer.

Some of these effects may be a by-product of relative novelty. After all, the car existed for quite a while before it made much impact on our patterns of living because of all the support services that had to be developed first. Without car dealers, a network of garages, motorways and motoring organisations, motoring would not have become a major means of commuting nor the focus of so much leisure activity. In the same way, we are only on the brink of finding out how IT affects the ordinary family's way of life.

Many predictions have been made about the house of the future and the *wired society* has become a catch-phrase. Figure 148 illustrates some of the possibilities for an information 'ring-main': the computer acts as a central controlling device and information processor; the television displays teletext and electronic mail, broadcast and interactive television programmes, closed-circuit security pictures of the outside of the house, and acts as a monitor for the computer; the telephone and cable TV wires link the household to the outside world. Whether people will prefer their doors to be controlled by voice recognition rather than keys remains to be seen.

Finally, IT may create entirely new forms of leisure, as surprising to us now as activities like personal computing and home video would have been to our great-grandparents. One of the most sinister examples is the sad figure of the computer junkie – a person who is obsessed by computers to the exclusion of all other interests, sometimes even to the extent that their health and work suffer because of lack of food and sleep. Although only a small minority of computer users is affected in this way, their behaviour is as compulsive as that of drug addicts. Some computer junkies are obsessed by programming. Others remain 'hooked' on the passive pastime of playing commercial arcade games, an alarming number of which are based on violence and warfare and promote values which most people find disturbing.

Interactive video provides further examples of new leisure activities. The coin-in-slot video juke-box (Figure 129) provides the appropriate video images for the record selected. Another pastime already popular in Japan uses interactive video for *karaoke* – a form of pop video without the lead singer. Customers in clubs queue up to take the microphone and sing along with the backing, prompted by the lyrics which are overlaid on the video picture – a bit like a teleprompter.

Another interesting application is the *Tour of the Universe*, which opened in Toronto in 1984 (Figure 147). This provides a 75-minute session in which visitors experience a simulated space flight not only visually but also through the 'seat of the pants': advanced flight simulation techniques ensure that the motion is realistic! Visitors participate in pre-flight procedures before entering the space capsule and the whole itinerary and storyline is

designed to be authentic at every stage. The backers predict that by 1989 there will be 23 different tours in operation in major cities world-wide, and that the operation might earn revenues of US $60 million per year. Whether or not this particular idea catches on, there can be no doubt that information technology will create many novel forms of entertainment.

Inside information technology

Information is funny stuff. You can't touch, see, taste or feel it, yet it makes the world go round. Processing, packaging and selling it occupies over half the workforce in most developed countries. Mastery of information technology confers power. IT is potentially an immense force for good or evil. Its influence on the world in the 21st century will be decided by those of us who have acquired inside information and who understand how computers and communications affect us all.

Figure 147 Will electronic media create new forms of leisure? This artist's impression of the *Tour of the Universe* suggests the flight-deck on a simulated space flight. But no illustration can convey the realistic motion participants will experience in the specially built vehicle.

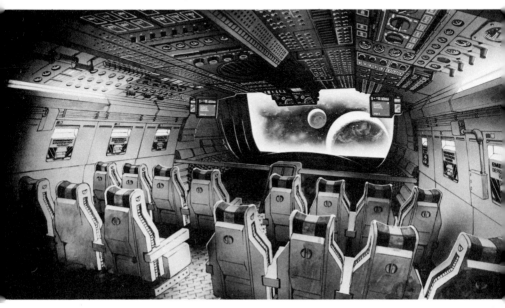

Part

Major landmarks in information technology

Note

It is sometimes debatable who should take credit for a particular invention, with competing claims depending on precise wording and technical interpretation. The dates below are simply intended for general guidance on the sequence and timing of major landmarks.

1833 Charles Babbage outlined design for Analytical Engine, a general-purpose computing device (never built).

1842 Publication of Menabrea's paper describing Babbage's invention, subsequently translated from the Italian by Lady Ada Lovelace. She also corrected Babbage's first program and explained how his Engine could be programmed for non-mathematical purposes.

1843 First telegraph message sent from Washington to Baltimore by Samuel Morse.

1858 First transatlantic telegraph cable laid.

1874 Emile Baudot's wheel allowed multiplexing of telegraph messages.

1876 Telephone demonstrated and patented by Alexander Graham Bell.

1878 Telephone mouthpiece patented by Henry Hunnings.

1884 First telephone handset to combine mouthpiece and earpiece produced by L M Ericcson in Stockholm.

1888 Almon B Strowger built first automatic telephone exchange (patented in 1891).

1891 First telephone cable laid between England and France.

1894 Oliver Lodge demonstrated first wireless (radio) transmission.

1901 Guglielmo Marconi transmitted first transatlantic radio signals.

1904 J A Fleming invented thermionic valve, marking the beginning of the age of electronics.

1907 Teletypewriter using 5-bit code and start-stop signals introduced – forerunner of modern teleprinter.

1913 First long-distance telephone cable in Europe laid in England (between Leeds and Hull).

1927 Regular transatlantic telephone service began, using radio waves.

1935 Speaking clock service began in Britain.

1936 Pulse code modulation (PCM) invented by Alec Reeves at Standard Telephones and Cables (STC). BBC gave first television broadcast.

1943 Colossus I, world's first electronic programmable computer, built in Britain for wartime code-breaking.

1946 ENIAC, first general-purpose computer, built in USA.

1948 Transistor invented at Bell Telephone Laboratories in USA.

1951 Ferranti Mark I, first commercial computer, sold in UK. Also Lyons Electronic Office (LEO), first office computer, built by J. Lyons.

Figure 148 Information technology and the house of the future? Cables from the outside world bring electric power, telephone and television. The household computer controls heating, lighting and security, and also provides information services through its links to computers elsewhere in the world.

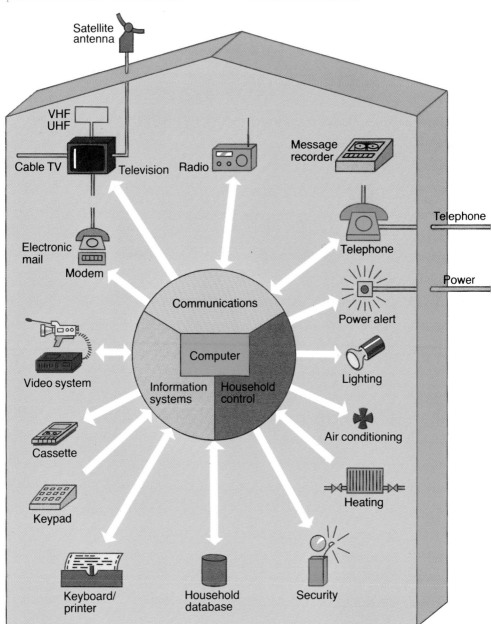

Figure 149 Electromagnetic waves carry energy and information. All travel at the speed of light (300 000 km/s); the shorter the wavelength, the higher the frequency. Wavelengths range from less than a millionth of a metre to many kilometres. The shorter wavelength (higher frequency) waves tend to have most importance in information technology because they have more bandwidth available for transmitting messages. The microwave band normally used is 2000 times broader than the medium wave radio band but still offers only a tiny fraction of the space available using fibre optics.

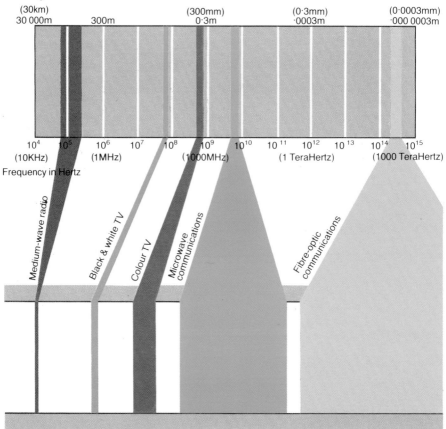

Wavelengths in metres

| (30km) | | (300mm) | (0·3mm) | (0·0003mm) |
| 30 000m | 300m | 0·3m | ·0003m | ·000 0003m |

10^4 (10KHz) 10^5 10^6 (1MHz) 10^7 10^8 10^9 (1000MHz) 10^{10} 10^{11} 10^{12} (1 TeraHertz) 10^{13} 10^{14} 10^{15} (1000 TeraHertz)

Frequency in Hertz

Medium-wave radio

Black & white TV

Colour TV

Microwave communications

Fibre-optic communications

The figures below the symbols show how much space, in terms of the bandwidth of one telephone channel, other channels of communication need.

Telex

1/20th

Telephone

1

Stereo hi-fi broadcast

14

B&W TV

1000

Colour TV

2000

High-definition TV

10 000?

1953 RCA introduced colour television in US. National Television Standards Committee defined NTSC colour standard.

1954 First transistor radios.

1955 Transistorised television cameras.

1956 First transatlantic telephone cable laid between Scotland and Newfoundland (2240 miles). Early videotape recorders.

1957 Sputnik I launched by USSR: beginning of age of satellites and space flight.

1958 First automatic telex exchanges. Subscriber Trunk Dialling (STD) service began in Britain. First integrated circuit produced at Fairchild Camera and Instrument company.

1960 Light emitting diodes (LEDs).

1962 Early electronic calculators.

1962 Telstar launched from Cape Canaveral: first broadband active communications satellite. Also first international direct dialling between London and Paris.

1964 First word processors. International Telecommunications Satellite Organisation formed.

1965 Launch of INTELSAT I (Early Bird): first commercial communications satellite in geostationary orbit.

1966 Idea of using ultra-thin strands of glass for transmitting digital information proposed by Charles Kao and George Hockham at STC.

1967 Electronic cash dispensers.

1968 Early industrial robots. Europe's first PCM digital exchange installed in London.

1970 Electronic pocket calculators. International direct dialling between London and New York.

1971 Early domestic video recorders. Confravision, world's first public two-way conference television system, linked 5 studios in Britain. Intel produced first computer microprocessor on single chip of silicon.

1972 Early video games.

1973 Teletext service (Oracle) launched in Britain.

mid-1970s First microcomputers.

1976 Optical character recognition (OCR).

1977 World's first optical fibre link installed between Hitchin and Stevenage in England.

1977 Early videodisc players in Japan and USA.

1978 First optical cable in Europe to form part of public telephone system laid between Martlesham and Ipswich in England.

1979 World's first viewdata service (Prestel) launched in London.

1980 World's first digital exchange opens in London. First unmanned factory opened by Fujitsu. First deep-water optical cable laid in Loch Fyne, Scotland.

early 1980s First pocket and lap-held computers.

1981 Telesoftware trials in Britain.

1982 British Telecom achieved transmission of data at 140 million bps over 102 km of continuous optical fibre without using regenerators.

1983 British Telecom satellite earth station enabled ship-to-shore direct dialling for telephone calls and telex world-wide.

1986 INTELSAT VI due to be launched.

1988 First transatlantic optical fibre cable (TAT 8) due to become operational.

The five 'generations' of computing

The terms 'fourth generation' and 'fifth generation' tend to be used very loosely, and there are no clearly agreed dividing lines between any of the 'generations'. Nevertheless, in a field where the hardware has changed so fast it may be useful to try to identify some features characteristic of typical mainframe computers at each stage. It must be remembered, however, that all figures are just a rough indication and that within each generation there was and is a tremendous variety of computer systems.

	FIRST 1940s-1950s	SECOND 1950s-1960s	THIRD 1960s-1970s	FOURTH 1970s-1980s	FIFTH 1980s-1990s
HARDWARE BASED ON	VALVES	TRANSISTORS	INTEGRATED CIRCUITS	LSI and VLSI	ULSI
TYPICAL MEMORY SIZE	1K	16–64K	128K–1Mb	1–10Mb	10–100Mb
TYPICAL PROCESSING SPEEDS	10 kips	50–500 kips	1–5 mips	5–50 mips	1–1000 gips
ENTRY COST AT 1980 PRICES	£10 000 000	£5 000 000	£1 000 000	£100 000	About £10 000 or less?
OPERATING SYSTEM	NONE	BATCH PROCESSING ONLY	TIME SHARING	FLEXIBLE	?
PROGRAMMING LANGUAGES	MACHINE LANGUAGE	AUTOCODE	FORTRAN, COBOL, SOFTWARE PACKAGES	INTEGRATED SOFTWARE, PROLOG, ADA, EXPERT SYSTEMS	NATURAL LANGUAGE PROCESSING, COMPUTER VISION, VOICE RECOG-NITION
COMMUNICATIONS	TELEPRINTER, TELEPHONE LINES	VDU's PCM	PACKET SWITCHING, NETWORKS (LAN, VAN, WAN)	ISDN, FIBRE OPTICS, CELLULAR RADIO	?
TYPICAL USER	RESEARCHER	TECHNICAL SPECIALIST	APPLICATIONS SPECIALIST	COMPUTER LITERATE USER	ORDINARY PERSON

Counting in twos and sixteens

Binary numbers

Everyday numbers are based on tens – the denary system. Each column of a long number represents a power of ten: units, tens, hundreds, thousands, tens of thousands and so on. Computer processors handle numbers in a different way, using the binary system. Binary numbers are expressed as powers of two: units, twos, fours, eights, sixteens and so on. To convert binary numbers into their decimal equivalent, refer to the table opposite or the diagram below.

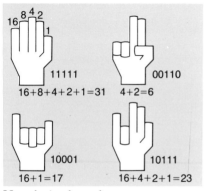

11111
16+8+4+2+1=31

00110
4+2=6

10001
16+1=17

10111
16+4+2+1=23

Hexadecimal numbers

Binary numbers quickly become very unwieldy: they are difficult for humans to read and take up a lot of space. Another counting system called hexadecimal (hex for short) is sometimes useful: it's compact enough for humans and also very easy for computers to translate into binary automatically. It uses powers of sixteen: units, sixteens, 256s, 4096s and so on. Because we run out of single-figure numbers at nine, hex uses the letters A to F to represent the numbers 10 to 15. This may sound confusing, but if you study the table opposite you should see a pattern emerging.

The figures in this table show ordinary (base-10) numbers next to their binary equivalents (base-two) and also their hexadecimal equivalent (base-16).

Base –10	Binary	Hex
0	0	0
1	1	1
2	10	2
3	11	3
4	100	4
5	101	5
6	110	6
7	111	7
8	1000	8
9	1001	9
10	1010	A
11	1011	B
12	1100	C
13	1101	D
14	1110	E
15	1111	F
16	10000	10
17	10001	11
18	10010	12
30	11110	1E
31	11111	1F
32	100000	20
33	100001	21
34	100010	22
62	111110	3E
63	111111	3F
64	1000000	40
65	1000001	41
128	10000000	80
256	100000000	100

Common prefixes for units

Units such as metres, Hertz and seconds are often too large or too small to be expressed in convenient figures, so they are commonly divided up or multiplied by adding prefixes. For example, a kilometre is a thousand metres, a MegaHertz is a million Hertz and a nanosecond is a thousand millionth of a second. Here is a list of some of the most useful prefixes:

Multiples

thousand	10^3	kilo-*
million	10^6	Mega-*
thousand million**	10^9	Giga-*
million million**	10^{12}	Tera-

Sub-multiples

one thousandth	10^{-3}	milli-
one millionth	10^{-6}	micro-
one thousand millionth	10^{-9}	nano-
one million millionth	10^{-12}	pico-

* In base-10, kilo- means exactly 1000 times. In base-two, it actually means 1024, which is a more convenient unit since it happens to be 2^{10} or, in binary, 100 0000 0000. Thus a kilobyte is 1024 bytes. Similarly, Mega- does not mean exactly one million; it is 1024 times 1024 or 1 048 576. So a Megabyte is 1 048 576 bytes (which happens to be 2^{20}), and a Gigabyte is 1 073 741 824 bytes (or 2^{30}).

** The term billion tends to mean a thousand million in North America and a million million in Europe, and is therefore best avoided.

ASCII code table (opposite)

The American Standard Code for Information Interchange is a 7-bit code for keyboard characters that has also been widely adopted by European and Japanese computer manufacturers. (IBM use a different 8-bit code called EBCDIC.) Most commercial VDUs and printers use the ASCII code, which is also important in telecommunications. Of the eight bits, seven are needed to represent the various characters and the extra bit can be used for parity checking.

In the table opposite the spare bit has been omitted. Also, the first 31 codes have been left out since they do not represent characters but are used for various functions, eg line feeds, printer control codes, signalling the end of a transmission etc.

The figures in the column between the binary numbers and their decimal equivalents are given in hexadecimal (base-16). The relationship between these three counting systems is explained on page 195.

Conversion table for tape widths and disc diameters

Tape thickness

Inches	Centimetres	Examples
0.125	0.318	Audio & micro-cassette
0.25	0.635	Reel-to-reel audiotape
0.5	1.27	Domestic video-cassette
0.75	1.905	Industrial video-cassette
1.0	2.54	Broadcast-standard
2.0	5.08	videotape

Disc diameter

3.5	8.89	Microfloppy disc
4.72	12.0	Compact (audio) disc
5.25	13.3	(Mini) floppy disc
8	20.3	Floppy disc, mini-videodisc
10	25.4	VHD videodisc
12	30.5	Laservision videodisc
14	35.6	Fixed disc/disc-pack

Character	ASCII code binary	hex	decimal
[SPACE]	0100000	20	32
!	0100001	21	33
"	0100010	22	34
#	0100011	23	35
$	0100100	24	36
%	0100101	25	37
&	0100110	26	38
'	0100111	27	39
(	0101000	28	40
)	0101001	29	41
*	0101010	2A	42
+	0101011	2B	43
,	0101100	2C	44
–	0101101	2D	45
.	0101110	2E	46
/	0101111	2F	47
0	0110000	30	48
1	0110001	31	49
2	0110010	32	50
3	0110011	33	51
4	0110100	34	52
5	0110101	35	53
6	0110110	36	54
7	0110111	37	55
8	0111000	38	56
9	0111001	39	57
:	0111010	3A	58
;	0111011	3B	59
<	0111100	3C	60
=	0111101	3D	61
>	0111110	3E	62
?	0111111	3F	63
@	1000000	40	64
A	1000001	41	65
B	1000010	42	66
C	1000011	43	67
D	1000100	44	68
E	1000101	45	69
F	1000110	46	70
G	1000111	47	71
H	1001000	48	72
I	1001001	49	73
J	1001010	4A	74
K	1001011	4B	75
L	1001100	4C	76
M	1001101	4D	77
N	1001110	4E	78
O	1001111	4F	79
P	1010000	50	80
Q	1010001	51	81
R	1010010	52	82
S	1010011	53	83
T	1010100	54	84
U	1010101	55	85
V	1010110	56	86
W	1010111	57	87
X	1011000	58	88
Y	1011001	59	89
Z	1011010	5A	90
[	1011011	5B	91
\	1011100	5C	92
]	1011101	5D	93
^	1011110	5E	94
–	1011111	5F	95
£	1100000	60	96
a	1100001	61	97
b	1100010	62	98
c	1100011	63	99
d	1100100	64	100
e	1100101	65	101
f	1100110	66	102
g	1100111	67	103
h	1101000	68	104
i	1101001	69	105
j	1101010	6A	106
k	1101011	6B	107
l	1101100	6C	108
m	1101101	6D	109
n	1101110	6E	110
o	1101111	6F	111
p	1110000	70	112
q	1110001	71	113
r	1110010	72	114
s	1110011	73	115
t	1110100	74	116
u	1110101	75	117
v	1110110	76	118
w	1110111	77	119
x	1111000	78	120
y	1111001	79	121
z	1111010	7A	122
{	1111011	7B	123
|	1111100	7C	124
}	1111101	7D	125
~	1111110	7E	126
DEL	1111111	7F	127

Glossary

This Glossary includes all the technical terms introduced in the text, whether they were italicised or not.

8-bit processors deal with information in 8-bit 'chunks', ie one byte at a time.

16-bit processors deal with information in 16-bit 'chunks', ie they process two bytes at a time. In theory, 16-bit processors can work faster and address more internal memory (typically 256 K instead of 64 K of RAM). In practice, it greatly depends on the supporting software.

40-track Data is stored on a disc in concentric circular tracks. Normally a 40-track disc can only be read by a 40-track disc drive.

80-track discs can generally hold around twice as much as discs with 40 tracks (see above). 80-track disc drives cannot normally read 40-track discs, though special software can make this possible.

A

abbreviated dialling The facility to code long telephone numbers so that they can subsequently be dialled just by pressing one or two keys.

access The retrieval of information from wherever it is stored, eg on floppy disc or videodisc. See also serial access and random access. Also used as a verb (meaning 'get access to'). Access to a computer system may be open to anyone who knows how to work it, or may be controlled by formalities like passwords, logging-on procedures, and so on.

acoustic coupler A sort of cradle for a telephone hand-set which can also be linked to a computer through a cable. The coupler turns computer information into sound signals and vice versa. This method is not as fast as using a modem, and is sometimes unreliable, but couplers are cheaper and more flexible.

ADA Real-time programming language developed by US Defence Department and recognised by ANSI. Named after the first computer programmer, Ada Augusta, Countess of Lovelace (Byron's daughter).

address Code that identifies a particular location in a computer memory or videodisc. Also used as a verb: the processor 'addresses' a particular disc drive when it reads from or writes to it directly.

ALGOL Early high-level programming language designed mainly for scientific applications; suitable for structured programming. ALGOL is short for algorithmic language.

alphanumeric Literally, alphabetic or numeric; an alphanumeric character can be any letter, number or symbol on a typewriter or computer keyboard.

AM See amplitude modulation

amplitude Technical word for size. The amplitude of a wave is the height of a crest.

amplitude modulation Method of encoding information on a carrier wave by varying its amplitude.

analogue This refers to real-world quantities, eg temperature, time, pressure, weight, which have not been translated into digital (numerical) form. Digital computers can only handle these quantities by assigning numbers to them. This usually means translating them into binary 1s and 0s.

analogue-to-digital converter A device that converts analogue information (eg time or temperature) into digital form (eg an on/off control signal). Converters allow digital devices to interact with real-world analogue quantities.

animation The arrangement of a sequence of separate pictures, eg computer graphics, made to follow each other so quickly that they appear to the viewer as continuous movement.

ANSI American National Standards Institute, an influential body that publishes standard versions of selected programming languages from time to time, setting the seal on their respectability.

answerback Code sent by telex machine to show that a message has been received.

APL Compact high-level programming language used mainly for engineering, business and scientific applications. APL just stands for A Programming Language.

applications software Any program that applies the computer to a real-world problem, eg accounts. This includes all software except systems software.

architecture The way in which a circuit, computer system or cable network is laid out.

array A list of numbers or words laid out in an orderly way.

artificial intelligence Some computer programs appear to be 'intelligent', eg they can add to their 'knowledge' on successive runs or can interpret information they receive using 'knowledge' already stored. Examples of artificial intelligence include programs which diagnose diseases or electrical faults. See also expert system.

ASCII American Standard Code for Information Exchange: an internationally accepted system for coding keyboard characters for computers. For example, the letter A is always coded as 65 (base 10) and B as 66. (In binary form these ASCII codes may be written 100 0001 and 100 0010 respectively.)

aspect ratio Ratio of width-to-height of a single frame or screen. For example, video pictures are 4 units wide to 3 units high, whereas film and 35 mm transparencies are 3 units wide to 2 units high. Most VDUs have the same aspect ratio as televisions, though standard A4 and A5 paper has a ratio of 7.1 units wide to 10 units high.

assembler Program that translates assembly-language program into machine language.

assembly language A low-level programming language that uses shorthand versions of English words to give instructions to the processor. These are automatically translated into machine language by the assembler. Assembly language is harder for humans to work with than high-level programming languages.

A-to-D Short for analogue-to-digital.

attenuation Loss of quality and strength in a signal transmitted over a distance. A shout sounding faint at a distance is an example of attenuation.

authoring language A very high-level programming language designed to speed up and simplify the job of writing applications software for computer-based systems. Authoring (or author) languages may also have special editing facilities and software tools to enable people who are not professional programmers to write their own software, eg for training: they are then sometimes called authoring systems. Modern authoring systems are often used for the control of presentation systems that include videotape or videodisc.

B

backing store External memory which supports and communicates with computer's internal memory. Back-up equipment duplicates crucial items in case of break-down. Back-up discs are kept in case of damage to the originals. To back-up a disc is to copy it in its entirety.

bandwidth Measure of the information-carrying capacity of a communication channel. The higher the frequencies used, the more bandwidth is available. See broadband and narrowband.

bar code Pattern of printed lines often seen on books and groceries. Can be used for direct input of data to a computer.

BASIC Beginners' All-purpose Symbolic Instruction Code. A very popular programming language for beginners, almost universally available on microcomputers. Exists in many incompatible dialects.

BASICODE A set of ground rules for programmers which, together with special loading programs for specific microcomputers, overcomes differences between dialects of BASIC. BASICODE users in different countries with different machines can exchange software, and can record computer programs from the same radio sound broadcast.

batch infill Process of filling in standard details on a batch of documents in word processing.

batch processing Computer processing in which jobs with common features are collected up and run in one batch. The opposite of interactive processing.

baud A measure of the rate of transmitting information within or between computers, eg telex operates at 50 baud; programs are often loaded from cassettes at 300 baud; teletex operates at 1200 or 2400 baud. For most practical purposes, 1 baud can be taken to be 1 bit per second.

BIOS Short for basic input/output section, the part of the operating system CP/M that deals with input and output and is specific to the processor.

bit A bit is a binary digit, 1 or 0.

binary system A method of counting which uses only two digits (1 and 0) instead of the usual ten (0 to 9). All digital computers work in binary deep down.

bootstrap (boot) Programs can be made to load other programs automatically so that the system 'pulls itself up by its bootstraps'. This is known as booting.

bps Short for bit per second.

broadband (wideband) General term for a communications channel with plenty of bandwidth. Usually taken to mean at least enough to transmit television signals at normal speed. Contrast narrowband.

broadcast Process of distributing signals to a wide audience, often by radio or television, usually financed by some blanket method of payment or advertising. Contrast narrowcast.

BT British Telecom, the United Kingdom's PTT.

BTG British Telecom Gold, the electronic mail service offered by BT, based on the American Dialcom system.

bubble memory A compact and robust form of non-volatile mass memory which depends on storing information in magnetic 'bubbles' (domains) in a thin film of material such as garnet.

buffer Temporary memory, eg for storing a document until the printer has completed the print-out, thus releasing the processor for other tasks. More generally, any electronic protective device.

bug A mistake, usually in a program. To debug is to remove mistakes.

bulletin board A communal electronic noticeboard that allows people to dial in and exchange news, views, sales and wants. Some are operated commercially, others by hobbyists 'after-hours'. They can be a cross between a magazine, noticeboard and exchange and mart.

bus A common path linking different parts of a computer system to allow them to exchange data. Everything is connected to the bus all the time, but each device only takes data from the bus, or puts data onto it, when necessary.

byte Group of 8 bits that can represent any keyboard character. An 8-bit processor handles information 'by 8s', ie in bytes.

C

cable TV Television distributed through wires rather than broadcast using radio waves. In areas with poor reception, a cable operator may erect a high-performance aerial to receive a broadcast signal and then distribute it by cable to local viewers. In other circumstances, cable TV may offer a whole new approach to financing and distributing TV.

call-connect Modern digital type of Private Branch Exchange offering a flexible range of facilities.

capacitance Ability to store electrical charge. In some videodisc systems, the varying capacitance between pick-up and disc is used to code and decode audio and video information.

CAPTAIN Name of viewdata system developed in Japan, with better resolution than, for example, Prestel.

carrier wave A wave which carries information by having variations of some kind (for example, in amplitude or frequency) imposed on it.

cartridge Software for some microcomputers is sold as a sealed plug-in cartridge. Popular for arcade games and personal computers without disc drives.

cassette An ordinary audio cassette can serve as external memory for most microcomputers, though short high-quality tapes (called data cassettes) are preferable.

catalogue Place on a disc that lists its contents. Also called directory.

CCITT International Consultative Committee for Telephones and Telegraphy. A body which issues standards for telecommunications and data transmission.

CCTV Closed circuit television: video cameras relay pictures either to a central point where they are monitored by people or to a videorecorder where they are stored for various periods according to the application. CCTV is mainly used for security purposes and for training.

Ceefax Teletext service provided by the BBC in Britain.

cell A particular item in an array. Each 'square' in a spreadsheet is known as a cell. Cells that make up a computer picture are called pixels.

Central Processing Unit (CPU) See processor.

Centronics interface A standard parallel interface widely used by microcomputer manufacturers for connecting printers to processors.

channel A path for communication. A channel is whatever connects an information source to an information receiver: a single channel may consist of several circuits and several bits of equipment.

character A number, letter or symbol on the keyboard, screen or printer. The collection of all symbols that can be displayed or printed is called the character set.

chat mode Electronic mail systems are designed to allow the sender to transmit a message to someone who may not be available at that time. However, if both parties *are* on-line at the same time they may communicate in chat mode, each

seeing each other's words on the VDU screen and typing in the reply immediately, like a typed-out telephone conversation.

check digit A digit conveying no information except to confirm whether the other digits it accompanies are likely to be valid.

chip A tiny sliver of silicon that can contain complicated electronic circuits.

chrominance Information about the colour signal in each part of a TV picture.

circuit-switching Linking two devices directly using exchanges or switching centres, as in the public telephone network. Throughout the duration of a telephone call, the two parties occupy the switched circuit exclusively, even if neither is speaking. Contrast packet-switching.

clock The basic rhythm of a processor is controlled by a clock that keeps its activities in step. Its frequency is measured in millions of cycles per second (MegaHertz or MHz). 8-bit microcomputers usually have a clock frequency in the range 1 to 8 MHz.

Closed User Group (CUG) A group of subscribers to a system like Prestel that has access to the public pages but can also exchange private messages.

coaxial cable (co-ax) Wire with an envelope of braided metal screening to prevent interference with the signal it carries. The wire connecting a television aerial to the receiving set is normally coaxial cable.

COBOL Short for Common Business Oriented Language. A high-level programming language used widely in business computing.

code (1) The process of writing out a computer program is called coding; chunks of program are called bits of code. Thus code generators are simply software generators (see software entry). **(2)** Codes are a way of compressing information so that it takes up less space in the computer.

COM See Computer Output to Microform.

COMAL High level programming language that is easy for beginners to learn (like BASIC) and also encourages structured programming (like Pascal).

command mode A style of software in which the user controls the program by typing in commands (instructions), as opposed to choosing options from a menu. Contrast menu-driven.

common carrier Provider of basic telecommunications facilities who takes no particular responsibility for the uses to which it is put.

communications software Programs that enable a computer user to exchange messages and data files over a distance, often using a telephone link.

compatibility Capable of working in combination. Refers to the ability (or otherwise) of computers and other equipment to be linked together or to run software designed for other makes of machine.

compiler A piece of software inside the computer that translates a program written in a high-level language like COBOL into machine language. Compilers do this as a once-and-for-all job, unlike interpreters.

Computer Output to Microform A process whereby microfiches can be produced directly instead of having to be photographed from printer output.

Concept keyboard Input device that is especially valuable for users who find a QWERTY keyboard an obstacle. Instead of having to spell out words letter-by-letter, the user presses the part of the 'keyboard' that bears a picture representing a particular concept. It accepts a variety of overlays so that it can be adapted to different software.

concurrent Literally, occurring at the same time. Concurrent programming is a technique for making a number of programs seem to run in parallel. Concurrent CP/M is a version of the CP/M operating system designed for this purpose.

conference call A telephone call in which more than two people can participate.

configuration The particular combination of equipment that makes up a system.

consumables Floppy discs, paper and ribbons – generally anything that you need a regular supply of.

control codes These are used to make printers produce a variety of effects like margins, boldface and underlining.

convergence The catch-word for technologies that were previously separate coming together and making use of the same basic principles (eg digital coding of information) and sometimes the same equipment (eg receiver/monitors, compact disc/videodisc).

corruption Unwanted changes to data or programs within a computer system or during transmission over a distance. Data may be corrupted as a result of software mistakes, interference or attenuation.

CP/M The nearest thing to a standard operating system for 8-bit microcomputers. It's always known by its initials (or sometimes as CP/M-80 to emphasise the processors for which it is designed); you can think of it as Control Program and Monitor or Control Program for Microprocessors. The 16-bit version is called CP/M-86 (which has not achieved the same monopoly) and the multi-user version MP/M.

crash When a program stops and cannot be restarted, it is said to crash. If good software design prevents this, it may be described as crash-proof.

cursor Something on the screen to show you where you are. Cursors may be square blobs or underlines; they usually flash.

cut In video editing, to jump straight from one scene or camera angle to another without anything in between.

cycle time Delay in teletext between when the user calls up a page and when it appears on screen, caused by the time taken for the teletext magazine to cycle through the pages before it.

D

daisy-wheel printer A printer that uses characters held on interchangeable wheels (like typewriter golf-balls). Usually slower, higher-quality and more expensive than a dot-matrix printer.

data Generally, information in the form of letters or numbers. Sometimes restricted to mean information after it has been prepared for computer processing or transmission.

databank A collection – usually a large one – of data held in a computer. The term is sometimes interchangeable with database (see below).

database A collection of data files organised systematically so as to make processing easy. Database management systems (DBMS) are computer programs for designing and managing a database.

data haven A country where there are no restrictions on the processing, exchange and sale of data. Countries with data protection laws may restrict the export of data since their laws could be evaded so easily in data havens.

data processing Loosely, the handling of information by computer. In practice, usually refers to batch processing of large volumes of prepared data, eg telephone bills, payroll.

data protection Procedures and laws designed to ensure the privacy and security of personal data.

data skew When data is sent over a long distance, bits that set off together do not always arrive exactly together. This lack of alignment is called skew.

data subjects Anyone on whom information is stored.

data user Anyone who stores or processes information.

DBS Direct broadcast satellite, ie one that transmits a signal direct to a local or domestic antenna.

debug To remove mistakes.

dedicated Specially designed for, or limited to, a particular purpose.

default The value or behaviour that a computer system assumes unless it is otherwise instructed.

demodulator Device that reconstructs the original signal from a modulated version, for example digital computer data from the analogue version sent down the telephone.

Dialcom An electronic mail service developed in the USA by the International Telephone and Telegraph (ITT).

dialect A variant of a programming language. For example, BASIC exists in hundreds of different dialects, most of them incompatible to various degrees.

dialogue An exchange of questions and answers between a computer program and a user.

digital Anything that can be counted in numbers; the opposite of analogue.

digital-to-analogue converter A device that converts digital information into analogue form. D-to-A converters allow the output of digital computers to control analogue devices like televisions and traditional telephones.

direct-connect modem Same as modem. 'Direct-connect' simply emphasises the fact that it connects directly to the telephone network, unlike an acoustic coupler.

directory Place on a disc that lists its contents. Also called catalogue.

disable To prevent from operating; sometimes it is useful to disable a key (eg the BREAK key which may wipe out a program) or a device (eg a printer, if printout is unnecessary). Opposite of enable.

disc A flat circular sheet of magnetic material used to store information. Sometimes called floppy disc or spelled disk.

disc drive A device that retrieves (reads) information from and records (writes) on to a disc. Disc drives only work with discs of a suitable size, density and number of tracks.

disc operating system (DOS) A program inside the computer that controls the storage and retrieval of programs and data on discs.

disc-pack A stack of magnetic discs.

documentation Printed instructions and manuals that are vital if a user is to get the best out of any software. An important – but often-neglected – part of a software package.

dot-matrix printer A printer that forms characters from a matrix (grid) of dots; the more dots, the better the shape of the character. Generally cheaper and faster than daisy-wheel printers, but only the best can produce remotely comparable quality.

download Transfer of programs or data from one computer to another, typically from a mainframe to a micro.

DP Short for data processing. Large firms often have separate DP departments with DP Managers at their head.

D-to-A Short for digital-to-analogue.

dual sound Two independent sound tracks, so that the same video material can be viewed with a choice of sound track, eg in different languages or aimed at different levels of audience, or the second sound track can be used to provide stereo.

duplex A communications channel is duplex (or full-duplex) when both parties can send and receive information at the same time. Contrast half-duplex and simplex.

E

EBCDIC Short for Extended Binary Coded Decimal Interchange Code. An 8-bit code for exchanging data used mainly on IBM equipment. Rival to ASCII.

edit To improve, cut or rearrange text, programs or videotape.

electromagnetic waves Vibrations of electrical and magnetic energy that travel together through space.

electromagnetic spectrum The full range of electromagnetic waves, usually divided up according to their frequency and wavelength (see page 192).

electronic mail Immediate transmission of messages or data across a distance. May use telephone lines, broadcast waves or satellites.

enable To make a key or device operate; opposite of disable.

enter To put instructions or data into the computer. The ENTER or RETURN key sometimes has to be pressed afterwards.

EPROM Stands for Erasable Programmable Read Only Memory: a ROM chip which can be loaded with a program that can subsequently be erased. This is usually done by passing ultra-violet light through a circular window over the circuit. EPROMs are a useful way of distributing firmware that is still being developed and refined.

ergonomics The study of the relationship between the design of equipment and the comfort and efficiency of those who use it.

execute The stage when the processor actually obeys the instructions in a program is called execution.

expert system Software that builds up expertise in making judgements and displays artificial intelligence. Some expert systems can converse with humans in a relatively natural way, and some can explain and justify their line of 'reasoning'. So far, the most successful ones tend to operate in a restricted field of knowledge; they are sometimes called (Intelligent) Knowledge Based Expert Systems (IKBES or KBES).

external memory The storage of information outside the computer, usually in magnetic form, eg on tape or disc.

F

fade In video production, the transition from one scene to another may be made smoother by fading the first scene down to blackness before bringing up the second.

fan-fold Paper folded in a long zig-zag consisting of thousands of sheets joined end-to-end by perforations.

Faraday Cage Total metal enclosure to screen a computer installation from interference or electronic eavesdropping.

fax Facsimile transmission: the entire contents of a sheet of paper (including letterhead, signature etc) are scanned, coded and sent through a telecommunications link to a remote terminal where it is printed out. The receiving and sending fax terminals must be compatible.

FDM See frequency division multiplexing.

feeder Device for feeding paper to a printer automatically (see hopper).

fibre optics The use of ultra-thin flexible strands of very pure glass to communicate information at high speed.

field (1) One complete scan of a television screen, covering every alternate line. Two interlaced fields together make a single frame of video. **(2)** A single item of information in a data base, eg a name or address. Each field may need a large number of bytes to store its information.

file A collection of instructions, text or data. A text file might be a short letter or a book chapter; a data file could consist of a handful of items or a hundred thousand.

filename The name by which a file is known to the computer system; this may be an abbreviation of the name by which the user normally knows it.

firmware Intermediate between software and hardware, firmware instructions are fitted to the computer semi-permanently, usually in the form of ROM chips.

flicker A shimmering instability in the image on a computer screen; can be tiring or even unhealthy in prolonged use.

floppy disc or **floppy** See disc.

floppy tape Form of external memory that is a halfway-house between disc and cassette tape in speed and cost.

flowchart Method of showing logic of a computer program or sequence of operations in a data processing system using boxes and arrows.

FM See frequency modulation.

footprint (1) The area of the earth's surface to which a satellite can transmit.

(2) The area on a desk-top that a computer system occupies.

format (1) The format of a piece of text means its headings, spacing and margins. The format of data means its arrangement in a file, on a disc or on a screen. The format of a videotape or videodisc includes its physical size and colour standard.
(2) As a verb, to format a floppy disc means to prepare it to receive information in a way appropriate to the disc drive and computer in use; this process deletes any information on the disc already.

FORTRAN Short for formula translations. A traditional programming language used mainly for scientific applications.

frame grabber Device that captures a frame taken by a television camera and turns it into digital form so that it can be displayed and manipulated by a computer.

freeze frame A single frame from a moving sequence held motionless on the screen. A frame frozen this way was not designed to be viewed in isolation. Contrast still frame.

frequency The number of complete cycles performed in each second. See also Hertz.

Frequency division multiplexing (FDM) Method of sending several messages down a single communications channel by letting each source use a different frequency.

frequency modulation (FM) Method of encoding information on a carrier wave by varying its frequency.

G

Gateway A system that gives viewdata users access to other computers and their databases. The data has to be rearranged into a suitable page format.

geostationary If a satellite circles the earth at a height of around 35 780 km (22 240 miles) it takes 24 hours to complete its orbit. It therefore appears to hover over the same place on the earth's surface and is said to be geostationary.

Gigabyte (Gb) Around a thousand million bytes (actually 2^{30} or $1\,073\,741\,824$ bytes).

gips Giga-instructions per second: a measure of the speed of computer processors in thousand million instructions per second.

GOTO A BASIC instruction to jump to a different part of the program.

graphics Pictures that the processor can draw on the screen or print onto paper. The higher the resolution, the better the picture.

graphics tablet An input device on which the user traces a shape that is coded in digital form for the computer to process.

H

hacker Computer enthusiast who breaks into public and private databases. Hacking is sometimes just for fun and sometimes to show how vulnerable the databases are; occasionally it has criminal intentions and effects.

half-duplex A communications channel is half-duplex when both parties can send and receive information, but not at the same time. Contrast duplex and simplex.

handshake An agreed convention for control signals so that two electronic devices can communicate with each other.

hands-on Practical experience of using or 'getting your hands on' a computer.

hard-copy Printed output; jargon word for print-out.

hard disc A high-speed, high-density form of external memory. Hard discs hold much more information than floppy discs, but because they are fixed into the computer, they cannot easily be duplicated for back-up. Removable hard disc cartridges may overcome this problem.

hard-sectored Some floppy discs have the boundaries between their sectors marked by the punching of holes (hard-sectored). This leaves all the disc space available for storage. Contrast soft-sectored.

hardware Equipment that makes up a computer system: processor, memory and input/output devices.

help menu Feature of a software program which reminds the user what options are available in menu form.

Hertz Unit of frequency, equal to one complete cycle per second. Radio frequencies are often quoted in Kilohertz (thousands of Hertz). Processors usually have clock frequencies measured in Megahertz (millions of Hertz).

hex or **hexadecimal** Number system based on 16 (see page 195).

high-level (programming) language A language such as BASIC, COBOL or ADA in which instructions are written in words resembling English for subsequent translation into machine language.

high resolution graphics Computer-generated pictures with very sharp definition which can, for example, show smooth curves. Professionals usually mean at least 500 × 500 pixels but computer salesmen use the term much more freely.

I

icon A picture that represents a particular function: for example in the Apple Macintosh system you point to a rubbish bin icon to delete a file.

information manager A program to help the user to create, edit and update files of information.

Information Provider Individual or organisation providing data for a database, usually used in the context of viewdata systems.

information technology (IT) Modern methods of collecting, handling and transmitting information whether as text, pictures or sound. IT is used in different ways in different contexts; in this book it is taken to consist of computing, video and telecommunications.

input Anything you put into the computer. Also used as a verb meaning to feed in. A keyboard is an example of an input device.

INPUT A BASIC instruction to read in.

integrated services digital network (ISDN) A digital network that combines voice and data traffic so as to allow a wide range of communications options. For example, subscribers might be able to call up information from a remote computer database using a data channel and discuss it with a colleague using a high-quality voice channel at the same time.

integrated software Programs which are designed as a collection so that the output of one can automatically be fed into another.

INTELSAT Short for the International Telecommunications Satellite consortium; also used to refer to satellites themselves.

interactive Two-way communication in which what the user does depends on the response just received. Thus interactive computing is the opposite of batch processing.

interactive video (IV) A new medium combining features of computing with those of video presentation. Instead of viewing a programme (ie a linear sequence of pictures and sound planned in advance by the producers), users choose their own route through the material. They may view still or moving video, hear stereo or dual sound, or see and hear pictures and sounds generated by computer. Sometimes they may see and hear a combined effect: eg computer graphics with video sound, or computer subtitles overlaid on a video still.

interactive videotex Another name for viewdata.

interface Junction between two things; for example, a beach is the interface between sea and land. To interface two devices is to do whatever is necessary to make them communicate. Computer interfaces often involve software as well as plugs and cables, and can be expensive.

interference Loss or alteration of a signal caused by noise (other unwanted signals).

interlace The process of lacing two fields together to make a complete video frame.

internal memory The store of information inside the computer, information. This is of two types: RAM and ROM. Internal memory is more limited and expensive than external memory.

interpreter Software that translates a program written in a high-level language like BASIC line-by-line into machine language. Each line of an interpreted program has to be re-translated every time it is obeyed.

ips Instructions per second: a crude measure of computing power, especially applied to mainframe computers. Computing speed is normally quoted in kips or mips (thousands or millions of ips).

IPSS International Packet Switching Service: international network for computer communications that gives higher speeds and reliability than public telephone lines, often at lower cost.

ISDN See integrated services digital network.

IT See information technology.

ITA2 International telex alphabet: a character set consisting of capital letters only and a restricted set of symbols, reflecting the limits of the five-column paper tape used in telexing. Contrast teletex.

J

joystick An input device for a computer, consisting of a short lever which can be moved freely in any direction. Often used in place of a keyboard in video games, computer software and interactive video. Also known as a games paddle.

jump An instruction to pass control to a different part of the program. Unconditional jumps are always obeyed, conditional ones only sometimes.

junkie Someone whose enthusiasm has developed to an abnormal and sometimes unhealthy level: computer junkies are often completely obsessed with computing to the exclusion of other interests.

justify The text on this page is unjustified, ie it has a ragged right-hand edge. Word processing software sometimes rearranges the spaces between words automatically (justifies the text) so that the lines are all the same length.

K

K See Kilobyte

Karaoke Form of entertainment popular in Japan: means 'empty orchestra'. Video shows popular singer with full orchestral backing, giving user option of turning off voice track and singing in place of star. Words of song may be displayed on top of video pictures as a prompt.

KBES Knowledge Based Expert System. See expert system.

keyword (1) Some databases can be researched by keywords that 'unlock' their contents; each item is known to the system by a number of keywords that convey the gist of what they are about. **(2)** In programming, keywords are words that have a special meaning to the computer.

Kilobyte or K Usually taken to mean one thousand bytes (actually 2^{10} or 1024). Since 1 byte is needed to store each character, 1 K holds 150 to 170 words of text.

kips (1) Knowledge Information Processing Systems: name given by the Japanese to the fifth generation of computers to emphasise how different their role will be from traditional computation and data processing. **(2)** Thousand instructions per second, a measure of the speed of computer-processors. See ips.

L

LAN See local area network.

laser A narrow high-energy light beam with important applications in computing and telecommunications. Laser printers are very high-speed and high-quality computer printers. Some videodisc systems depend on lasers.

laser disc See optical videodisc.

Laservision The trade name for Philips' videodisc system.

LCD Liquid Crystal Display. Liquid crystals do not give out light, but can switch from opaque to transparent. This can provide quite a legible display in suitable lighting conditions, as used in many digital watches. LCD displays need little power, and are used in many lap-held computers.

LED Light Emitting Diode. Element of a display that gives out light when activated by an electric current. LED displays usually look brighter than LCD displays, but require more power to drive them.

light pen A pen-shaped pointing device which can be used to select from choices displayed on the screen, or (sometimes) to draw shapes directly onto the screen.

line printers High-speed computer printers that print a whole line, as opposed to a single character, at a time.

LISA A microcomputer produced by Apple (later re-named Macintosh XL) that started the fashion for icons, overlapping screen windows and mouse input.

list As a verb, to make the computer display all the instructions of its current program. If a program is printed out, this is referred to as a listing. LIST is the relevant BASIC instruction.

list processing The processing of data arranged in the form of lists. In word processing, sometimes used to describe the insertion of standard information into mass mailings.

LOAD A BASIC instruction to copy a program or data from disc or tape into the computer's RAM.

local area network (LAN) A method for linking computers and peripherals that are nearby, usually within the same building. Contrast wide area network (WAN).

LOGO A powerful and easily learned high-level programming language developed in the USA by Seymour Papert and widely available on microcomputers. Used to develop learning in people of all ages through programming and de-bugging. See also Turtle.

log on To register your presence on a system, perhaps by identifying yourself as an authorised user.

logic programming Approach to programming developed by workers in artificial intelligence. The programmer supplies facts and rules about the problem to be solved, stated in a formal way. The programming language (eg Prolog) then 'deduces' the consequences.

long wave Electromagnetic waves with a long wavelength and low frequency.

loop A section of program that is repeated over and over again, sometimes using different values or data.

low resolution graphics Crude pictures in which individual pixels are clearly visible. Resolution might be 40 across by 20 down, fine for bar charts but not curves.

LSI Large Scale Integration: method of packing a large number (100 to 1000) of electronic components (and their connections) onto a single chip. (See also VLSI and ULSI.)

luminance The signal that carries information about the light and shade at each point in a television picture. Colour information is carried separately as a chrominance signal.

M

machine language The language of binary numbers in which the processor works. Instructions in machine language are also known as machine code.

Macintosh A popular micro made by Apple sharing most of the features of its more expensive forerunner, the LISA.

Magnetic ink Character Recognition (MCR) Automatic recognition of characters printed with special magnetic ink.

mailbox Space in the memory of a computer reserved for user to store incoming and outgoing messages.

mail merge A word-processing facility

where details from a customer file are merged into a standard letter.

mainframe A large powerful computer with many users, often spread over a distance, sometimes using a variety of different languages or software at the same time (see time-sharing).

Maltron An experimental keyboard with a more ergonomic lay-out than the standard QWERTY arrangement.

medium resolution graphics Pictures of medium quality, adequate for diagrams but not good curves; technically, around 300 pixels across by 200 down.

medium wave Electromagnetic waves with a medium wavelength and medium frequency.

Megabyte (Mb) Usually taken to mean one million bytes (actually 2^{20} or 1048576), enough to hold the text of this book over 20 times.

MegaHertz (MHz) Measure of wave frequency in millions of cycles per second.

memory A computer's memory is a device or series of devices capable of storing information temporarily or permanently. Internal memory contains standing instructions and temporary working space. External memory stores larger volumes of information.

menu-driven A style of software in which the user controls the program by choosing options from a menu, as opposed to typing in commands (contrast command mode).

microcassette A small audio cassette, common on dictation machines, sometimes used as external memory especially for hand-held computers. Compared with standard cassettes, the information can be packed more densely and the motor controlled more precisely.

microcomputer (micro) Any computer you can easily carry. Nowadays, some are quite fast, powerful and may have sizeable memories (see also minicomputer).

microfiche A rectangle of film, usually around 6 in by 4 in, on which tiny photographic images of pages of text or drawings have been arranged. Each microfiche might hold anywhere between 60 and 300 pages depending on how much they have been reduced.

microfilm A roll of film on which tiny photographic images of pages of text or drawings have been arranged in sequence.

microfloppy A floppy disc of diameter less than 5¼ in, generally 3½ in.

microform General term for minaturised storage of documents using a photographic process, eg microfiche and microfilm. Humans need a special magnifying device to be able to read documents in microform.

Micronet 800 A club for microcomputer users that operates as a Closed User Group under Prestel. Provides a software preview service, bulletin board and commercial telesoftware.

microprocessor A computer processor on a single tiny chip of silicon.

MicroProlog Version of Prolog programming language scaled-down to fit micros.

Microtext An authoring system developed at the National Physical Laboratory in the UK and available on a wide range of microcomputers.

microwave Very short wavelength radio waves used in radar navigation, burglar alarms and microwave ovens.

Microwriter A hand-held keyboard with its own system of coding characters using only one hand.

minicomputer (mini) More compact and cheaper than mainframes, but more likely than microcomputers to have several users at a time. There is no sharp division between the power, speed and memory of top-range micros and bottom-range minis.

minifloppy A 5¼ in. floppy disc.

mips Million instructions per second; a measure of the speed of computer processors. See ips.

mix In video production, a shot can be gradually dissolved into another shot by mixing the two: the proportion of the second shot increases as the first fades.

modem (MOdulator/DEModulator) A device that allows computers to transmit information through a telecommunications link by turning it into an analogue signal. Modems can be built into computers or connected to them separately. See also acoustic coupler.

modular A module is a self-contained unit that can readily be added to or built on. Computer hardware, telephone systems and structured programming are all modular in this sense.

modulation The encoding of information onto a carrier wave by changing it in some way. For example, amplitude modulation (AM) depends on changing the size of the carrier wave, frequency modulation (FM) works by varying its frequency.

monitor (1) A high-quality screen designed to display computer output. It gives a steadier display than a television. **(2)** Set of basic systems software to control and monitor overall operation.

monochrome One-colour only: for example, a black-and-white television or an amber or green monitor.

mouse Input device about the size of a cigarette pack, which the user rolls around on a desk-top to control the movement of a pointer on the screen. Choices are made by pressing buttons on the mouse.

MP/M A multi-user operating system derived from CP/M.

MS-DOS A 16-bit operating system commissioned by IBM for its Personal Computer (on which it is known as PC-DOS). Its main rival is CP/M-86.

MSX A standard for microcomputers developed jointly by an American and a Japanese company in 1984. It covers the operating system, programming language and control of peripherals. Any MSX computer should be able to work with any MSX equipment and any MSX software.

multiplex To transmit more than one message at a time using a single channel. One method is to split up the frequency band available into several narrower bands and allocate one to each source; this is called frequency division multiplexing or FDM. Another method is to allocate the whole channel to several sources in turn by dividing up each second into short time-slots; this is called time division multi-plexing or TDM.

multi-tasking A system that can deal with more than one program at a time.

multi-user A system that can deal with more than one user at a time.

N

narrowband General term for a commu-nication channel with restricted bandwidth and limited capacity for carrying informa-tion. May mean as little as 300 Hz or as much as 3000 Hz (enough for telephone conversations). Contrast broadband.

narrowcast Transmitting signals intended for a specific and relatively small audience, using cable, satellite or radio waves. Likely to be financed differently from broadcasting, eg by subscription or a charges related to connection time.

network System for linking one or more computers and terminals so that they can communicate with each other and share facilities like disc drives and printers.

noise Any unwanted signal that dimi-nishes or alters the wanted signal.

NTSC The colour standard established by the National Television Standards Committee in the US. It is applied to video systems that handle colour in this way and use a 525-line screen running at 30 frames (60 fields) per second. Used throughout N America and Japan.

O

object program The machine-language instructions into which the source program must be translated before the processor can obey them.

on-line Connected to a working computer system.

operating environment A comprehen-sive operating system complete with integrated software and special hardware, eg Apple's Macintosh system.

operating system (OS) Vital program in overall control of the computer whenever it is operating. Without the OS, the computer could not load programs, process data, retrieve from disc or send output to prin-ters: it would be useless. Personal micros often have resident operating systems on ROM chips. CP/M-compatible micros load the CP/M operating system from disc. Many 16-bit micros give the user a choice of operating system. The characteristics of the OS determine how the user regards the computer and how easy it is to use.

optical To do with light. Light waves have very high frequencies compared with radio waves, giving far greater bandwidth and information-carrying capacity. Optical fibres are very important in modern tele-communications. Many videodisc systems, eg Laservision, also depend on the reflec-tion or transmission of laser light.

Optical Character Recognition (OCR) Automatic recognition of characters by their shapes, using special alphabets.

optical fibre Flexible strand of very pure glass drawn out to be finer than a human hair. Compared with traditional metal cables, optical fibres are very light and fine, and they have a much higher bandwidth.

Oracle Teletext service provided by the Independent Broadcasting Authority in Britain.

output Any result which comes from the computer; usually it is in the form of text and graphics displayed on the screen and/or printed on paper.

overwrite To record on top of. In word processing, it is a mode in which the letter typed in replaces what is there already.

P

package Program or set of programs complete with documentation, designed for a particular application.

packet-switching A digital method of transmitting messages electronically by dividing the signals into little packets of information, each of a standard size and format, and labelled with its source and destination. The packets are then transmitted in whatever way makes most efficient use of the network, and they are reassembled into the original message at the other end. Contrast circuit-switching.

PAL Colour TV standard developed in W Germany. Widespread in Europe, Middle East, Africa, Australasia, S America. Short for phase alternating line.

parallel interface Connection between two devices capable of parallel processing, ie handling information more than one bit at a time.

parity check A method of checking whether the number of ones in a set of binary digits is odd or even. Sometimes a bit (known as a parity bit) is added to the set to ensure that the total is always even (even parity) or always odd (odd parity). This makes it easy to check data for simple input or handling errors.

Pascal A high-level programming language that evolved from ALGOL and is well-suited to structured programming. Named after mathematician Blaise Pascal.

password Secret word to prevent unauthorised use of a computer or private viewdata system. Passwords can give different categories of user access to different levels of privileged information.

PCM See pulse code modulation.

peripherals Any computer equipment other than the processor, eg input/output devices.

persistence of vision Inability of our eyes to follow very rapid changes in what we see. Thus a light that flashes rapidly enough – for example, more than 50 times per second – will appear steady. This is the illusion on which films and video depend.

personal computer Computer that is small enough or cheap enough to be used mainly by one person.

phosphor coating The layer on a monitor screen that produces the display. Different coatings produce displays of varying colours and legibility.

PILOT Authoring language developed at the University of California in the late 1960s and available on microcomputers in various versions, eg Apple SuperPILOT.

PIN Personal Identification Number to identify the user of a bank cash-dispenser or computer system.

pixel Picture cell: tiny squares of light that make up pictures on the screen. The more pixels, the higher the resolution.

PLATO A mainframe authoring system developed at the University of Urbana-Champaign, Illinois by Control Data Corporation in the 1960s. Cut-down versions called MicroPLATO have been produced for some microcomputers.

PL/1 Short for Programming Language 1: a high-level programming language designed by IBM for commercial and scientific applications.

PL/M Programming Language for Microcomputers, a language derived from PL/1 to run on smaller computers.

plotter Output device for drawing and lettering in which the movement of pens is controlled directly by the computer.

port A place where electrical connections can be made with the central processor of a computer.

portable (1) Easy to carry, like a small microcomputer. (2) Capable of running on other equipment, like a standard CP/M program.

Prestel A public viewdata system which contains large amounts of information in page format. Subscribers can order goods and catalogues as well as getting up-to-date information. Prestel subscribers with microcomputers only need an acoustic coupler and some software to be able to access, save and print Prestel frames.

PRINT A BASIC instruction to display something on the screen.

printer A machine like a typewriter without a keyboard that prints computer output. Dot-matrix and daisy-wheel printers print one character at a time, but line printers print a complete line as one unit.

print-out Output from a computer printer; same as hard-copy.

procedure Self-contained mini-program typical of structured programming (sometimes called a module or routine). A procedure is called up by name from the main program to do any task which is likely to be needed several times, eg setting up a screen display, performing a calculation, producing a sound effect. After it has been carried out, control is returned to the main program.

processor The part of the computer that actually does the arithmetic and makes the decisions. In mainframes sometimes called the central processing unit. In micros, often consists of microprocessors.

program A list of instructions for the computer to obey, written in a special language (see below).

programming language A special language for giving instructions to computers. There are hundreds of different ones available. All have to be translated into machine language before the computer can obey the instructions.

Prolog High-level language devised by artificial intelligence workers, and suited to developing expert systems.

prompt Any sign given by the computer (a symbol on the screen or an audible beep) to indicate that it is waiting for a response from the user.

proportional spacing Method of printing letters so that the space for each character is proportional to its width when handwritten eg m is wider than i. Proportional spacing is generally more legible than uniform spacing; although some computer printers can produce proportional spacing, it often cannot be combined with justification (see justify entry).

protocol A set of conventions about the format of messages and how they are exchanged.

PSS Short for Packet Switching Service: a network dedicated to computer communications that gives higher speeds and lower error rates than the PSTN (see below). PSS charges often reflect the length of the message rather than its destination. For overseas communication it is often far cheaper than post or telephone.

PSTN Public Switched Telephone Network – the ordinary telephone system. It can be used to transmit data in addition to speech using a dial-up connection charged like an ordinary phone call.

PTT Authority that co-ordinates Post, Telegraph and Telephone in a country. For example, in Britian the PTT is British Telecom (BT).

pull-down menu Computer displays sometimes show reminders of facilities available along the top of the screen. The user positions the pointer over his choice and 'pulls down' the full menu; eg the reminder might be 'shading' and the menu would show shading styles available.

pulse code modulation (PCM) A method for sending analogue information in digital form. The analogue signal is sampled frequently, and the readings are converted into binary numbers.

Q

Q-23 A protocol established by CCITT for interpreting the tones produced by each key on a digital telephone keypad. Used in voice response systems.

QWERTY The standard arrangement of keys on a typewriter or computer keyboard in the English-speaking world is known by its top row of letters: QWERTYUIOP or QWERTY for short.

R

RAM See Random Access Memory

random access This means that any part of a floppy disc or videodisc can be found quickly without having to read through all the other parts. It is the opposite of serial access as in a cassette that has to be wound through from beginning to end.

Random Access Memory (RAM) The storage space inside a computer where software is stored while it is being worked on. Its contents are constantly being over-written when different programs are running and are often lost altogether when the computer is switched off.

raster Pattern of lines on a TV screen.

read (1) A disc drive is said to 'read' information from a disc when it retrieves it (and to 'write' to a disc when it records it). **(2)** The BASIC instruction READ is used to enter data.

read-only Anything that can only be read, not written on, eg a protected disc, ROM (see below).

Read Only Memory (ROM) Part of the computer's internal memory that stores software in frequent use. Unlike RAM, the contents of ROM are not forgotten when you switch off. See also EPROM.

real-time Used to describe when a computer obeys each instruction as soon as it is received, eg in interactive use or when controlling events as they happen.

record (1) Each file in a database consists of a number of records, each of which contains a number of fields of information. For example, a business's customer file might contain thousands of individuals and firms, with a separate record for each one. **(2)** To record information on a disc or tape is to overwrite whatever is already there with fresh information.

redundancy The extent to which parts of a message can be predicted from a knowledge of the other parts. In a highly redundant message, a large proportion of it can be deleted without loss of meaning.

refresh rate The frequency with which the contents of a screen is refreshed (renewed). If too low, a flicker may result.

reflective Dependent on light being reflected or bounced off a surface.

regenerator A device that detects, boosts and re-transmits a digital signal. Compare with repeaters. Because digital signals are more robust than analogue ones, regener-

ators can be spaced out at larger intervals than repeaters.

relay As a verb, to pass on a message. As a noun, an electromagnetic switch.

REM A BASIC instruction for REMark, ie a message left for humans to read.

repeater Devices placed at intervals in long-distance cables to strengthen the signal. Without repeaters, the signal would quickly get too faint to detect. Repeaters work on analogue principles, and tend to amplify any noise together with the signal. Contrast regenerators.

replicate To reproduce a message, formula or experiment. In setting up a spreadsheet, the user often wants to build in similar relationships between different rows and columns of figures. A replicate command makes the software fill in the appropriate entries automatically.

resident Permanently fitted to a computer, eg held in ROM.

resolution Measure of quality in computer graphics. The higher the resolution, the finer the detail. See also pixel.

RF Radio frequency: electromagnetic waves of frequency suitable for radio transmission (roughly in the 10 KHz to 10 million MHz range).

RGB monitor Short for red-green-blue: a colour monitor in which the three primary colour signals are handled separately. Gives excellent displays for coloured graphics compared with a colour TV.

rigid disc Another name for hard disc (as opposed to floppy disc).

robot A machine that can be programmed to do a variety of jobs automatically; often controlled by microprocessors.

robust Adjective used to describe software that is unlikely to crash (fail) or signals that are unlikely to be corrupted.

ROM See Read Only Memory.

RS-232 A standard developed by the Electronics Industry Association for tele-communications equipment. Transmission is serial, at one of a standard range of speeds. The standard has been widely adopted by computer manufacturers, so that many computers have an RS-232 port for connecting processors to peripherals.

RUN A BASIC instruction to make a program start running, ie working.

run-time The stage when a program is being run (as opposed to being written or tested).

S

satellite Unmanned device put into orbit around the earth for monitoring purposes (eg the weather or flying objects) and for bouncing signals off the earth's surface. Modern communications satellites are active, ie can pick up and boost signals before re-transmitting them.

satellite TV The relay of television signals by communications satellites.

save To record a copy of a program, text or data file (usually in magnetic form, eg onto a disc).

scout Type of message sent along a network to check whether a terminal is ready to receive or not.

scramble To disguise a message or program so that only authorised people can unscramble it.

screen Output device that shows what the computer is doing. The term is often used generally to mean either a monitor or television set used this way.

screen dump The contents of a screen (text and/or graphics) printed onto paper.

scroll When a document is larger than the screen, the processor makes the text seem to move up so that the screen can display the next 'page'. Most systems scroll up and down when required; some also scroll from side to side.

SECAM Short for sequential couleur à memoire. Colour TV standard developed in France and adopted by the Soviet Union and its satellites, also parts of the Middle East and North Africa.

sector Smallest area on a disc that can be addressed individually. The boundaries between sectors may be hard (permanently punched holes) or soft (magnetically recorded and erasable).

sensor Device that detects touch, temperature, sound, smell or other sensory information. Sensors allow computers and robots to react to their environment.

serial access When you have to search through something from beginning to end, as with a cassette tape, instead of being able to jump to any part of it at random, as with a floppy disc.

series interface Connection between two devices capable of handling information only one bit at a time.

shared-logic When a number of terminals share the same processor, the system may be called shared-logic. Now that processor power has become so cheap, networked microcomputers are often preferred to shared-logic systems.

short wave Electromagnetic waves with a short wavelength and high frequency.

shredder Machine that shreds paper, eg computer print-out after use so that it cannot be read by anyone unauthorised.

signal Anything carrying information, a radio broadcast, voice on the telephone or computer data.

signal-to-noise ratio Whenever a signal is transmitted, it will pick up noise which affects its reception. The higher the signal-to-noise ratio, the clearer the signal will be at the receiving end.

simplex A communication channel in which messages can be sent only in one direction. Contrast half-duplex and duplex.

simulator Device that accurately represents something that is too large, expensive, dangerous or difficult to practise on directly. Used for training and sometimes also for research.

slow-scan TV Television pictures shot at one frame every few seconds instead of 25 to 30 per second. The effect is like a rapid succession of still photographs, and the pictures take far less bandwidth to transmit than normal-speed television. Slow-scan TV is useful for security purposes, and in situations where the cost of transmitting true moving pictures is not justified, eg a business teleconference.

Smalltalk A programming language developed by Xerox and used in artificial intelligence and the development of micro-computer systems.

soft-sectored Some floppy discs have 'soft' boundaries between sectors, ie they are recorded onto them by software. The same disc can thus have its boundaries changed by re-recording. The price of this flexibility is having slightly less space for data. Contrast hard-sectored discs.

software Programs and data. A software generator is a program that reduces the labour of routine programming. A software tool is any utility that helps to make programming faster and easier.

source program The instructions written in a programming language before they have been translated into an object program for the processor to obey.

SPC See stored program control.

speech synthesis The production of sounds resembling human speech by artificial means.

spreadsheet A software package that displays a set of entries (such as a firm's accounts) and allows the user to define and re-define the relationships between those entries, calculating the consequences of any changes automatically.

sprite Computer graphic that the user can control and move easily. Some games computers have built-in colourful sprites of animals and people; others allow users to design or adapt their own sprites.

stand-alone A computer system used on its own as opposed to being part of a network or telecommunications link.

standard A set of rules and conventions about hardware, software or communi-cations that allows easier exchange between those who adopt it.

still frame A video picture or diagram deliberately presented as a single static image rather than as moving footage. Contrast freeze frame.

store-and-forward Form of electronic communication in which a message is not sent directly to its destination but is stored in computer memory and forwarded later. Many electronic mail systems work thus.

stored program control (SPC) Telephone exchanges that are controlled by a computer program rather than by permanent wired connections.

string A set of characters one after the other. The last sentence is an example of a string; note that it includes spaces and a full stop as well as letters. Strings can also consist of numbers or a mixture of characters.

structure chart A diagram that displays the structure of a computer program using boxes on a number of different levels; lower-level boxes spell out the details of the higher-level boxes.

structured programming A method of programming in which each section consists of clearly defined and labelled units, which can be written and revised independently.

switched star Network layout for cable TV that is specially suitable for interactive services, but tends to be expensive to build.

synthesizer Device for producing artificial speech or music electronically.

systems analysis A skilled task involving analysing an information-handling need and preparing detailed statements specifying what programs would be suitable. Systems analysts often have professional programmers working under them.

systems software Software such as the operating system and programming languages that the computer needs to allow it to do anything useful.

System X British Telecom's high-speed high-capacity digital telephone network.

T

TDM See time division multiplexing.

telecommunications Transmission and reception of information at a distance.

telebanking Process of instructing bank payments and getting account information from a distance, often using viewdata from a terminal in the home.

telegraph Early electric method of transmitting signals using on/off codes.

teleshopping Ordering goods at a distance, often using viewdata from a terminal in the home. Has proved valuable for the elderly, disabled and housebound.

telesoftware Software that is sent straight into a computer's memory over a distance, using telephone lines or broadcast waves.

teletex The CCITT system for transmission of text and data between terminals using the public telephone network. Likely to supersede telex.

teletext Information broadcast as part of a television signal, eg Ceefax, Oracle. Televisions with built-in teletext decoders are known as teletext televisions.

telex A worldwide telegraphic service that allows communication between special printers. By modern standards it is slow and inflexible, but it is well-established and widely available.

Telidon Canadian viewdata system with comparatively high-resolution graphics.

Tempest Standard defined by the North Atlantic Treaty Organisation (NATO) for shielding a computer installation from electronic eavesdropping.

terminal Equipment that allows the user to communicate with a remote system. It might consist of any combination of a screen, keyboard or printer.

thesaurus Dictionary of keywords in a database showing related meanings and relationships.

time division multiplexing (TDM) Method of sending several messages down a single communications channel by giving each source a slot in turn.

toggle Switch or key which reverses its effect when pressed twice, eg light-switch you press once for 'on' and again for 'off'.

touch screen A touch-sensitive screen allows the user to make choices by pointing with a finger, thus making the screen act as an input device as well as displaying output. Some touch-screens detect pressure, others sense the interruption of a criss-cross grid of infra-red beams. They are used in computer and interactive video systems aimed at the general public and anyone for whom the traditional keyboard presents a barrier.

track Complete circular path on a disc where data is stored.

transborder data flow The transmission of information (as text, broadcast or data) across national borders.

transportable More accurate name for microcomputers that are too big and heavy to be truly portable. Also used to describe software that will run on a different computer.

tree-and-branch Method of arranging viewdata pages or cable TV networks that resembles the trunk and branches of a tree.

triad Group of three.

time-sharing Whenever a processor works on several jobs at once, it shares its time between them.

transmissive Depends on light being shone (transmitted) through something.

turnaround Time between when a job is submitted and when the results are ready.

turtle Remote-control floor robot shaped a bit like a turtle, whose movements can be controlled by young children using the language LOGO.

TV/monitor Screen that can either display television pictures or act as a computer monitor. Some can do both jobs at once and show computer text and graphics on top of the video picture.

U

UHF Ultra high frequency, usually meaning electromagnetic waves.

ULSI Ultra Large Scale Integration: method of packing an ultra-large number (more than 1,000,000) of electronic components (and their connections) onto a single chip. See also LSI and VLSI.

Unix A popular and sophisticated operating system for 16-bit microcomputers that allows multi-users and multi-tasking.

upgrade Process of improving or adding to the original hardware or software. A good system will have a well-planned upgrade path so that software can be transferred onto expanded hardware easily.

upstream Messages sent by TV viewers to the cable TV providers are referred to as upstream messages. The transmission speed needed depends on their nature.

user-friendly Overworked adjective to describe IT systems believed by their designers to be easy to use. In practice many of them turn out to be user-hostile.

utilities Programs that allow users to do useful jobs such as copying discs or recovering deleted files.

V

VAN Value added network: a network that provides subscription services like electronic mail and viewdata in addition to basic telecommunications facilities.

variable A labelled 'pigeon-hole' that can stand for different values at different times. In school algebra, x is a common name for a variable. Variables in computer programs may contain numbers or strings, and are called numeric or string variables.

VCR See video cassette recorder.

VDU See visual display unit.

verification Process of checking computer input or software for mistakes. 'To verify' means to check whether the process of saving a file or formatting a disc was successful.

VHD Short for Video High Density, a videodisc system developed by JVC of Japan and marketed in Britain by Thorn-EMI Videodisc. It is based on the

capacitance principle and can cope with the different colour standards (NTSC, PAL and SECAM) in a single machine.

VHF very high frequency, usually meaning electromagnetic waves.

videocassette Cassette containing videotape.

videodisc Plastic disc, usually 8 in to 12 in in diameter, which can store large numbers of moving or still television pictures with sound. Unlike videocassettes, some videodiscs can be accessed at random and can store digital information. They have great potential as a medium for computer memory because of their enormous capacity. At present, videodiscs cannot generally be recorded onto by the user.

videocassette recorder (VCR) A machine that records and plays back videotape packaged in cassettes.

videotape Magnetic tape on which video pictures and sound can be recorded. Generally wider than audio tape (from 1/4 in up to 2 in).

videotex An electronic method of receiving information at a distance and displaying it on a screen. Videotex may use broadcasting (teletext) or telephone lines (viewdata). Teletext may be referred to as one-way or broadcast videotex, and viewdata as two-way or interactive videotex. Videotext is the spelling common in the US.

viewdata Two-way transmission of electronic information using telephone lines, television sets and a keypad or computer. Local users can not only retrieve information from large databases but also send messages back. Prestel was the world's first public viewdata system.

VisiCalc The first and most famous electronic spreadsheet.

visual display unit (VDU) Device that displays computer output on a screen (monitor). Also used loosely to mean screen and keyboard unit.

VLSI Very Large Scale Integration: method of packing a very large number (1000 to 1,000,000) of electronic components (and their connections) onto a single chip. See also LSI and ULSI.

voice-grade Communication channel capable of transmitting speech.

voice recognition units Computer input device that can be programmed and trained to identify words spoken by humans.

voice response systems (VRS) Computer-based information systems to which users can send messages, orders and questions using a telephone and touch-keypad. The computer responds immediately in a high-quality synthesised voice, delivering information or confirmation in the appropriate language.

voice traffic Use of telephone to carry conversations as opposed to data.

volatile Computer memory that is lost when you switch off is called volatile.

VRS See voice response systems.

W

WAN See wide area network.

wavelength The distance between two peaks (or troughs) on a wave. All electromagnetic waves travel at the same speed (300,000 km/s). The longer the wavelength, the lower the frequency.

wide area network (WAN) Method for linking computers and terminals that are widely separated, often using telephone lines. Transmission speeds are often lower than in a LAN, but WANs often span immense distances.

wideband Same as broadband: communications channel with plenty of bandwidth.

Winchester A type of sealed hard disc unit becoming very popular for use with microcomputers. Originally 14 in in diameter, Winchesters have become progressively smaller despite greater capacities and faster access times.

wipe In video production, a transition from one scene to another in which a moving line appears to reveal the new scene, a bit like a wiper moving across a windscreen.

wired society Catch-phrase to suggest the social implications of improved modern communications.

word Computer processors do not deal with individual bits of information; they group them into 'words' and process them as a single unit. Personal computers generally have a word length of 8-bits, while newer business computers tend to work on 16-bit or even 32-bit words. There is no direct relationship between the processor's word length and how many English words a computer can deal with!

word processor Strictly, a machine dedicated to word processing, but loosely used to describe any computer that is running word processing software.

word processing A system for editing, storing and rearranging text so that it can be perfected before it is finally printed out. Word-processed text can be produced easily and without errors to give (for example) 'personalised' letters containing variations on a standard text. Any computer can run word processing if it has suitable software and peripherals.

wp Word processing.

write-protected You can make a $5\frac{1}{4}$ in disc 'read-only' (ie nothing can be recorded onto it) by sticking a bit of paper over a notch. It is then write-protected. (In the case of 8-in floppy discs you take the sticker off.)

X, Y, Z

X-25 One of the best-known of the X series recommendations from CCITT, X-25 lays down standards for the use of terminal equipment on the public packet-switching service.

The Inside Information project

This book is just one part of the *Inside Information* project which provides a basic grounding in information technology for adults and young people. It is mounted jointly by BBC Education and the City and Guilds of London Institute.

The other three parts of the *Inside Information* package are

1 A ten-programme radio course, presented on BBC Radio 4, available in an edited version on two C60 cassettes from:
BBC Publications
PO Box 234,
London SE1 3TH.

2 Software pack for the BBC Micro from:
BBC Publications
PO Box 234,
London SE1 3TH.

3 Assessment and certification by:
City and Guilds of London Institute
(Section 18)
46 Britannia Street,
London WC1X 9RG.

The radio series offers a lively, general introduction to the whole field of Information technology, while the software pack enables the user to explore this area in greater depth, to get 'hands-on' experience of computers and to gain some insight into their workings. Finally, the City and Guilds assessment provides an opportunity to gain a nationally recognised qualification. Brief details of these three elements of the project are provided below. For further information please contact the addresses above.

Assessment and certification

The scheme is intended for anyone who wants to improve his or her understanding of information technology. There are no restrictions on the time taken to complete the course or the method of learning, but candidates will need to have access to a BBC Micro either at a local college, school, training or adult education centre, at work, or at home. Once candidates have completed the course and passed the computer-based assessment (see below), they will be awarded a City and Guilds certificate.

Note for prospective centres

The flexibility of the *Inside Information* scheme will enable centres to plan their own courses which can also incorporate additional objectives. Indications in 1985 were that centres will offer the scheme within a Certificated Prevocational Education or Youth Training Scheme framework, as a pre 726 Information Technology course from City and Guilds, as a Sixth Form General Studies course, as an evening adult education course, in Information Technology Centres (ITeCs) and as part of an in-service scheme for school teachers.

The syllabus is presented in an objective-type format and draws on the other three parts of the *Inside Information* package. Cross-references are given to the radio programmes by number, to the BBC software pack by programme and to this book by chapter.

The assessment is on BBC format computer disc. The disc contains a bank of multiple-choice questions, testing familiarity with IT concepts and basic practical skills. Candidates who answer sufficient questions correctly will be awarded a City and Guilds certificate.

INDEX

Italic page numbers indicate relevant illustrations which appear away from the main text reference.